SEARCH FOR
A NEW HUMANITY

SEARCH FOR A NEW HUMANITY

A Dialogue Between
Josef Derbolav and Daisaku Ikeda

edited and translated by Richard L. Gage

New York   WEATHERHILL   *Tokyo*

First edition, 1992

Published by Weatherhill, Inc., 420 Madison Avenue, 15th Floor, New York, New York 10017, and Tanko-Weatherhill, Inc., 8–3 Nibancho, Chiyoda-ku, Tokyo 102. Protected by copyright under the terms of the International Copyright Union; all rights reserved. Printed in Japan.

Library of Congress Cataloging-in-Publication Data: Derbolav, Josef. [Auf der Suche nach einer neuen Humanität. English] Search for a new humanity: a dialogue between Josef Derbolav and Daisaku Ikeda / edited and translated by Richard L. Gage.–1st ed. / p.   cm. / Translation of: Auf der Suche nach einer neuen Humanität. / ISBN 0-8348-0252-X : $32.50 / 1. Humanism.   2. Manners and customs. 3. Ethics.   4. Buddhism–Relations–Christianity.   5. Christianity and other religions–Buddhism.   6. Education.   7. Civilization, Modern–1950–   / I. Ikeda, Daisaku.   II. Gage, Richard L.   III. Title. / B821.D3913   1992 / 144–dc20 / 91-46150 CIP

CONTENTS

FOREWORD

In meetings in both Germany and Japan, the two authors of this book decided to undertake a dialogue similar in general plan to those already conducted between Daisaku Ikeda and such leading thinkers as Arnold J. Toynbee, René Huyghe, Aurelio Peccei, and Brian Wilson. Hoping that their dialogue would become a bridge between Asiatic and European cultures, in November 1982, they put the idea into more concrete form and determined discussion themes.

They decided that the dialogue should include a treatment of fundamental issues, including tradition and modernization, humanism in the East and West, the role of ethics and religion, and a systematically viewed encounter between Buddhism and Christianity. After a section on education, which is prerequisite to understanding what is to come, they concluded the dialogue with a glimpse into the conceivable future on the basis of an analysis of the crisis-laden present.

After initial meetings, in which topics were agreed upon, the dialogue was carried out in written form. Daisaku Ikeda, as a representative of Oriental culture, was responsible for the exposition of the main themes of each chapter and the sub-themes generated by them. As a representative of European culture, Josef Derbolav undertook the systematic explication of those themes. Then both the Japanese and the German partners went through the dialogue again to deal with still unsettled problems and to put the whole into relatively complete form.

Both authors have striven for clarity in their arguments, although, given the fullness, richness, and complexity of the issues, attaining it has not always been an easy task. They are fully aware of not being specialists in all the aspects dealt with in this *tour d'horizon* of European and Asiatic cultures. Moreover, they do not agree on all points. Nonetheless, their common spiritual basis is sufficient to enable them to produce reliable conclusions.

Confident that the themes of this book are not only highly interesting, but also of explosive urgency, the authors hope that, in discussing them, they can somehow contribute to the improvement of the current human situation.

Although it might seem slightly presumptuous, the title, *Search for a New Humanity*, at least indicates the orientation of the authors' questioning. As should be apparent, the title makes reference to that of Marcel Proust's famous novel, *A la recherche du temps perdu*, but differs from it in direction. In other words, the search for a new humanity deals not with things past that are to be recalled, but with things to come that must be undergone.

It might seem strange that, with the exception of a few concluding remarks, practically no mention is made in the book of the "new humanity." But this is easily explained. Humanity, as the object of the search, can be encircled and enclosed but cannot be directly defined. Even the chapter on humanism deals, not with a new humanity, but with old and sometimes already outlived forms and leaves the future dark. This is as it should be, for, given the evolutional pressure on our entire technological and political development, the constantly increasing drive for progress, and the intensifying complexity of our living conditions, it is no longer possible to make fairly reliable prognoses even for the next 10, let alone the next 50 or 100 years. Futurology has lost itself in abstract philosophizing, with which it attempts to conceal its own confusion.

Without attempting to reveal their conclusions ahead of time, the authors feel that, here, the following can be said: for the first time in history, humanity realizes that further technological advances could lead to the annihilation of the human race. Excessive technological efficiency threatens to cut the ground out from under human feet. And, should the end come, to some imagined observer in outer space, the self-destruction of Homo sapiens probably would be no more startling than the extinction of an animal species is to biologists on Earth.

Clearly, if we intend to last into the future, we must find answers to the increasing challenges facing us in what remains of the twentieth century. Both authors are convinced that these answers will be forthcoming only from a new, still undefined humanity.

This is why, instead of using a phrase like "on the way to a new humanity" in our title, we have chosen to rely on the dialectic inherent in the word *search*. This is the dialectic that Plato originated and that Saint Augustine employed in his search for God. In Oriental tradition, the bodhisattva is a being in search of the perfect wisdom (enlightenment) that, once attained, constitutes Buddhahood. The dialectic inferred by these terms is set forth in the Lotus Sutra.

The searcher misses the object of his search but must nonetheless know what he seeks and must in this way, at least, anticipate his own fundamental tendencies. It is because this is true that Saint Augustine was able to write about his relation to God, "I would not have sought you, if I had not already found you."

In an interesting parallel, Nichiren Daishonin (1222–82) the great Japanese religious reformer and the founder of Nichiren Buddhism, says that common mortals born in the Latter Day of the Buddhist Law can believe in the Lotus Sutra because the world of Buddhahood is present in the world of Humanity.

Today, we human beings already know, or at any rate can formulate, the outline of the answers we must give. We know that we can hope to be ready for what the future holds in store only if we have substantial expertise, the strongest sense of responsibility, and the highest degree of self-control.

It is true that we can to a large extent make our own futures, but frequently we carelessly allow the reins to slip from our hands and act without thinking. Then, our actions come back on us in the form of rigid structures of recalcitrant facts that make it seem as if the future had been preordained.

In interpreting the title of the book it is necessary to remember that attaining a new form of humanity entails an inner revolution—a radical alteration of our way of thinking—that will free us from prominent egoistic, commercial, and ideological motivations and at the same time liberate us to the deep and genuine claims of Eastern and Western cultural traditions and such of their treasures as Buddhism and Christianity.

In conclusion, the authors should like to express their deep gratitude to Mr. Richard L. Gage, Dr. Elke Jarnut and Mr. Carlos Cooper for their hard work in translating the texts.

Josef Derbolav
Daisaku Ikeda

June 1987

POSTSCRIPT

On July 14, 1987, when our dialogue had been concluded and late corrections were being made to the typescripts, I received news of Professor Derbolav's sudden death.

I am told that during the preceding month, though ill and hospitalized, he had kept our text by his side constantly and had read it often. After his death, his daughter Dr. Elke Jarnut was kind enough to put the text in final form; and, in March of this year, the German-language version was published by Nymphenburger under the title *Auf der Suche nach einer neuen Humanität*. At present the English-language version, *Search for a New Humanity*, and the Japanese-language version,

Atarashii Ningenzō o Motomete, have been completed and are being prepared for publication.

The successful conclusion of this extensive and important project is certainly a fine tribute to Professor Derbolav's memory.

Daisaku Ikeda

May 1988

SEARCH FOR
A NEW HUMANITY

CHAPTER ONE

TRADITION AND MODERNIZATION

1. Reactions

IKEDA: The wave of modernization–or perhaps Westernization is the more apt term since the intellectual and scientific revolutions on which it rests originated in Europe–now sweeping the world conflicts with traditional ways of thinking and behaving in many fields of activity. Nor does modernization always have the right answers to the problems sparked by such conflict. Nietzsche pointed out many of the contradictions and dangers inherent in modern rationalism. After World War I, Oswald Spengler caused an international sensation with his idea of the decline of the West. And, from the commanding viewpoint of his own immense knowledge of history, Arnold Toynbee attempted to view the modern West in relation to the traditional cultures of the rest of the world. In my estimation, internal criticism of this kind demonstrates the depth to which peoples of the West are rooted in the past on which modernization rests. Furthermore, objective critical examinations of the present show that the ancient and medieval past were not times of ignorance and intellectual darkness, as some people have described them, but had brilliant moments of their own. Such a view indicates that, while distinctive in itself, the modern age is not a unique instance in the general current of human (European) history.

3

What is your opinion of the criticisms of Westernization and modernization men like Nietzsche, Spengler, and Toynbee have made?

DERBOLAV: If we follow the thoughts Oswald Spengler expressed in his epoch-making book, *The Decline of the West*, cultures can be seen to grow like plants, each from different soils, introducing the genetic heritage of its people into its growth. Culture-plants, or as Spengler calls them "culture souls," are, therefore, more or less related or alien to each other, depending on the extent to which the character of a nation develops in isolation from, or in loose or close contact with, other nations.

Undeniably, the European peoples are geographically far removed from the peoples of the Far East and contacts–especially with Japan, owing to her own temporary self-isolation–came about relatively late and sporadically, even in the Middle Ages, which you quite rightly defend against accusations of being an age of darkness and ignorance. Although development in the Middle Ages progressed differently in East and West, there were certain similarities with respect to habitat, population structure, and culture–in other words, with respect to the characteristics we today would ascribe to premodern society.

The first attempt of the West to widen its sphere of influence in Japan occurred in the fifteenth and sixteenth centuries with attempts at Christian missionizing. Afflicted by many setbacks, the venture was rather unsuccessful. I mention this only to demonstrate that Westernization and modernization cannot simply be equated. It is true that modernization is a product of European history, as you have said; but it has structurally changed traditional European culture as much as it has the Oriental cultures that imported it from the West.

IKEDA: I agree. The Industrial Revolution, in which England took the lead, came along later to alter everything in Europe. But, in the fifteenth and sixteenth centuries, when Japan was first influenced by the West, Spain and Portugal were the prominent nations in European affairs. As is well known, at that time, the thing the Japanese imported most eagerly from the Spanish was the rifle, which attracted the military leader of the nation, Oda Nobunaga, because of the supremacy it promised to give his forces over those of his opponents in the struggle to control the nation.

But the West with which Japan came into contact in the middle of the nineteenth century had already acquired tremendous powers of production through the Industrial Revolution. And the European national states were already compound bodies of military, political, and economic elements pervaded by traditional rationalism.

DERBOLAV: You quite correctly attribute modernization to the positive relationship to rationality, something especially characteristic of European man. Continuing along these lines, I should like to hazard the opinion that rationality was already an implicit element in European antiquity and in the Middle Ages, before its characteristic use of numbers, measurements, and construction transformed it into technology, and, with its special ways of organizing, molded traditional customs.

A well-known Classicist termed the rise of the world of antiquity as the path "from mythos to logos" and described this transformation from a mythopoetic to an abstract-constructive way of thinking, as it appeared expressly in Greek philosophy. Anthropomorphic representations were progressively replaced by more rational concepts. Earth, water, fire, wind, love, and hate as constituent elements of the world were replaced by idea and phenomenon with Plato, and *eidos* and *hyle* with Aritstotle. Both thinkers introduced a teleological interpretation of the world-whole that was then adopted–including its critical sense of method–into Christian theology and the dogmatic explication of the elements of its belief.

In antiquity and the Middle Ages, the thing that prevented this rational, fundamental attitude from turning into sheer rationalism was the coherence of the Christian cosmological order, which gave all creatures, nonhuman as well as human, places and roles in that order and compelled them to remain where it put them. Still a constant trace of this rationality persisted in the exclusiveness of Christian doctrine, as the following comparison demonstrates.

In Christianity, man is committed to one God, next to whom he may have no others. On the walls of a Hindu temple, on the other hand, all indigeneous earth-deities are shown united with Christ as if all of them represented parts of the truth of salvation.

In the final analysis, the step into the modern world required fundamental supersession of the theocentric cosmological order of antiquity and Christianity, which placed man himself as the creative organ in the center of the universe. Only from the perspective of the transformation of the human position is it possible to understand the achievements of modern times: substitution of the number for the idea; of mechanics for teleology; and of laws of cause and effect, which, instead of merely clarifying the universal structure, make its movements and changes predictable, for the older, intuitively transmitted, coherent order of things. By applying the principle of causation, it becomes possible to trace a process not only to its beginning, but also to its final end. In short, knowledge allows itself to be employed. This is the point at which technology comes into being as a mechanical-constructive procedure.

Still, the building of machines or mechanical automats alone would not have led to the genesis of the chain of renewal demonstrated by modernization. In premodern times, astounding things bore witness to technical perfection in the East and West; for instance, the pyramids in Egypt, ballistically sophisticated defense weaponry in Greece, and the complicated aqueducts of ancient Rome. Only by uniting technology and industrial production, only by releasing the fundamental economical structure–that is, by a transition from a need-oriented to a market-oriented economy–could the traditional world be changed. Owing to its strict progressiveness, the technological and economic way of thinking cannot be bound to tradition and steadfast customs. Machinery turns out more quickly and efficiently things that once demanded difficult manual labor to produce. And rapid distribution methods get these products to market more easily. The structural transformation from a need-oriented to an intensive, expansive, mass-production industrial economy lifted a great burden from human shoulders and seemed to free us from the bonds of matter.

IKEDA: The modern national state may be compared with a vast, complex mechanism, composed of highly rationalized parts and motivated by the driving force of human desire –especially the energy of material demands. Consequently, this has brought the blessing of liberation from material poverty.

DERBOLAV: The necessity of the working population to relocate near production facilities had led to urbanization and the abandonment of the country. As the organizational structure of all facets of life became increasingly complex, administration was forced to rationalize. This meant expanding a bureaucracy that operated mainly–as it still does today–in accordance with the Parkinson principle: the more clerks there are on the job, the more work they have to do. On the other hand, the distribution of labor and the simultaneous differentiation of the working process soon meant professionalizing many easily learned occupations. In other words, all this led to the formation of a technical administration aristocracy, whose ways of thinking could no longer be discerned by the common man. Coeval with this, commercialization in most areas of life–including rec-reation–reached the extent where, stimulated by sophi-sticated advertisements, people began replacing natural needs with artificial ones and demanding more and more of only the best.

Dismembered from their historical origins, these modern-istic structures join to form a kind of social superstructure that, to a certain extent, can be transferred to other cultures and that appeals to needs inherent in most peoples: the need for *enlightenment* and the use of the intellect, and the desire to have more and more (pleonexy).

IKEDA: Westernization, or modernization, in areas where the traditional culture is very different from that of Europe and the West–for instance, China and Japan–generates problems that fall outside the range Western thinkers work in when analyzing their own tradition. Jung said that, confronted with a totally alien culture, the European intellectual may take one of two courses. He may reject his own tradition and attempt to assimilate with the alien culture. Or he may reject the alien culture and close himself up in the traditions of the West, to which he is accustomed by birth and breeding. Jung went on to express the opinion that European intellectuals find it difficult to sustain the effort required to walk a path between two cultures since this entails tolerating the tremendous complexities cultural differences inevitably generate. While making this point, however, Jung said that attempting to find a middle road among these complexities is one of the major tasks facing the contemporary Western intellectual.

I agree with this view. It seems to me that, allowing worldwide modernization (Westernization) to come into contact with non-Western (specifically Oriental) cultures in such a way that each adopts the worthwhile and abandons the useless from the other's approach would contribute to the evolution of a more widely accepted understanding of the universality of humanity. Do you agree that this is the course we ought to strive to follow in the future?

DERBOLAV: Advocates of modernization in all nations, Western or Eastern, can cooperate in the area of the technical, economical, and cultural superstructure. The actual difficulties arise only when the fundamental structures of a culture gain relevance in deep-rooted forms of life and demand mutual understanding.

This is where Jung is quite accurate in defining three ways

to confront this task: one can retreat fully into one's own culture or envelop oneself completely in a foreign one. But it is possible to try somehow to bear the tension between two cultures and find mediating solutions in making contact with foreign ones. The result will probably be the one you consider most recommendable: that each nation adopt the things that prove worthwhile, that support and help that nation further along, and abandon the rest. Virtually all historicocultural encounters have proceeded in this way; that is, in a slow, provisional manner that could certainly be expedited with guided planning and insight.

2. Japan as an Encouraging Experiment

IKEDA: Accommodating the scientific and technological innovations accompanying the modernization that originated in Europe inevitably involves severe problems for non-European nations, as I have implied in the preceding question. At present China, India, Iran, the nations of Southeast Asia, and the nations of Central and South America are being forced to try to harmonize conflicts arising between their non-European traditions and the need to modernize. The same kind of difficulties in the political, economic, and other fields await other developing nations of the world.

It can, however, be said, that in terms of superficial life-style, social system, and scientific technology, Japan, where the process started earlier than anywhere else in the non-Western world, has virtually completely modernized.

DERBOLAV: Quite evidently, modernization in Japan did not originate in the history of the nation, as it did in the West, and, therefore, it created a number of serious conflicts within tradition. No matter how different the cultural background of each region is, the difficulties of adapting are the same everywhere and cannot simply be done away with by using superficial methods of harmonizing. Having taken on the role of a pioneer-nation in this respect, Japan is capable of benefiting other peoples–especially those of the developing nations–through its own experience.

IKEDA: Perhaps no other non-Western nation has become so completely modernized, in some respects, as Japan. Nonetheless, the Japanese people preserve parts of their ancient traditions. We Japanese are sometimes described as living in a two-story house, the first floor of which is purely Japanese in style and the second floor of which is purely Western. We do this skillfully enough to avoid all sense of rejection or contradiction. I point to this not to emphasize the astuteness of the Japanese people, but to suggest that our national experience offers an illustration of the way in which a people can thoroughly modernize while preserving its own deeply vibrant ethnic tradition. Although, like many other countries, Japan offers many instances in which over-modernization has led to errors and contradictions, the Japanese experience is a potentially important experiment in connection with the problem of modernization and tradition.

DERBOLAV: If, as you say, within the last 100 years, your country has been modernized enough to compete easily with Western nations, it is probably due to Shintoism and Buddhism, the two most widespread religions in Japan: Shinto is oriented toward the veneration of nature, and Buddhism toward meditative self-realization. The two have created no barriers in the struggle of coming to terms with the rationality of modern times. That is why I can see nothing objectionable to your simile of Japan as a two-story house, the first being in a traditional, the second in a modern form. This complies exactly with the kind of modernization I described as a superstructure neutral toward tradition and customs.

   This superstructure cannot be made to fit all peoples and cultures; antagonisms invariably arise. I remember in Nepal encountering local scientists or managers, who, having long since assimilated the principles of rationality, in critical moments of their lives preferred to turn, not to modern technology, but to magic practices handed down from the past. I can imagine that, in Islamic countries as well, tensions may arise between the demands of the working world and religious fasting practices. Japan has been spared all this.

Indeed, an astounding capacity to adopt foreign civilization and technology has brought Japan under the unfounded suspicion of being talented only in copying. The many Nobel prizes Japanese scientists have won are evidence to the contrary; but it is true that everything the Japanese adopt is brought to a certain perfection. As an example, you will find Japanese musicians in almost every orchestra in Germany; the number of Japanese concert masters is constantly growing, and Japanese conductors are entering the ranks of the great representatives of this art in Europe. Nonetheless, at home, traditional Japanese music is still cultivated with no sense of competition between the new and the old. What is true of music no doubt applies to other cultural fields as well.

IKEDA: The nineteenth century was not the first time the Japanese have been called upon to preserve their indigenous culture while importing cultural elements from abroad. The situation was very much the same in the sixth century, when Buddhism and much of the culture of the Chinese mainland was introduced into Japan. At that time, the Japanese people combined their own distinctive native (Yamato) vocabulary with vocabulary and a writing system borrowed from Chinese. In addition, they worked to bring about a fusion of indigenous Shinto with the religions they imported from the continent. In these distant times, the traditional was preserved while the new was being adopted. The same thing can be said of modern Japanese cultural importations.

DERBOLAV: Certainly tradition is preserved in the hearts of the modern Japanese. A European invited to visit a Japanese family must first remove his shoes. After being greeted by his hosts, in kimono, he sits cross-legged on the tatami–if he is supple enough. Finally, he is catered to in the Japanese style; that is, his eyes as well as his palate are gratified by the foods presented to him. Then he begins to realize how vibrant tradition is in every moment of Japanese life. Perhaps, however, the things I mention are only consciously cultivated superficialities. Perhaps one can experience the Japanese as they really are only in a Shinto shrine or a Buddhist temple.

In my many trips to Japan, I have never had the impression that my hosts suffered from a frustrated attempt to reconcile tradition and modernization. Of course, however, there must be purists for the Japanese tradition as well as radical modernizers.

I consider the virtually complete replacement of laborers with robots in Japanese factories sometimes shown on television a sign of overmodernization. Such plants are, no doubt, more efficent than those in which human errors are constantly being committed. But they fail to awaken feelings of human familiarity and have only dubious social consequences.

Quite clearly, in coming to terms with tradition and modernization, justice must be done to both sides. Above all, in both Japan and Germany, positive relations with religion have prevented the spiritual roots of our highly complex modern world from being completely desiccated. It is difficult to say how far still-developing countries will be able to emulate the Japanese experience of successful synthesis. In any case, it will be difficult, since the cultural background of each people is different. For that reason, most probably, each nation will react to the challenges of modernization in a different way.

IKEDA: Although it may be unable to serve as a model, the Japanese success can certainly give psychological encouragement to other peoples wishing to create a better society. The Japanese process of modernization has not been free of such errors as incursions into neighboring Asian lands and oppression of our domestic poor. And today we are still plagued by serious industrial pollution of the environment. The important thing is to examine our historical mistakes coolly and to avoid repeating them. To help developing nations avoid making similar ones, we must rely on personal exchanges among peoples to disseminate the truth about prevailing conditions.

3. The Nature Tradition

IKEDA: Some of the primary goals of modernization are greater productivity, increased material wealth, and improvements in the general living standard. In the industrialized nations, these aims have to some extent been reached, but often at a tremendous cost in the loss of what I might call mankind's nature tradition.

The great forests, sources of oxygen in our atmosphere, are being ruthlessly felled in the name of development. Our rivers are being polluted. Aside from the effect loss of timber has on economic growth, the destruction of the natural environment is profoundly disturbing on the psychological level. For instance, who can restore the thousand-year-old cedar trees that once stood on the southern Japanese island of Yakushima but that have been cut down? And in many other parts of the world, the general citizenry has stood by, apparently unaware, while their forests, part of the priceless, irreplaceable treasure of nature, have been destroyed. In my opinion, the natural environment is one part of our worldwide human tradition that deserves the greatest respect and the most jealous protection in the face of the onslaughts of materialistic modernization.

I understand that Germany's Schwarzwald, or Black Forest, and the Wienerwald, or Vienna Woods, in Austria are officially protected. Do you countenance governmental controls in cases like these? How can we awake developing nations to the danger of losing their natural wealth if they blindly pursue the course of modernization without carefully gauging the effects human actions have on the environment as a whole?

DERBOLAV: In the final analysis, so-called modernization is

unimaginable without industrial civilization, which has, of course, positive and negative aspects. Thanks to it, our economic productivity has grown, material wealth has increased, and our living standard has improved. The loss of what you call "nature tradition" is one of the terrible side-effects of this development. *Nature,* from a purely economical viewpoint, indicates nothing but the means without which the purposes of production and profit-maximizing cannot be served. You consider deplorable both the felling of the thousand-year-old cedar trees on the island of Yakushima and the destruction of forests, lakes, and rivers that, as part of the natural environment, made human life richer through their beauty and conducive to human health because of their pristine purity.

It must be remembered, however, that, even in the preindustrial world, clearing of forests in Europe was in full swing, especially in the Romance countries of southern Europe where the value of wood as a construction material and a fuel was recognized very early. Where it was allowed, forests were felled. The ancient Greeks put carved reliefs of gods in certain special groves, which were spared out of reverence for these venerated objects. But, aside from cases in which inhibitions or taboos of this kind prevailed, driving economic interest motivated attitudes toward nature. Only political influence puts a stop to exploitation of nature. Consequently, I consider nature conservation a legitimate concern of the state and am personally very glad to see that Austria's Wienerwald and Germany's Schwarzwald have been spared the fate of the forests of southern Europe.

IKEDA: In the past, the beauty of mountain and valley elevated the spirit of man, liberated it from the sorrows and worries of daily life, and inspired hope and courage. Eternally flowing streams brought psychological release from the constraining patterns of social living. Profound forests filled the mind with a sense of the mystery of the source of all things and encouraged respect for all forms of life.

Though the spiritual uplift nature provided could not have

solved all social problems, it was an important psychological sustenance. By robbing much of humanity of that sustenance, modernization has contributed to the mental insecurity prevailing in modern society and, in so doing, helps stimulate both crime and reliance on such things as narcotics as escapes from that insecurity.

A good part of the man-made cultural tradition of the past has been sacrificed to modernization, too. And this urgently demands our attention; at the same time, however, the harm that has been done to nature must be reckoned with.

DERBOLAV: A stop can be put to the destructive capriciousness of forest clearing. On the other hand, it is not easy to limit the destructive side-effects of the industrial economy, which are summarized in the term *environmental pollution*. River and lake pollution by industrial wastes and the much-talked-about dying out of forests, which seems to be preceding a general impoverishing of the soil, can, at most, be decelerated with the help of certain measures like the compulsory introduction of unleaded gasoline and more rigid regulations for the disposal of industrial wastes. It cannot, however, be stopped or reversed. Not all sources of damage have as yet been recognized or discovered; and, even if they were, we would be unable to take drastic measures against them, as each infringement upon the trends of the open-market economy has undesirable social consequences. Too many restrictions with regard to environmental protection would threaten the existence of many financially weak enterprises and would inevitably increase the unemployment rate.

Everyone agrees that measures must be taken against environmental pollution, but no one is willing to accept responsibility for the pernicious econopolitical consequences of such measures. If we of the industrialized nations are in such a dilemma in this respect, developing countries will find it much more difficult to avoid endangering their natural resources in striving for modernization. They must learn from our mistakes; but, as it is, no people can be hindered from making their own mistakes or repeating those of others.

IKEDA: Ironically, though they are the ones often mentioned in connection with nature conservation, most of the currently developing nations still possess great tracts of pristine natural environment. The industrialized nations, on the other hand, long ago carried out their processes of environmental destruction. It is unfair to attempt to deprive Brazil of current opportunities for developing economically in order to save the Amazon rain forests, which are, undeniably, a great source of oxygen for the entire planet. Instead, we should devote attention to trying to discover ways to aid Brazil in developing while minimizing harm done to the rain forests. In addition, it is important to adopt a broad global view and attempt to find ways to compensate in other countries for the loss of the natural environment in places like Brazil.

4. The Family Group

IKEDA: Of the many influences modern society exerts on individual character formation, perhaps one of the most significant arises as a consequence of changes in family structure, especially prominent in the industrialized nations. Of course, the family shows no signs of disappearing; but it has greatly diminished in scope from the expanded family group of the past, in which three or more generations lived under one roof, to the so-called nuclear family of the present, which usually consists of two generations only.

This reduction in scope concerns everyone but has its most pronounced effects on children and old people. Children are deprived of the stabilizing wisdom that association with grandparents makes available. In their early years, children are incapable of understanding or appreciating fully what they derive from close acquaintance with people of greater age and infinitely greater experience. But infancy and early youth are the times when the foundations of character development are laid; and, at that stage, observing the actions and hearing the words of people nearing life's end provide material that will transcend all other knowledge and technical skill to help cultivate understanding of the significance of living and of what it means to be a human being.

DERBOLAV: Changes in the modern family have been greatly influenced by urbanization, one of the most significant consequences of the modernization process in our society. In preindustrial times, Germany's rural-agrarian substructure and even urban life were not very dissimilar from Japan's, apart from differences in crops and agricultural technology. In a rural residence, or in a city craftsman's home, the family group lived together, with the servants, in a regulated order. Downstairs was the workshop; upstairs, parents, grandparents, and servants lived in concord. Significantly, even children occupied an important place in the structure of duties and tasks. They grew up quite naturally in rural everyday life. And, even in the city, they at least saw the full spectrum of their father's trade, to which, usually, one of them would some day succeed.

IKEDA: Under such circumstances, German family life was a period of occupational training for children, who were called upon to do their part in supplying the economic needs of the group. The same system prevailed in Japan. For instance, as a child, I helped in our family business, which was cultivation of edible seaweeds.

DERBOLAV: As you may know then, this form of family group had its advantages. Of course, it had its disadvantages too. Often enough, the younger generation had to share the hard work of adults, and even mandatory schooling was often seen as an impairing disturbance in the routine of the workday. Because they grew up in a functional and more-or-less impersonal relationship to a certain extent distancing them from their parents in their development, children were valued for what they achieved, a criterion otherwise applied only to adult society.

As in Japan, so in Germany too, the social process of class changes in the age of industrialization led to a concentration of city dwellers and rural inhabitants in small, inexpensive city apartments. And this made way for the end of the family group. Out of the separation of the grandparents' generation from the generations of the parents and children grew the smaller, so-called nuclear family. This was the beginning of a new situation for social existence as a whole. But sociologists see positive aspects in this shrinking process. They point to the advantage of parents having a greater chance to direct more attention and affection to their children outside the work routine. Spoken of as the *emotionalizing of the nuclear family*, this trend is seen as a substantial gain.

Family research has clearly shown that both mother and father are significant, in different ways, to growing children. First of all, in the words of Fromm and Erikson, children need the loving affection of a mother, in order to overcome the fear of isolation and to gain a fundamental trust of the world. The father helps children in the process of leaving home and entering society. In other words, he supports them in gaining self-assurance. When both tasks are adequately fulfilled, children are less likely to be led astray in life, as is often enough the case in broken homes. But these tasks are not centered entirely on mother or father together. They can be fulfilled by either one. Unless they are fulfilled, however, sooner or later something will go wrong.

IKEDA: You are absolutely correct, and this is a very serious problem. In Japan today many fathers either lack or are unwilling to find the time to be with their children as much as they should. The children, consequently, are left virtually entirely in the care of the mothers, on whom they become so dependent that separation is difficult, sometimes even after the children have grown to adulthood. It is said that excessive dependence results from small families in which mothers have only one or two children on whom to lavish attention. Perhaps in more numerous families, children are left on their own enough to generate a sense of independence. Of course, in the older expanded family, the grandparents, too, played a part.

DERBOLAV: Yes, the emotionalizing of the nuclear family by no means necessitates the grandparents' losing their place in the household and in raising the children. Often they help by taking care of the children and even assuming the responsibilities of parents who are too occupied with their own work. Grandparents' success in these endeavors depends on experience in life and their reflections on it. Wisdom does not come automatically with old age, but requires long, deep pondering on experience. Be that as it may, children love grandparents, who manifest a forecast of what they themselves will be later in life. At the same time, from grandparents they learn to hear and observe things parents fail to show them.

IKEDA: The growing tendency for young families to live apart from grandparents means that older people are being isolated from much of society. In pursuit of wealth and comfort, men and women in the prime of life sometimes regard old people as hindrances with whom they do not want to live. For the sake of work efficiency, population concentrates in urban areas where housing is so cramped that the extended family cannot be comfortably accommodated under a single roof. Consequently, in many instances, in Japan at any rate, grandparents remain alone in the country, while children and grandchildren live far away in city apartments.

It is true that social security, annuities, and other similar programs provide old people with a certain amount of assurance of relative ease even when their offspring have moved away. But the quality of life possible under such systems is usually minimal. Furthermore, put at ease by the very existence of such a welfare system, children feel relieved of responsibility toward their elders, who must therefore live sadly and in far less than luxurious circumstances on what funds are made publicly available to them or on what savings and annuities they have themselves amassed.

Perhaps old-fashioned expanded families in East and West differed in some particulars, but I feel certain that the good effects the presence of old people in the home had on the development of children have been and are the same everywhere.

DERBOLAV: In the German family tradition, the grandmother commonly takes on the role of storyteller, whereas the grandfather is seen as the suitable guide in all kinds of hobbies.   Before they can read or write, children are introduced to the world of fairy tales by their grandmother; and, when they go for walks together, their grandfather teaches them to recognize and name plants and animals.   Or he shows them how to use tools and materials to make simple things.   As you have said, quite often grandparents are discerning counselors and sources of life's wisdom for children.   Occasionally, by means of their own piety, they can awaken dormant religious feelings in children.

All of this is impossible, however, as long as the first thing a newly married couple strives to do is to build a home apart from their parents.   Such a step might be understandable in children who have been constantly regimented by their parents.   But, in today's Germany, such regimentation is becoming rare because most growing children want to be independent as soon as they begin a training or study program.   To the great dismay of their parents, who would be more than happy to care for them if they would remain at home, at such times, children often rent a room or small apartment.

It is understandable for young couples to want their own intimate sphere, free from parental hindrance.   As soon as they have children of their own, however, and need grandfather or grandmother to babysit, these same young people are quick to see the value of older people.   As long as they live not too far away and especially if they are widowed or alone for some other reason, grandparents are frequently called on to perform such tasks as babysitting.   Frequently enough, however, in Germany, grandparents are put into sanitariums or old folk's homes, where, complaining of the aches and pains of age, they usually sadly vegetate away, like the old Japanese people left behind in the country as you mention.

I agree with you that the situations in Japan and Germany are not dissimilar and that separation from grandparents means certain disadvantages for small children.

IKEDA: Actually, as an awareness of the harm separation from grandparents can do grows stronger, many newly built houses and apartments are being planned to include rooms for the elderly. In most parts of the industrialized world, the nuclear family is now the norm. What do you think of the possibilities of returning to the older, expanded family system?

DERBOLAV: Although in both Germany and Japan a return to the old-fashioned extended family group is probably impossible, a secondary community including three generations can be created. For instance, in Germany, too, with appropriate planning, a young couple who decide to build a house can provide room for their parents and, in this way, combine separation and a partial community. A student of mine has done this very thing. Since he and his wife needed help caring for their children, they lived with his parents for a while. He later built a two-story house that would make it possible to maintain this same small community at a later time. As he said to me, "They were good enough to be our babysitters, and we'll have to take care of them later on." His approach is a way of reviving, at least partly, the three-generation family. Surely this would be far from the worst solution from the standpoint of both grandparents and children.

IKEDA: I agree. Furthermore, willingness to care for parents demonstrates a natural gratitude. Children who fail to be grateful to their parents lack a human essential. Oriental philosophy–Buddhist and Confucian alike–teaches the importance of gratitude to parents, as I am certain do Western religion and philosophy, though perhaps to different extents. Indeed, such gratitude is deeply related to the dignity of humankind.

The steady increase in numbers of nuclear families in Japan following the end of World War II has tended to weaken the bonds between man and wife and, therefore, to increase the divorce rate. Ironically, the nuclear family was preferred by many people as a way of avoiding the antagonism that so often characterized relations between bride and mother-in-law in the old-fashioned Japanese expanded family. Living apart from inlaws meant less chance for friction; and this in turn would, it was hoped, strengthen the bonds between man and wife. In actuality, however, such has not been the case. Whereas most marriages in the past were arranged, today men and women choose marital partners on the basis of affection alone. When the first fires of passion die out or when one partner becomes increasingly dissatisfied with the other, love is not enough: understanding and forebearance are essential if the marriage is to survive. In such cases, the absence of a sympathetic, understanding third party, in the form of older, more experienced parents to give counsel and advice to a much less experienced young couple can lead to either separation or divorce.

The United States has one of the world's highest divorce rates, and Japan is catching up. In the Soviet Union, too, divorce is becoming a serious problem, and in Catholic nations otherwise apparently faithful believers divorce spouses in spite of strict Church condemnation. Is a growing divorce rate a problem in Germany today? What are your opinions of divorce as such, of the relation between the nuclearization of the family and the increasing divorce rate, and of the influence divorce has on children?

DERBOLAV: In premodern times, in European countries as in Japan, marriages were commonly arranged by parents, with more emphasis given to economic than to personal considerations. Thus it was ensured that the rational was given preeminence over the emotional.

Nonetheless, even when the increased danger of divorce is taken into account, we should not simply dismiss the modern, so-called love-match marriage. Some people will always prefer to annul marriage when disappointment sets in after extinguished passion. I share your opinion that much of this could be avoided if young people had older, more experienced people–grandparents for instance–to turn to for counsel.

Still, deceptions of the emotions are not the only cause of the increasing numbers of divorces in East and West. An important causative element is longevity. People today live longer than they did a century ago. This, together with numerous educational opportunities making possible greater development, means that, as they grow older, husband and wife can grow far apart in terms of educational level and interests. In addition, today we face what is called the midlife crisis. When children of couples who married early become independent, the parents are still relatively young and feel justified in thinking about themselves and making up for what they might have missed in their first years of marriage. They may turn to other partners or may select different, more satisfying kinds of work. I recall an Austrian diplomat who, because of his travels from one embassy to another all around the world, was able to offer his family a diversified way of life. Nevertheless, his wife divorced him because she suddenly no longer wanted to "see things through her husband's eyes" and believed she could cultivate her artistic talent better alone. In instances of this kind, because traditional religious and moral values have to a great extent lost their binding power, not even the verdicts and sacramental taboos of the Church can prevent divorce.

IKEDA: But, as I have said, when married couples live in one place and parents live in some distant other place, counsel is not forthcoming; and man and wife separate, for their own reasons, with sometimes traumatic effects on children. When one parent dies, children can devote all the more love and care to the remaining parent and grow up strong and sound. But, when the selfish interests of the parents split the family, children may come to distrust not only all adults, but all human beings as well and may be irrevocably warped thereafter.

DERBOLAV: As bitter as a divorce can be for young children and as great as the suffering it brings can be, in some situations divorce offers the only reasonable solution to the problem. When a couple constantly battles and each partner wants sway over the children, a bitter end is better than endless embitterment. The separation of parents improves the atmosphere for the children, who must then decide whether they want to live with mother or father and must limit contact with the other parent to occasional visits.

IKEDA: Although I agree that divorce can reduce the scale of unhappiness for both parents and children, I insist that parents must remember that the family they have brought into being exists for the sake of more than their own interests and that, conceivably, their children are part of a generation much more valuable than the one to which they themselves belong.

5. The Community

IKEDA: In addition to the family, the community played a major part in supporting the traditional way of life in societies all over the world and was especially strong in Japan. Rice cultivation requires concerted effort, which in turn demands a strong sense of devotion to the community. In Japanese villages, extensive irrigation systems had to be prepared to water the paddy fields of all the farmers equally. Planting rice seedlings and harvesting the ripe grain are exhausting tasks the successful completion of which inevitably entails pooling of efforts. On one day everyone in the village helps farmer A plant or harvest. On the next, everyone, including, of course, farmer A, helps farmer B with his work, and so on until all the work is done. Under such circumstances, while preserving its own independence, each family must become a member of the larger community family. To strengthen the bonds holding that community together–or perhaps as an outcome of those bonds–all villagers worshiped at a single Shinto shrine or Buddhist temple and participated together in seasonal religious services and other communal events.

The sense of community prevailing in the traditional Japanese agricultural settlement expanded to include the clans of the feudal period of our history. All the people living in the domain of a given lord felt a powerful bond of devotion to his clan, which was a kind of extended family. Since the Meiji Restoration, the Japanese people have come to regard their entire nation as an even wider family group. As an illustration of the way they feel, I might mention the detailed information the mass media in Japan give whenever an aircraft accident or other disaster involving Japanese citizens occurs anywhere in the world. Of course, this is done primarily to inform relatives of the fate of their loved ones. But, in a broader, deeper sense, it reflects the concern felt for all members of the Japanese family for all their fellow family members. (Obviously, if family-like community bonds have their good aspects, they have their bad ones too, since they often limit the freedom of individuals and suppress the manifestation of original creativity.)

DERBOLAV: Since the time of Aristotle, in a number of overlapping, intermediary stages, the community–or, to use Aristotle's words, the village population–has played an important role. Problems and tasks transcending and demanding pooling of efforts–you mention the example of planting and harvesting rice, for instance–constantly arise. In such tasks, inhabitants of the community must mutually assist each other. Though it occurs in Germany to a lesser extent than in Japan, we term such help as neighborly.

But not even rural substructures remained untouched by industrialization and urbanization. As rural population increased, a growing number of local tasks had to be organized at the communal level; they could no longer be solved by improvisation on the part of individuals. Furthermore, the greater the number of difficult organizational and financing tasks that the state shifted on community administration, the more active the community bureaucratic administration became.

Today, in Germany as in Japan, the community persists as a unit only in certain instances like church functions, festivals, and so on. Above the communal administrative level in Germany is the echelon referred to as *Länder*, which are subdivided into greater administrative districts including structural elements persisting from older traditions. The Swiss educator Johann Heinrich Pestalozzi, who made parallels between rural and reigning families, has shown the extent to which, at the beginning of the nineteenth century, it was common to view the reigning prince as the principality's father and to interpret the form of government as patriarchal. Father, prince, and God stood side by side in ascending order.

IKEDA: Similar attitudes are to be found in the thought of Chinese and Japanese philosophers and religious leaders and may have been considered part of the natural order of things by all peoples of the distant past.

But modernization has mechanized many of the tasks for which people once pooled efforts. And young people today pursue liberty so ardently that they can tolerate no restrictions on their activities. The outcome of both trends is the weakening of the old traditional community bonds to the point where they now persist as no more than memories in the minds of a few and are especially tenuous in large cities. It is good that individual freedom has grown, but the loss of community bonds has generated a cold society devoid of a spirit of mutual concern and assistance.

I believe that human beings ought to demand to be free. But, since I also believe that, to preserve spiritual equilibrium and be more than merely materially wealthy, human beings must mutually assist and support each other, I think we must strive to create a new sense of community in our society, a sense that will suit our times as the traditional communal spirit suited the purely agricultural age. Assuming that you share my opinion, I should like to know what kind of community spirit you consider best suited to modern society. With special reference to Germany and other Western countries, how do you think we can generate such a sense of cummunity?

DERBOLAV: The patriarchal mentality has long since been replaced by a more functional approach, in which politicians are judged according to two criteria: suitability for the job and the image they present to the people governed. But, even in the late nineteenth century, quite a different approach prevailed. Certainly the old family-group structure echoed in the patriotic spirit that animated the Austrians throughout the nearly 70 years of the reign of Franz-Josef I and the Germans in the time of Bismarck's empire.

Nowadays we live in what you call a cold society because community bonds among citizens of the same nation, believers in the same religion, and even members of the same household are barely alive.

This development is due not only to the functionalism of the impersonal consumer trends dominant in our society, but also to the growing individualism of young people who prefer to be single personalities instead of parts of a whole.

Since the community spirit, a willingness to tolerate subordination, and a desire to be helpful all belong together, it will be difficult to reawaken the old community spirit, which, to a great extent, has been either relaxed or done away with. Not even modern administrative unions, of which there are many, can fill the gap. One can point to a secondary restitution of the community experience in such things as the groups young people and adults form to carry out certain projects. But such groups lack permanence and mutual bonds.

In addition to this, however, spontaneous, neighborly help is forthcoming in cases of unexpected mishap, catastrophe, and political crisis. In 1945, in the little city of Durnstein on the Danube, I, for example, was asked to stand guard against infringements by the Russians, who had occupied the area. I am sure that many other German citizens had similar experiences at that time.

6. Dealing with Stress

IKEDA: To round out our discussion of the effects of the collapse of traditional values, I should like to examine stress resulting from this phenomenon and problems connected with it. In Japan today, a number of conditions contribute to the generation of stress in many realms of daily life: urbanization of population and consequent depopulation of rural settlements; the formation of an impersonal, administration-dominated society; and the demands of high-speed economic growth and rapid technological innovations. Stress generated by these factors causes both psychological and physical disturbances. For instance, stress aggravates cardiac ailments, ulcers, and conceivably cancer. In addition, it causes neuroses and other pathological psychological states that are especially evident in the high ratio of depressed people and even suicides among middle-aged Japanese.

DERBOLAV: In considering the negative aspects of modernization, we must remember the ill effects that have contributed to the decline of physical and mental health. Three or four generations, depending on age group, often live together in a given population, though the burdens of each are different. Each generation differs from the others in both experience and maturity.

   In Germany, for example, the generation that reached adulthood before World War II now constitutes only a small group. Those who built the postwar economy are mostly near retirement age, though the youngest of them–for instance, young men who were inducted into the military just before the end of the war–are now in their mid-fifties. Many people now in the prime of active life and filling positions of paramount political responsibility know of World War II and the subsequent reconstruction from hearsay only.

Each of these generations had its own tasks to fulfill as well as they could and came to know the phenomenon you call stress, initially in reconstruction, then in the period of economic boom, and finally in the phase of initial indication of imminent economic crisis, with its heated competition among powerful rivals. All working peoples must withstand the progress of technological development and competitive efforts that strain every nerve.

IKEDA: The causes of neuroses, depression, and even suicide in middle-aged people–especially men–are related to place of work and to the home and to the characteristics of this age group. In the traditional Japanese system, employees are hired for life, seniority is highly important, and family-like attitudes pervade human relations at the workplace. But in recent years, this system has begun to give way gradually in favor of a system oriented toward emphasis on performance only. This stimulates a gap between older and younger employees and compels middle-aged administrative personnel to try to iron out inevitable differences.

Nor do middle-aged fathers find solace in the family since the home has ceased to be a place of ease and comforting tranquility. Divorce rates among the middle-aged are rising, and parents and children find themselves separated by a rift of misunderstanding. The insecurity and unhappiness bred in children by these circumstances lead to domestic juvenile violence and in extreme cases to patricide or matricide.

The third contributory factor to stress in middle-aged Japanese has to do with the peculiar historical experience of this age group, which has lived through periods of extraordinary upheaval and change. They spent their early youth in the time of misery brought on by Japanese militarism and World War II and their early maturity in the conditions of hunger and hardship that prevailed in the immediate postwar period. Though their efforts made possible Japan's economic recovery and speedy growth, they now find themselves in peril of being made obsolete by the dizzy pace of technological innovation. Finally, as most physicians agree, being caught between traditional values imbibed in childhood and early youth and the new value criteria of today greatly lowers such people's resistance to stress-related illness and psychosomatic disturbance.

DERBOLAV: *Stress* is a frequently used catchword for situations of utmost exertion. It must be remembered, however, that doctors do not always interpret stress as negative. Everyone needs a good measure of stress and challenge in order to realize themselves. But it should be kept within bounds.

Stress becomes understandable when its nature is clarified. Stress is nothing more than a neurological-physiological mechanism triggering a charge of energy by means of adrenaline secretions into the blood stream. In animal and primitive human life, this expresses itself in aggression, flight, or other deferring activity (sometimes in the form of depression). Stress may have both exogenic and endogenic causes: difficult work, unexpected and unavoidable occurrences, hectic business routines, imperative needs, and so on. The stress mechanism accumulates energy for later consumption and involves both tensing and relaxing reflex conditions that are inseparably bound together.

Seen from this vantage point, the negative elements of stress become clearer. Whenever stressful situations occur–and, in the modern business world, they occur in a vast array–they produce energy that, because of social taboos and other considerations, cannot be released. Stored up, this energy either seeks outlets offering minimum resistance–anger, aggression, flight, and so on–or manifests itself in psychosomatic disturbances. Everyday language contains many expressions indicative of this situation: "That makes me sick" or "That knocks me off my feet" to name only two.

Undue, extended stress leads to unbalanced exertion of the heart, the circulatory system, and the digestive system or may cause excessive irritation, aggressiveness, and depression. In the light of the already burdening complications of the everyday business-world routine, plus such social grievances as rising unemployment, the eagerness of older people to hang on to their positions, tough competition in finding jobs, and frustration caused by failure to find work, it is very difficult indeed to believe in the possibility of a magic formula to rid ourselves of the present dangers of stress.

Our only practical outlets are unyielding self-control in resisting unreasonable demands at work, efforts to relax stored-up pressure in ways that have no ill effects on the self or others, and attempts to preserve one's own self-balance.

I believe it is of the utmost importance to be alone with ourselves and to associate with ourselves in a meaningful way. Two of the many effective ways (the two are related) of achieving this are meditation, common in Japan, and autogenic training, practiced in Germany.

IKEDA: Though they may have a degree of psychological effect, in work and actual living, Zen meditation and autosuggestion are escapist and limited. There are Buddhist teachings, however, that stimulate human beings to strive to manifest what are called the Buddha and bodhisattva states of life. In these conditions, the individual experiences a powerful upsurge of wisdom and compassion that assist development and convert stress into hope and joy. It should be recalled that meditation is only one of the so-called Six Practices for Perfection (almsgiving, keeping the precepts, forbearance, assiduousness, meditation, and wisdom) that a bodhisattva must carry out for the attainment of Buddhahood. All six—not just meditation—are required for a truly fulfilled life.

CHAPTER TWO

HUMANISM IN
THE EAST AND WEST

1. Background of Western Humanism

IKEDA: In addition to the meaning of faith in man's ability to work out his own fate without the aid of supernatural beings, the word humanism is used in the, of course related, sense of the interest in and study of the Greek and Roman classics that was one of the factors leading from the medieval period into the Renaissance. Though I realize that learned men have discussed this topic countless times, perhaps my view is somewhat different from the usually expressed ones: I see a possibility that this return to the writers of classical times is a reflection of man's need to examine himself and a turn away from a remote, superhuman god.

DERBOLAV: A revealing fact about the many-sidedness of the basic idea of humanism is its appearance in the form of so-called scholarly or learned humanism, which expresses its interest in man by studying the Greek and Roman writers and by cultivating the ancient tradition they represent. This classical humanism is not a one-time phenomenon; it appeared in several forms: initially in Roman humanism, which was the introduction of leading examples of Greek thought into Latin culture. Rome's literature shows distinct signs of Greek influence; Greek philosophers were most welcome in Rome, especially in Scipio's circle; and the teachers of Roman youths were often enough *graeculi*, or well educated slaves from conquered Greece. Later came Carolingian humanism, Ottonian and Renaissance humanism, which we understand to be the break with the Middle Ages that led to the modern enlightenment. Finally, at the beginning of the nineteenth century, classical humanism or neohumanism evolved; and paideutical humanism developed in the 1920s.

IKEDA: In other words, the Greek and Roman classics have constituted the mainstream of much of European thought. The research of the Greek philosophers on universal phenomena has been an inexhaustible source of material.

DERBOLAV: The alliance of the European spirit with antiquity needs to be elucidated. Greek and Roman cultures were regional, ethnic cultures, like all others of their time, from which they differed only in creative achievements anticipating further developments. Later they gained a universal-human character, since occidental man saw reflections of himself again and again in the problems, conflicts, fates, and ideals of the classical peoples.

Pursuing their literary legacy became a favored medium of education for many generations. Cicero gave a well-founded reason for this. According to him, all prehuman life forms are either born into or grow into their essential natures. Only man is left unfinished by providence and must, therefore, complete himself through the genesis process of education and upbringing. And what could be a better way of doing this than acquiring knowledge of the Greek tradition, the form of study that appeared to be most capable of making man more human through its exemplary spiritual content? Indeed, in the Renaissance, such study was called *studia humaniora* or *studia humanitatis*.

In the framework of our earlier discussion, classical humanism represents the educational level. It shows how it is possible to uplift natural man to a spiritual level but does so in a way that simultaneously makes clear the danger that educational efforts can run aground and miss their goal. In such a case, instead of *humanitas*, or the perfected human character, the educational process would produce the kind of mere social affability called *urbanitas*. In other words, if it misses its mark, the study of man can sink into mere scholarly pedantry or a cultivated sociability finding fulfillment in flowery words and noncommittal dialogues that neglect creative action. Ambivalence in the reception of antiquity persists into our own times. Time and again, Greek and Roman culture have been interpreted as an ideal education oriented toward true humanity. Time and again, new justifications for choosing this ideal have been sought. But equally as frequently, our encounters with Greek and Roman culture have run the risk of degenerating into formalization.

IKEDA: Whether book learning is assimilated to perfect the human character or ends up mere social affability (*urbanitas*) is an important issue in all fields. In the Orient, mention is made of people who read the Confucian Analects without ever understanding their meaning. Of course their pantheons played an immense role in the lives of the ancient Greeks and Romans and figured large in all of the philosophy, literature, and art that remain from their times. But the classical deities indispensable to the Greek and Roman ways of life are always as human as we human beings–if not more intensely so–though projected on a huge scale.

In contrast, the God of medieval Christianity is the almighty, absolute creator before whom man is a frail, sin-stained creature with no hope but divine salvation. Even Jesus Christ, who was born a human being on this Earth to atone for the sins of mankind, strongly partakes of the absolute nature of his heavenly father in the medieval interpretation and is a far cry from the vulnerable, fallible gods of Greece and Rome.

But later, people like Dante, who judged the personages of classical literature in Christian terms, directed popular attention to the ancient Greek and Roman views of the world and, in doing so, reawakened the Western world to the glory of being human. When this happened, not only the gods of the classical past, but also the prophets and personages of the Old Testament and Jesus and God himself were depicted–as, for example, in Michelangelo's paintings for the Sistine Chapel–in the warmest, most full-blooded human terms. But man's favorite study is himself; consequently, the people of the Renaissance were strongly attracted to the Greek and Roman classics, in which even gods are conceived of in human terms. The tendency to measure everything by humankind extended to Christianity and gave birth to the kind of art represented by Michelangelo's frescoes of the Creation on the ceiling of the Sistine Chapel.

DERBOLAV: You have rightly emphasized the attractiveness the authors of Antiquity held for Renaissance man, delighted in the this-worldliness they affirm. You underscore the humanness of the classical pantheon and the anthropomorphic influence humanistic studies themselves exerted even on the religious ideas of their times.

But in antiquity, the world had its dark side, which often manifests itself in the Greek tragedies, where man is confronted only in extreme situations with an unpenetrable fate. In most other aspects of their culture, however, the Greeks enjoyed a thoroughly liberal relationship with the world of the gods. The established order included heroes, demons, semi-divinities, and the gods but did not disclaim man's place as a self-responsible being. The Greek gods were anything but transcendent entities. Even Homer, Virgil, and other poets portrayed them with vibrant plasticity as closely entangled in the world of human affairs.

IKEDA: The ways of life of the Greek and Roman gods were very much like life in the actual human world. The only differences are of scale and in the ability of the gods to appear among and associate with human beings.

DERBOLAV: The Christian world of the Middle Ages was something very different from the world of classical antiquity. In medieval times, transcendence and immanence, the remoteness and proximity of heaven and hell, intermingled. Christian theology struggled for a rational understanding of God in various ways and could not prevent the divine from floating away into otherworldliness. It is to the credit of Christian theology that good use was made of the struggle. In the Middle Ages, the classical approach to divinity by advancing from the lowest to more complete levels of perfection (the *via eminentiae*) proved impassable because the most sublime link in the chain was still bound to the sensible world. The opposite procedure of the *via negationis*, a systematic negation of all attempts to determine the nature of God conceptually, led, if not into a void, then at best only to an approximation growing simultaneously more distant. In this perspective, relations between man and God remained very problematical.

The search for analogues took its most acute form at the fourth Lateran synod of 1215 in the formulation that there could be no similarity between the Creator and a created being that failed to include an even larger dissimilarity between the two. This was, of course, a less than satisfactory solution. For that reason, in our own times, even the leading Protestant theologian Karl Barth replaced the *Analogia-entis* doctrine with another analogy, the *Analogia verbi*, which simply jumps over barriers: because God speaks to us (in other words, because there is divine revelation) we are able to talk to and about Him.

IKEDA: In Christian teachings, too, in addition to being a transcendent being, like the deities of Ancient Greece, God was familiar and ready to be talked to. In other words, in the lives of the ordinary people, He was believed to lend an ear to all prayers addressed to Him.

DERBOLAV: Yes. Furthermore, the problems of divine transcendence, however, were very alien to the simple medieval Christian, who experienced the reality of good and evil in much more concrete ways. Recently the difference between the medieval and the modern consciousness became very apparent to me after I read the best-selling novel *The Name of the Rose* by the excellent Italian scholar Umberto Ecco. Medieval man believed in the presence of God and Jesus Christ and that of the Devil or demons in all human things, and in the final analysis could only understand his own activity as either something supported by the divine or a fall to the satanic-diabolical principle. That is why the Church considered the sentencing and burning of heretics possessed by the Devil justifiable, although doubts were often entertained and occasionally decisions were revised.

Even Luther rejected the idea of human freedom as propounded by Erasmus of Rotterdam, because he was convinced that man's will was either directed by God or driven by the devil. Nevertheless, he did not consider himself able to see through God's–the dark-removed one's–plans and only pleaded despairingly for a "merciful God." You have rightly pointed out a certain lack of self-responsibility in this connection during the Middle Ages.

The turn to the Roman and Greek classical writers in Renaissance-humanism meant rejecting scholastic transcendence speculations, which had come to appear to be fruitless subtleties, and bondage to Christian beliefs in demons (the radical dualism of heaven and hell). You have convincingly pointed out the glorification of man in Renaissance art and quite rightly traced it back to the adoption of Greek and Roman models. Renaissance artists took their motives not only from Greek and Roman mythology, but also from the biblical tradition and, in this way, glorified Christian symbols, too, relieving them of much of their dark horror and obscurity.

IKEDA: Whereas the simple people of the Middle Ages looked on God as part of the ordinary world they understood, in orthodox Church doctrine, the scholastic theologians interpreted Him as transcendent. The Renaissance humanists, on the other hand, even within the orthodox church, envisioned God as a very real-life part of the world and depicted him boldly in murals and other forms of paintings, which are manifestations of the Renaissance tendency to regard God as human.

DERBOLAV: Now I should like to examine the further history of the adoption of humanistic ideas–mainly neohumanism of Humboldt's time and the paideutical humanism of our century. I have already spoken of the epoch-making renewal of education in Germany with Humboldt in another context. In the case of neohumanism, in contrast to the Renaissance practice, most scholars went directly to Greek culture–without resorting to Latin intermediaries–and delved even deeper than their predecessors into the soil of the human spirit. We owe thanks to neohumanism for many valuable things. The neohumanists not only gave us a translation of Plato's writings that almost converted the Greek into a German philosopher, but also imbued our language and art with their standards and allowed a humanistic spirit to flow into education and the schools.

The classical high school (*Gymnasium*) is evidence to this, as Hegel's *Schulreden*–his regular addresses to the students of the Aegidiusgymnasium in Nuremberg, where he was principal for seven years–clearly show. Hegel, whose point of departure is the relatedness of the German soul with that of the Greeks, proclaimed Greek artistic standards as absolute and their representation of an intact public life as indispensable for his own times. No one has ever spoken so intensely of the close union between the modern and the antique worlds; no one has ever so urgently recommended pupils to house themselves in these tremendous models of thought as Hegel himself did.

Goethe's *Iphigenie,* a unique example of German Classicism attesting to the close alliance between the Greek and German souls, is the drama in which graecophilia (the glorification of everything Greek) achieves its most complete expression. In addition, however, it clearly shows the point where graecophilia threatens to degenerate into graecomania, an imitation, even a servile one, of the Greeks. Indeed, classical standards and images faded relatively quickly in the following decades under the influence of utilitarianism and economism and of historicism.

IKEDA: The important thing is maintaining balance between idealism and realism. Studying the way of life and thought of the ancient Greeks ought to be done not in mere imitation divorced from reality, but for the sake of improving actual philosophy and society. Idealism that ignores the real world can cause harm. On the other hand, merely conforming to reality with no ideal for reform or ennoblement descends into selfishness and economism.

DERBOLAV: Only in the 1920s did the so-called third, or paideutic (derived from the Greek *paideia*, education) humanism try to revive Greek and Roman writings by defending them against the historical criticism that had robbed them of their exemplary character and by bringing to light their impact on history. Although paideutical humanism was only a faint echo of its great forerunners, it nonetheless provided evidence for the unextinguishable presence of humanistic thought.

All of these versions of humanism contain in themselves their own dangers. As long as they concentrate on studying man only from a literary standpoint, they could easily run aground by cultivating formal knowledge and material erudition. When this happens, humanity becomes an empty word, and the education of man an ideology that no longer cultivates the real meaning of humanity and is, therefore, liable to criticism by people persistently hostile to humanism. Educational humanism can transform itself into a false consciousness, the form and matter of which if not artificially revived, would have long since been dead and forgotten. And as we have painfully experienced many times in the course of the centuries, the moral core of humanism can very easily lose valuable substance and lead to brutality and bestiality.

2. On killing

IKEDA: Criteria of judgment of the nature and value of humanity and of life in general have many ramifications, some of which obviously exert a profound influence on the attitude human beings take to other creatures. In Europe and the West in general, the tendency has been to consider human beings valuable because they are intellectually superior to other members of the animal kingdom. This attitude pervades European thought from the time of Thales and Anaximander through that of Plato and Aristotle, to the age of the medieval Christian philosophers including Augustine and Thomas Aquinas. Stress on the importance of thought as man's most distinguishing trait is especially marked in more modern philosophers like Descartes, who, as is well known, equated thought and existence (*cogito ergo sum*), and Pascal, who described man as a thinking reed. Certainly, the philosophical achievements born of this tradition have been great.

Still, it seems to me that overemphasizing intellectuality as man's major characteristic has had some results that are less than desirable. Considering himself generally superior because of the particular mental superiority he undeniably has, Western man has tended to look down on other living creatures, whom he believes exist for him to exploit. He, therefore, has felt justified in killing them as he wishes. Even worse, human beings of high mental ability have tended to regard those of less intellectual talent or of less education and training as inferior and exploitable.

The Buddhist view is entirely different. Buddhism puts great value in life itself, no matter what its manifestation. Each creature wishes to preserve its own life, and Buddhist thought regards it as wrong to take that life. The sin of killing is intensified when the victim is aware of the dignity of life and wishes to use its own life in a valuable and creative way. Consquently, it is worse to kill another human being than it is to take the life of a nonhuman being unaware that its life is of value. Since making life valuable consists in helping others and making them better and happier, it is a grave sin to kill a benefactor. It is bad to emphasize man's brain as his most salient characteristic without paying due attention to his other aspects.

DERBOLAV: I think you are correct in contrasting Western rationalism and its tendency to see the intellect as an absolute with Buddhism's way of turning to nature and all living things. You find intellectualism already pervading Greek philosophy and name a number of its more modern advocates like Descartes and Pascal. We have already quoted Pascal's famous aphorism regarding man's extraordinary place in the cosmos. Descartes goes even further than Pascal when he lets himself be seduced by the dualism of substances and subsumes the animal world under the mechanical one. One cannot go much further in estranging the natural world by claiming superiority for man's mind. In order to characterize appropriately the paradox of his position, anthropologists who are critical of rationalism have not hesitated to call man "an animal ill in mind" and a "predatory ape grown megalomaniac because of hypertrophy of the intellect."

With such an attitude, it is clear that arrogance toward both prehuman nature and less talented humans can emerge. This is why Western man so clearly and decisively dissociated actions toward his fellow man from those toward the world of nature. The hunting and slaughtering of domestic animals accordingly are considered essential to maintaining human life and are morally separated from the killing of a fellow human being: *murder*, one of the worst crimes one can commit. Of course, legal degrees like that between manslaughter and murder are taken into consideration in sentencing. Nevertheless, in the humanistic-Christian conception, human life itself is fundamentally inviolable and holy, and the question of from whom it has been taken or by whom it has been destroyed is of only secondary significance.

IKEDA: In the Buddhist gradation, patricide and matricide are considered especially heinous and are listed among the five gravest sins. The other three are as follows. Killing an arhat, that is a person who is disciplining himself in Buddhism and is, therefore, more aware of the precious nature of his own life than ordinary people. Causing a Buddha to bleed. Since Buddhas are the most precious of all beings, no one can kill them; but wounding them and making them bleed constitute a grave sin. Finally, disrupting the harmony of the Order; that is, breaking the unity of people who exert efforts for the salvation of the world.

Although sin is committed when human beings take the lives of other creatures for food, efforts to preserve one's own life are considered good. And the good is all the greater if the life preserved is used for the sake of the happiness of other people. Such taking of life must, however, always be solely for the sake of maintaining or improving the quality of life. Killing for pleasure is unjustifiable. Furthermore, killing for self-sustenance, too, is sinful if one's own life is not put to use in a valuable way.

DERBOLAV: I have already mentioned the possibility inherent in the ecology movement for stimulating a general sense of responsibility toward nature and, especially, respect for animal life. Such an approach could become one of the leading themes of our century. Some people do advocate doing without animal foodstuffs, pointing to the strict vegetarian habits of certain aboriginal peoples living in mountains. You have taken a middle path, with which I am thoroughly in accordance. In devotion to and caring for all creatures you see a possible moral counterbalance to the killing of animals for purposes of nourishment.

But beyond that, there might be other plausible ways of compensation. In undisturbed circumstances, nature regulates the growth and decline of animal species by keeping the proportion of each at such a level that none die out altogether. Old and sick individuals are weeded out, making room for the young and strong to take their places. Excess numbers of species that reproduce too vigorously are simply eaten by other species, whereas those that reproduce slowly are given more chances to survive.

Man has brought disorder into the natural regulations with either capricious or planned interference. Perhaps we could reverse the situation. Could we not require hunters to consider themselves executors protecting the natural order by allowing to be shot only those animals that would otherwise have little chance of surviving? Could we not also oblige animal breeders, without disclaiming their right to a profession by abstaining from eating meat, to treat and care for animals in ways corresponding to conditions in their natural environment? This is possible only in a limited way, as domestic animals have long since forgotten their wild-life origins.

Such professional rules would be an objective expression of regret for previous errors and of devotion to the world of creatures. In your view, such devotion might compensate for the injustice of keeping animals as food for humans. These precepts have, without any doubt, already been recognized to an extent and are followed in the parts of the professional world not wrenched by the demands of the market.

3. Variations on Humanism

IKEDA: The humanism of the modern West–that is, the nontheistic philosophy advocating the possibility of human self-fulfillment without reliance on supernatural beings–is different from what I call the humanism of the East largely because of differences in origin. Humanism in the West came into being as a reaction against the doctrinaire suppression of freedom of thought and expression imposed by the Christian Church. In that it inspired earnest striving for objective truth and encouraged creativity in artistic, literary, and social fields, it produced much of value. The way in which humanism recognized the dignity of humanity and liberated human beings from slavery to God is laudable. But this very liberation compels human beings to face two dangers. In the first place, it stimulates the use of reason in an insatiable search for truth; and this in turn stimulates pursuit of satisfaction of material desires. The search for truth has led us to scrutinize the world of nature in isolated segments and has destroyed the respect we once felt for the vital rhythm resulting from the actions of all things. In bringing about this state of affairs, humanism has generated an environment in which traditional ethical systems have been eroded and in which not only the dignity of man, but also his continued physical existence on the planet are in jeopardy. Furthermore, this situation is so apparent that most average people as well are aware of and concerned about it.

Christianity has lost its position of ethical leadership because, while insisting that human beings have the freedom and the right to govern all creation, it has imposed doctrines that restrain the search for truth, thus inviting hostile reaction against itself and leading many people to reject its ethical teachings.

In general, in the Orient, in spite of despotic politics, a tendency to formalism and ancient superstitions, religions have not attempted to put men's minds in bondage, to postulate faiths in absolute gods, or to impose ethical codes in an authoritarian manner. At least in the spiritual realm, they have consistently centered on humanity. In other words, the foundation of Oriental civilizations has been, in this sense, humanistic. But this Oriental version of humanism has never assumed the form of a philosophical movement and has never stimulated keen awareness nor upsurges of activity.

Far from attempting to impose bondage on the human mind, Buddhism, among the Oriental religions, teaches the importance of developing profound, rationally guided wisdom to overcome greed, the source of inner human bondage, and of harmony with the great rhythm of all things. This teaching has never, however, manifested itself as a consciously humanistic philosophy.

Nonetheless, realizing the nature of Western humanism, I

feel certain that the theory and practice of this Buddhist teaching could become the basis for a new kind of humanism manifesting true human independence and dignity. With your exhaustive knowledge of Western philosophical development and your awareness of the crisis philosophy now faces, what is your opinion of the role Buddhist ideas can play in this connection?

DERBOLAV: You see Western humanism as reflecting confidence in man's capacity to master his own fate without relying on supernatural help and as a reaction to the repression of liberty of thought and speech by the Christian Church. In your portrayal, Western humanism appears to be a weltanschauung of emancipation that, in spite of all its achievements in the cultural area, has gone astray, especially by subscribing to strict analytical thinking and by disregarding traditional values and man's dignity. In this way, it has degenerated into materialism of the worst sort.

Insofar as Buddhism–in contrast to Christianity–does not regiment its own followers or find itself compelled to struggle against regimenting contenders, it lacks the emancipating element of Western humanism and the need for dogmatical precision. Nevertheless, you have called it a kind of humanism–rightly so in my opinion–because it is imbued with esteem for man's dignity and also because it upholds the idea of man's self-perfectability by cultivating inner wisdom and striving to find his place in the great rhythm of nature and the cosmos. I have difficulty in equating Western man's renunciation of Christianity to a subscription to analytical philosophy and in ascribing his surrender to materialism to the historical phenomenon of European humanism. For this reason, I prefer to describe as rationalism, positivism, secularism, or anthropocentricism the Western attitude you criticize. Aside from the incidental application of the term in such things as humanistic psychology (Erich Fromm and C. Rogers) or humanistic pragmatism (F. C. S. Schiller), humanism can stand for a number of historical representations stemming from the idea of human self-understanding, which may be implemented in good or bad ways.

The idea of humanism is neither an anthropological theory nor a definite image of man. Instead, it is a relatively simple thinking model that grew out of differences in regarding or disregarding the dignity of man and can be interpreted on three levels: philosophical-anthropological, ethical, and educational.

IKEDA: I assume that the anthropological level is the one on which human beings attempt to discover the special characteristic that makes them human and sets them apart from the other animals.

DERBOLAV: The philosophical-anthropological interpretation is attested to again and again from Aristotle to Pascal: man is the being that has *logos* (Aristotle) or that is "kept" and "had" by *logos* (as Heidegger corrects Aristotle). In other words, man is aware of having the world (*Welthaben*) and of his knowing of the world (*Weltwissen*). Therein lies his greatness and his affliction. "Man is only a reed, the weakest in nature, but he is a thinking reed. It would not be necessary for the whole world to arm itself in order to crush him: steam or a drop of water would be sufficient to kill him. But if the universe would crush him, man would be nobler than what killed him; for he knows that he is dying and comprehends the superiority of the universe over him; the universe knows nothing of this." (Pascal).

The philosophical-anthropological interpretation implies that man is capable of distinguishing between the world as merely a thing known and himself as the (spirit) knower of this known world. Being a spirit means both existing in and transcending the world, being theoretically free of the world and practically dependent on it. Transcendental self-knowledge containing the concept of spirit is invariably accompanied by the practical meaning of conscience. By simultaneously separating themselves from and rebinding themselves to it, human beings move the world from the mode of reality to the mode of unreality. For man, the world is the object of acting, planning, and responsibility in which his conscience expresses itself.

The practical interpretation involves the duality between the world as a given fact and the world as a task or obligation; in other words, between the world's it-ness and thou-ness or, in still different words, between in its object-ness and personal attachment. Viewing the spirit at the level of a mere given entity and interpreting man's self-knowledge as no more than intellectual behavior is, theoretically, the same kind of offense against human dignity as reducing thou-ness as an end in itself and a self-imposed task to objectify it-ness; that is, to a sphere of mere means to given ends.

But man is not innately responsible to himself and the world but must be guided through upbringing and education until, in terms of insight and conscience, he has reached the philosophical-anthropological and the practical dimensions. This is the third or the educational interpretation of the humanistic idea. Since the educational formation process is long, man is always on the way to higher knowledge of himself and the world and to increasingly general as well as concrete self-determination. Consequently, humanity is an enlargeable concept; and humane or inhumane educations differ from each other basically in regard to the issue of striving for and supporting enlargement or remaining neutral or actually working against it.

IKEDA: You put the matter very clearly. The different levels of human understanding of the world and of self-determination depend, as I have said, on degree of dignity. I am completely in agreement with what you say about the role of education in deepening understanding and giving concrete expression to self-determination. This was the basis of the attitude of Tsunesaburō Makiguchi, founder of our organization, toward education which he called value-creating education. *Jinsei*

Chirigaku (Geography in Terms of Humanity), one of his major written works, explains geography in connection with daily human life.

DERBOLAV: Because its structural frame is relatively formal, humanism can be both meaningfully and inconsistently implemented. I should now like to investigate some possibilities of its implementation. In the spiritual tradition of antiquity, the birthplace of humanism, it is possible to see the first implementation of what I call classical humanism. At this point, I shall confine my discussion to four other implementations of the humanistic idea that have had a major impact on German and French intellectual history and that remain influential today: the positive humanism of Ludwig Feuerbach, the existential humanism of Jean-Paul Sartre, the historical (geschichtliche) humanism of Martin Heidegger, and finally the historico-materialistic humanism of the young Karl Marx. (This list is not historically chronological.) Many of the defects and achievements you attribute to Western humanism are more easily understood in the light of these four implementations.

For instance, both positive and existential humanism accentuate renunciation of Christianity and, therefore, represent the criticism of religion that you cite as the actual origin of humanistic thought. In contrast to these two, the historico-ontological humanism of Martin Heidegger demonstrates the extent to which secularized Christianity continues in the humanistic movement. Marx's historico-materialistic humanism takes as its task the further development of Feuerbach's criticism of religion: the criticism of religion for being compelled to employ the vale of tears and woe represented by society as its own ideological illumination.

IKEDA: Society always reacts against a philosophy that sounds an alarm. Indeed, hostile reactions account for the acuteness of philosophies of this kind. In their brands of humanism,

Feuerbach and Sartre criticized society, especially Christianity, in order to expose the oppressive effects they observed the Christian faith to exert on the world around them. The same thing can be said of Marx. Martin Heidegger, on the other hand, took a more severe view of psychological distortions caused by loss of religion and the oppressive social influence of absence of religious ethics.

DERBOLAV: Feuerbach's positive humanism frees itself from the dominance of the Christian doctrine by interpreting it as a subjective projection of human miseries and as the wish for happiness in a life to come. This wish is an illusion that, once seen through, dissolves and gives way to the tangible realm of the I-Thou community on Earth. As Hegel finds the Holy Ghost in the spiritual community of Christians, so Feuerbach insists that the divine is realized in positive relationships among human beings in the sensible world. And this is where the limitations of his humanistic approach become apparent. Feuerbach confines the spirit to the empirical world and thus allows the task-character of the human being to dwindle into a mere given proposition. In other words, this approach restricts humanism's ethical dimensions and severs its actual point of distinctiveness.

Sartre's existential humanism falls into the opposite fault in that it completely separates the determination of man from natural essence and transfers it into the realm of human autonomy–to the extent that humanity is considered to be absolutely self-creating. The denial of man's essence arises from a resolute decision for atheism. From the nonexistence of God, existential humanism concludes that a being exists but without determination on the part of a supernatural will. The being is man, who exists (is thrown into the world), comes into contact with the world and with other beings, and later finds meaning for himself. As the existentialist sees him, man is undefinable because initially he is nothing. Since no God created one, there is no human species "Man." Man is nothing but what he has made of himself.

In his historico-ontological humanism, Heidegger searches for a return to the divine, which he calls Being, and attempts to achieve this by way of a critique of traditional humanism, which conceives of man solely in terms of the logos and of technology, while completely forgetting man's calling to Being. Heidegger designates his approach humanistic in a deeper meaning. According to his view, science must return to the mythic. Man must consider himself a guardian of Being and must regain his land rights, in poetic language, as the "home of Being." In other words, Heidegger's historico-ontological humanism strives to return to the primordial paradise that precedes all branches of the humanistic concept.

IKEDA: In other words, whereas the humanisms of Feuerbach and Sartre lack the educational perspective, that of Heidegger contains it in the form of the self-reforming striving to return to a primordial paradise. No doubt Heidegger employed the idea of such a paradise since it was familiar to Europeans as a Christian idea.

DERBOLAV: Historico-materialist humanism has no doubt had the greatest influence on our times. By absorbing and realizing the principle of freedom on which European philosophies have expounded, Marx developed this kind of humanism as a theory of revolutionary practice. In doing so, as I have already said, he reverted to Feuerbach and located his heavenly kingdom on this Earth in the historico-social ambience of the world of the modern capitalistic industrial economy responsible for three alienations, which I shall mention later. Marx considered himself capable of criticizing, even of vanquishing, this development to resolve the alienation, and thus "to overturn all conditions in which man appears as a degraded, enslaved, abandoned, and despicable being." This, or what he called the emancipation of humanity, is the aim of his revolutionary theory. And this point reveals how Marx's position fails to do justice to the fundamental idea of humanism. Marx politically radicalizes the educational interpretation of the humanistic principle. From his viewpoint, not education, but the salvation of mankind is at stake.

Of these interpretations of the fundamental idea of humanism, only the interpretation of Karl Marx has succeeded in capturing the political awareness of the people and acquiring power as a mass movement. The others have never expanded beyond the limits of the small circles of their creators and their followers.

Your interpretation seems to consider Marxism as the primary representative of Western humanism. In fact, however, it represents only humanism's anti-religious and materialistic aspects. Moreover, since it attempts to assist humanity to assert itself against economic materialism, it represents materialism only in a formal sense (an economic frame of reference) and not in a truly material sense (the attitude of egoism and exploitation). To introduce an analytical philosophy into the picture would require combining Marx's thought with a completely unpolitical positivism, to some extent related to Feuerbach's humanism and its presumptions on sensibility. The other three versions of humanism stand at a critical distance from Marx, who finds a typically bourgeois-alienated attitude in positivism. Marx, in short, makes of Western humanism–in your sense of the term–no more than a cipher for various systematizations of the humanistic principle–moreover, a cipher containing elements actually alien to humanism.

IKEDA: My concern is not with evaluating the merits and demerits of the variations individual philosophers have worked on different brands of humanism, but with the way average Westerners have accepted and developed humanism, how they have put it into practice, and what results such practice has produced. In spite of the differences separating the interpretations of Feuerbach, Heidegger, and so on, the general European population seems to have regarded humanism as liberation from various kinds of oppression and to have attached to it meanings useful in their own actual circumstances. For the majority, liberation has been from the oppression of Christian ethics. In other instances, it has stimulated application of the power of science to develop–and in many instances to destroy–the natural environment in the hope of relieving the oppression of poverty.

While including in its own fundamentals certain humanistic elements, Christianity has striven to exert control over human society through its system and dogma. Once it achieved this goal, it began demonstrating marked anti-humanistic aspects. This is why, in their struggle to liberate humankind, modern humanists have often leveled their attacks at the Church.

Buddhism, however, has rarely restrained human beings through either system or dogma.

4. The Angel and the Devil

IKEDA: Many non-Europeans are disappointed by the discrepancy between the words and theories and the actual practices of Western humanism. During World War II, we Japanese, for instance, suffered atomic attacks on Hiroshima and Nagasaki. The costs in noncombatant dead and wounded in the bombing of such major cities as Tokyo, Osaka, and Nagoya were virtually incalculable. After the war, the Allies tried Japanese military leaders for atrocities. The contradictions inherent in all these things inspired distrust in our people.

It is scarcely surprising that still deeper distrust is felt by all those peoples of Asia and Africa who were once subjected to the colonial rule of European nations. Other examples of the same kind of gap between Western words and practices are the black people who were shipped as slaves to the United States in conditions of inhuman harshness and the American Indians who, deprived of their heritages of land and property by the white man, were forced to work and die in mines.

As the French rule in Vietnam and then massacres carried out by Americans in that same nation indicate, the inhuman Western attitude toward non-Western peoples remains essentially the same.

Of course, I realize that my line of reasoning in this instance is broad and that inhuman treatment of others is not limited to Europeans. Furthermore, only a very small number of Europeans have been guilty of such behavior. Japanese treated Chinese, Koreans, and Southeast Asians inhumanly during World War II.

All human beings can behave cruelly. In Christian terms, this is referred to as something like the cohabitation of the angel and the devil. Buddhism explains the breadth of human behavior in terms of what are called the Ten Worlds or Life-conditions (hell, hunger, animality, anger, humanity, heaven, learning, absorption, bodhisattva, Buddhahood), all of which are inherent in each human being. At one end of the scale are the bodhisattva and Buddhahood states, characterized by compassion and the desire to make others happy. At the other end is the hell state governed by violent anger making people sacrifice others in any way, including assault or murder, to satisfy their own desires.

DERBOLAV: It can hardly be denied that humanism and Christianity have been unable to improve Western man though they have kept a tight reign on him by means of many a moral codex, some more liberal and some more rigorous than others. But this does not present a contradiction. Both humanism and Christianity fully realized man's incorrigible condition as either a godless, blind creature or a sinner. In other words, even the best humanistic-Christian education could not prevent the Christian European from relapsing into barbarism, no matter whether it manifested itself in the eruptive form of a great tempest or in revolts, insurrections, and massacres. While pointing to a number of examples of such phenomena in the Western world, you have not forgotten the atrocities the Japanese committed on foreign soil in World War II. All this evidence signifies only that man's imperfection is by no means specifically Western, but runs through all religious and cultural worlds. Thus, wherever he appears in history, man remains confronted with his own dark side, where the floodgates of evil open up to him.

IKEDA: The important thing is to realize one's potential for both good and evil and to attempt to cultivate the former while suppressing the latter. Often people assume that they are totally in the right and their adversary totally in the wrong and, therefore, believe that any of their actions, even cruel ones, are justifiable. If such people bore constantly in mind the possibility of their own evil, they would be more critical of their actions.

The first step in improvement is awareness of the truth that anyone can be evil (wrong) as well as good (right). But this is not enough, for human beings can be driven by powerful emotions and hungers to act contrary to what they know is right. It is, as I have indicated, essential to strengthen one's good and minimize one's evil. (We Buddhists believe that self-training and the application of Buddhist teachings have this effect.)

To summarize, I believe that, to achieve the goal of making man happier and better, humanistic disciplines must both recognize the good and severely examine the evil in humanity. Christ's teaching, "Do unto others as you would have them do unto you," emphasizes the possibility of good. The Confucian dictum, "Do not do to others the things you would not have them do to you," suggests the possibility of evil and the need to avoid it. Do you agree that both views are essential?

DERBOLAV: The defects you want to overcome with the help of Buddhist practices and teachings seem to be placed on two levels. First, you cite the stubborn narrow-mindedness of many people who claim to be in the right and see their partner in the wrong. People who act in this way–and there are surely just as many in the West as in the East–simply lack education, the primary benefit of which is enabling us to objectify the world and place the claims and demands of ego in relative terms. Since it cultivates critical self-estimation, education is essential for all people.

You charge the second defect especially to the account of Western humanism, which you criticize for lacking a realistic view regarding the interrelationship of good and evil, in other words for blindness to the graduated levels of self-perfection that, according to the Buddhist interpretation, lead from hell upward to Buddhahood.

IKEDA: No, I do not indicate that this viewpoint is missing in Western humanism and am fully aware of the idea of the joint existence of the angel and the devil. I merely believe that in the West the idea is elucidated in less detail than it is in Buddhism.

DERBOLAV: In the Buddhist system, all levels are contained within each one of us and can compel us to worse or better conditions. A differentiated scale of ascension to self-perfection, as the Buddhists know it, is missing in Western philosophical thought. Its lack can, with good reason, be considered a deficiency. Nevertheless, I should like to show that, in articulating the areas of experience concerning good and evil, some European philosophies, from Socrates and Aristotle to Kant, approach the structure of Buddhist doctrine.

It is said of Socrates that he brought philosophy out of the stars and down into the market place; that is, he replaced the cosmological speculations of the Pre-Socratics with a "philosophy of man". In time, this anthropological turn in European thought led to the first systematic probing of the complex subject of virtue. In our present context, I attribute two things to Socrates: first, he emphasized the necessity of constant self-examination and considered an unexamined life not worth living and, second, he compared his educational task with that of a midwife who supports the learner in his spiritual births. (Both can be seen as intimations of the idea of individual self-perfection.) But it is true Socrates interpreted learning too intellectually, as a process of moral insight and not as one of moral improvement. This is because he considered wrongdoing an error no one consciously chose. With that, moral education reduced itself to theoretical education.

Aristotle first overcame Socratic intellectualism by analyzing the origin of the bad and then distinguished various conceptions of human existence. The bad can come about because of weakness of character, as when feelings or passions overpower the conscience. (You mention this as a possible human failing.) The bad can also grow out of an asocial environment or the complete lack of discipline. It can have its origins in educational deficiencies. (The Christian idea that Satan or demons possess man's spirit was foreign to Aristotle, who would hardly have accepted it. Probably he would have seen possession as an indignant degradation of man.)

As far as his second teaching is concerned, Aristotle differentiated among the life of *pleasure*, of practical *occupation*, (politics) and of *theoretical reflection*, considering them to resemble a scale of levels at least tending toward the Buddhist order of gradation.

IKEDA: Perhaps. But, before leaving this topic, I should like to say that, though the Ten Worlds were taught in fragmentary fashion by Shakyamuni and other Indian sages who followed him, it remained for the great Chinese monk and philosopher Tientai to bring them together into a system indicating the diversity within the individual human lives and providing a criterion for self-examination. As you have pointed out, Socrates and other Western philosophers have taught things that approach this system. But the vitally important thing is to have the entire system as a mirror in which the entirety of one's life condition is reflected and as a guide for self-improvement.

5. Lord or Creation?

IKEDA: Each living entity is at once a conqueror and a debtor to other living beings since, in addition to such elements from the physical environment as water and air, the sustaining of life demands nutrition. This means that, to survive, the carnivore must kill and eat the herbivore or the weaker creature.

In connection with the environment and other forms of life, humanism may adopt one of two approaches. It may assume that human beings alone are worthy, physically and psychologically, of respect and that therefore everything else in the environment and all other creatures as well are subordinate to them—no more than means to the accomplishment of the end of sustaining human life. Humanism of this kind is self-righteous, aggressive, and violent.

Or humanism may view everything in the environment and all other living creatures as supporters of human dignity and, therefore, deserving of gratitude and compassion. Humanism of this kind is harmonious, pacific, and open.

Though both of these attitudes toward the relation between human beings and the ecological system are found everywhere, I believe differences in nuance and emphasis can be traced in the Eastern and Western views of them. How do you evaluate the European interpretation of this relation?

DERBOLAV: Inherently all of the kinds of humanism I have described define man as having lost all interest in prehuman nature because he has turned inward to himself. Though far removed from them in all other consideration, humanism in all its forms shares this anthropocentric tendency with Judaism and Christianity (according to Judeo-Christian beliefs, man is the "crown of creation"). Surely no one can approve of the arrogance of self-estimation in both these approaches to prehuman life.

IKEDA: Yes, but this very tradition is given the highest authority when the omnipotent God himself, in the first chapter of Genesis, gives humanity ruling rights over all forms of life: "God created man in his own image, in the image of God created he him; male and female created he them.

"And God blessed them, and God said unto them, 'Be fruitful and multiply, and replenish the Earth, and subdue it:

and have dominion over the fish of the sea, and over the fowl of the air, and over every living thing that moveth upon the Earth.'

"And God said, 'Behold, I have given you every herb bearing seed, which is upon the face of all the Earth, and every tree, in the which is the fruit of a tree yielding seed; to you it shall be for meat.' "

DERBOLAV: Humanism is structurally disposed to show no solidarity with the natural world, which it recognizes only as an area of things and as a means for human actions. It is true that Judaism and Christianity regard the prehuman world as part of the divine order of creation that consequently cannot be considered valueless. Nonetheless, that world is placed at the disposal of man, who has the task of subjugating it. In Christian belief, the most that can be said for nonhuman animals is that they unconsciously strive after and want to be what man already is. Of course, their strivings are in vain since such elements of natural life as plants and animals have no part in the salvation of man and, therefore, fall into an ontological second rank.

Animals play no role in the holy scriptures. In Christian legends of the Middle Ages, they are occasionally portrayed as robust, good-natured helpers of anchorites that serve them but never enter into real partnerships with them. Only Saint Francis of Assisi, who called the animals of the forest his brothers and who preached to the birds in the sky, did away with the barriers between human beings and nonhuman animals. But the Franciscan spirit was felt very little in the Christian Church. Christian moral teachings lack the normative provision to have a binding, obligatory regulating effect on man's relations to the plant and the animal world and thereby further to enhance nature's brighter side.

IKEDA: Yes, few Christians have assumed an attitude similar to that of Saint Francis. Indeed, all too often, medieval Christians identified mountains and forests as nests of evil spirits and believed superstitiously that the devil assumed the forms of such animals as the goat.

DERBOLAV: Another of its gloomier aspects, however, reveals strong human connections with the world of nature. All living things exist in a state of interdependency. The natural order seems to require each species to hunt and devour others in order to survive. As a natural species depending on the plant and animal worlds for nourishment, humanity too is part of the overall balance. But the aspects of his nature that set him apart from all other beings change his situation in two ways. Human beings *know* what they do and may interpret their meddling in the natural world either as a natural right or as trespassing. That is, they may put their acts into juridical, moral, and even theological categories. On the other hand, human beings are capable of refining their methods of intervening in nature beyond all the possibilities seen in animals' struggle for existence.

And this brings us back to the topic of modernization. In the framework of the industrial-production economy, nature is transformed from a source of nourishment into the object of human exploitation and is, therefore, completely subject to calculating economic interests. The immense chicken farms supplying us with eggs, other profit-making animal-husbandry practices, felling of forests, covering the living earth with concrete, and the destruction of the ecological foundations of our existence by means of smog and other kinds of industrial pollution are the terrible consequences of the modernization processes that, as we have already seen, have imposed themselves as economical superstructures on cultural and religious systems in both East and West.

Though these superstructures can perhaps be controlled or modified, their basic tendency to transform nature progressively cannot be halted. All attempts to stop this trend not only meet certain failure, but also return humanity to a primitive condition. This is why neither humanism nor the Christian Church discredit the achievements and benefits of the industrial age. All that they criticize is the corruption, inhumanity, and perversity they find in the system.

Humanism and the Church cannot, however, prevent these perversions from occurring because they are programed to the pace of modernity–a pace that they themselves affirm. (Indeed, doing otherwise would be to deny man the right to progress beyond himself.)

IKEDA: I do not imply that Oriental history has known no tyrants or ruthless exploiters of the environment. But it does seem to me that approaches to the environment in the East, especially in India, China, and those regions that have come under Indian and Chinese influence, have been marked by a greater sense of gratitude and compassion than has been true in the West. Do you agree with this? What is your opinion of my idea that Westerners feel less gratitude for the physical setting and fellow living creatures on whom their lives depend because they consider it sufficient to be grateful to the God they believe created all things? Do you think it is possible to respect humanity in a broader humanistic way without callously exploiting–often to the point of extinction–the other beings with whom we share this planet?

DERBOLAV: When great teachers of Buddhism, like you yourself, travel throughout the world proposing peace and understanding–just as popes in their encyclicals or other religious organizations in their peace manifestos–they do not question the validity of the whole system of modernization, but plead only for a humane way of handling it. For this you believe there are reliable guidelines in Buddhist teachings, a conviction I wish not to oppose.

With this we return to Western man's *relationship to nature*. We failed to find signs of a bioethic in Christianity and saw that European humanism, too, with its anthropocentric attitude, has neglected morally defining its relationship to prehuman nature. This is its point of departure with respect to technological planning. Admittedly this might appear to be a regrettable shortcoming, but the deficiency does not preclude the emergence of private and group morals with productive and virtuous principles. For instance, groups for animal protection have taken the initiative and have made great efforts in limiting medical experimentation on animals. Other similar organizations have regulated care of pets, to the point of having animal cemeteries built. Along with this, the mass media have stimulated interest in animal research providing the already existing positive attitude with reliable knowledge and a good foundation for understanding.

I agree that Westerners, generally speaking, act more thoughtlessly than the peoples of India, China, and Japan in terms of gratitude toward nature because of an educational lack in our background. In addition, Westerners require more blatant, negative experiences to become aware of our dependency on and obligations to nature, both of which for Buddhists are self-evident. In the countries of the East, young children are taught to develop openness and devotion to nature and the cosmos. In contrast, Christianity and humanism show signs of the blindness of routine in that they neglect the caring for our natural sources and stress man's own anxieties.

The growing ecological movement, however, is a sign that people are starting to see through and criticize this negligence. This has motivated a kind of caring and responsibility for nature, primarily among young people. Consequently I cannot rule out the assumption that a sense of responsibility toward nature–in the form of respect for the conservation of plant and animal life–could become a great ethical leading theme of the late twentieth century and could sting the public conscience as slavery did in the eighteenth century, and the inhumanity of torture and capital punishment did in the nineteenth century.

IKEDA: It is certainly a possibility. With no such conscious notions as those of love and protection for animals, peoples in the Orient have long considered it perfectly natural for human beings to coexist with nonhuman domestic creatures in one family. Europeans, it seems to me, are much more self-conscious and condescending in their view of coexistence with nonhuman animals. And as long as human beings continue to regard themselves as stronger and other animals as weaker, love and protection–even condescendingly given–are probably the best that can be expected.

6. The Six Wise Practices

IKEDA: To put total trust in human beings and their ability to work out their own fates, as a humanist does, requires definition of the optimum human condition. In the past, philosophers have often tended to lean too far in one direction in their estimates of what constitutes the essence of the best of the human condition. Some have emphasized reason to the exclusion of everything else. But surely a person who, no matter how rationally wise, lacks concern for his fellow human beings fails to set an ideal pattern. Similarly, a person who has all possible interest in the welfare of others but lacks self-control in the way he manifests his concern can become a pest instead of a blessing. This, too, is far from the ideal.

For the Buddhist, the ideal is self-cultivation, self-perfection, and ultimately the attainment of the Buddha state of total enlightenment or wisdom. As a practical training regimen for the attainment of this condition Buddhist teachings set forth what are called the Six Perfect Practices leading to enlightenment: charity, observance of moral precepts, endurance, spiritual diligence, meditation, and wisdom. In slightly expanded form, the practices entail assistance for weaker creatures (charity), self-control (observance of moral precepts), ability to withstand suffering (endurance), relentless effort for self-improvement (spiritual diligence), spiritual concentration and tranquility (meditation), and the ability to make appropriate judgments concerning all things (wisdom). Furthermore, Buddhism teaches that the attainment of perfect enlightenment is impossible if any one of these practices is neglected.

This makes very good sense. The wisest man cannot be

perfect if he is indifferent to the fate of others, since he is likely to be interested only in his own welfare. The person who ceaselessly tries to improve himself can, without the spirit of charity, sacrifice others, exert ill influences on his environment, or be unjust.

As I have said, the true humanist requires an ideal vision of human nature toward which to strive. Not solely because I am myself a Buddhist, but also because I think anyone can see the inclusiveness of the human condition that is its goal, I believe the system of the Six Perfect Practices suggests an excellent model for our emulation.

DERBOLAV: No humanism is possible or even thinkable without an optimum human image. You yourself adhere to the Buddhist ideal of self-perfection which leads to the attainment of Buddhahood: complete enlightenment or illumination and wisdom. Before final attainment can be achieved, a number of exercises and practices must be gone through. The practices you outline preserve the balance between inward turning and altruistic service, which is part of the essence of humanity.

I find many points of comparison between your remarks and the Western classical philosophy that has Socrates, Plato, and Aristotle as its sources. All three philosophers inquired into the best life, human perfection, and happiness as the greatest of all goods and all arrived at a gradation of goodnesses and virtues approaching your Six Wise Practices, even though they rather differ with regard to content.

IKEDA: As you say, Buddhism interprets existence as suffering. In addition, it considers sympathy with all suffering to be the basis of the training of the bodhisattva, in Mahayana teachings, a being who aspires to Buddhahood but delays his own attainment of it in order to save others. The practice of compassion consists of two aspects: the relief of suffering and the bestowal of pleasure. Compassion is both essential to the training of the bodhisattva and an attribute of a Buddha, who will, of course, have completed that training.

Although anyone can feel compassion for the weak, in general human beings limit their expressions of it to those closely related to them–family, relatives, friends, and loved ones–and remain indifferent to the trials of people outside their acquaintance. Indeed, it is not unusual for people to rejoice at the sufferings of people they dislike.

The bodhisattva and the Buddha, on the other hand, extend their compassion equally to all creatures and teach ways to overcome suffering, all of which they take as their own. For instance, Nichiren Daishonin said he thought of the suffering of all creatures as his own and added that the greater the hardship the greater the realm of wisdom and joy to be attained by overcoming it. He said that burning the firewood of delusion produces the compassionate flame of wisdom.

DERBOLAV: The West offers little that can be compared with your enlightenment. Medieval Christian mysticism cultivated the ideal of a vision of God (*visio beatifica Dei*), and Aristotle knew of a kind of happiness–next to practical happiness–that consists in the mind's recognizing itself. But since both presuppose a nondependent, removed divine principle that Buddhist teachings reject, neither the *visio Dei* nor the mind's recognizing itself corresponds to the Buddhist idea of illumination. As one of the most famous Catholic researchers in the field of Buddhism, Hans Waldenfels, put it, the personality of God, to which every Christian must adhere, is at best a term of limitation. This is why Buddhists practice meditation but no specific form of prayer. And the specific experience of Buddhist enlightenment remains foreign and inimitable to Westerners with their approach on philosophy and Christianity. Still many Europeans have found this nondualistic form of religion so attractive that they have converted to Buddhism.

Even if their points of departure differ, it is impossible to overlook a certain agreement between the initial steps leading to enlightenment in Buddhism and the Western gradation of good and virtues. In the East, compassionate aid and sympathy for weaker creatures take the place of *philanthropia*, as an attribute of man, which is a central prerequisite for all kinds of humanity in the West. On the basis of my own experience, it does not seem at all improbable that pity (*Mitleid*) and compassion are more elementary feelings preceding love in genesis and substance.

The Buddhist attitude presumes experiencing suffering as a characteristic of human life. Christianity, too, concerns itself with suffering but interprets the unavoidable sufferings of life as a test or trial. The Buddhist, on the other hand, regards suffering as fundamental to the human condition and as something that must be endured and overcome on the path to self-perfection as an outcome of following the teachings of the Six Wise Practices.

The most significant element in the Buddhist approach seems to be the meditative immersion leading to wisdom. Western–including Christian–ethics have no such remedy for suffering except prayer. If we exclude from consideration the mystical experiences of medieval Christianity, the virtue of meditation (as inactive immersion into the self) is foreign to Western thought. In Buddhism, on the other hand, it is a necessary requirement to the attainment of wisdom, which is understood as the capacity to make appropriate judgments on all things. The Western canon of virtues, too, is crowned with wisdom (*Sophia*). But in the Western context, the term means insight into the order of the cosmos and is distinctly separate from prudence, which is insight into the structures and conditions of practical situations.

In the West, too, self-perfection is a virtue, perhaps the most universal one conceivable. It stretches from unpretentious moderation as an element of ordinary morality to Socratic self-investigation and to the constant effort at self-cultivation that Kant considered a cardinal duty for each individual. In both Eastern and Western doctrines of virtue, since we have duties to others as well as to ourselves, no ethical system can be based entirely on self-perfection. I think that the remarkable thing is the absence of traces of hedonism in Buddhist aspirations toward self-perfection. Kant too decisively dismissed hedonism, perhaps because, for him, happiness is to be found in serving others and not in one's own self-pleasures.

In summary, I should like to stress my belief that the six Buddhist practices leading to enlightenment offer very stimulating alternatives to the ideal of humanity and Christian love and deserve to be given the most serious consideration by Western man.

CHAPTER THREE

THE ROLE OF ETHICS AND RELIGION

1. Origins of Ethics

IKEDA: Though they differ from culture to culture, most ethical systems are based in one way or another on religion. It is true that today virtually no such systems claim to be the actual word of a god; nevertheless, it is usually possible either to find religious elements in them or to see that their founders are regarded by their adherents as saints or inspired sages. This is no doubt either because determining absolute good and evil has been deemed beyond the powers of human empirical knowledge or because, in order to convince human beings to abide by them, ethical systems have required the dignity of divine institution. The codes set forth in the Koran and the Mosaic Ten Commandments are examples of how divine pronouncement has reinforced the applicability of given codes of ethics.

In the secularized modern world, however, fewer and fewer people believe in supernatural gods; and ethical codes based on divine authority are losing the power to compel. Instead of ideas about absolute good and evil, personal preference and considerations of possible profit and gain govern the ways most people behave. Indeed, it can be said that today society considers profit to be absolute good and loss to be

67

absolute evil. In a time when there is no longer a supernatural being capable of guiding human beings, where can man turn for help in respecting good and rejecting evil?

DERBOLAV: I quite agree with your statement about the interconnectedness of the origins of ethics and religion. None of the revealed religions is without an authorized moral codex like the Old Testament or the Koran; and, even in the (so-called) primitive religions, the promise of salvation is tied to the fulfillment of certain rules of conduct. Kant, the father of autonomy-ethics, too, was convinced that moral maxims acquire greater plausability for the average man in the role of divine commandments, although he did not try to legitimate them with the Christian faith. Traces of this theological context, however, can still be found in the holiness Kant attributes to a moral "shall and shall not" (*sollen*).

The argument for the divine decree of moral norms or the holy "shall and shall not" in Kant's sense finds hardly any resonance whatsoever for the average modern man, whose moral convictions are, as you have rightly underlined, utilitarian and pragmatic. The economistic way of thinking has so thoroughly moulded his disposition that not even the most insistent moral appeals can withstand it.

As a remedy against this decline, Buddhism recommends the law of cause and effect, which stands in close connection with the central Buddhist doctrine of Karma. (If I understand it correctly, Karma means the potential energy of man stemming from his own accumulated former actions and determining his momentary condition and, therefore, his future fate.) According to this, the law of cause and effect implies not only that good and evil are comprehended in a universal interconnectedness, but also that good and evil actions return in their original quality to make their perpetrator happy or unhappy. The insight into this interconnectedness compels me to accept the moral responsibility of my actions, just as insight into natural laws compels me to obey the physical order of things.

IKEDA: I think the Buddhist doctrine of cause and effect is convincing enough to be a very hopeful possibility. There are, of course, people who deny the law of cause and effect and insist that all apparent causal relations are coincidental. Certainly, in the world of phenomena, especially in the realm of consciousness, it is sometimes difficult to detect cause-and-effect relations. Good intent does not always produce good results. The wicked are often, at least superficially, richly blessed with wealth and apparent happiness. These considerations, too, cast doubt on the validity of the law of cause and effect. In spite of these objections, however, I am convinced that, in the long term and on a deeper plane than that of superficial phenomena, this Buddhist law is universally operative and that modern man can find it highly compatible. By learning the laws of nature, mankind has come to condition behavior to the natural world. By learning the law of cause and effect, mankind can develop a sense of responsibility making possible accurate judgment of good and bad. If it is overoptimistic to expect all human beings to make such an achievement, it is within the bounds of rationality to hope the majority can and does believe that this law can lead to the establishment of a new ethical code stronger and more durable than those of the past.

DERBOLAV: You of course concede that the law of cause and effect, which guarantees a balance of justice in this life, is not always confirmed by experience. Seen from an undistorted perspective, even the best intentions often do not bring success. Moreover, fortune and happiness seem unjustly distributed among mankind. In other words, human beings must believe in the validity of the law of cause and effect if it is to be upheld. Some reflections from European philosophy assist in showing how such belief can be justified.

Happiness and misfortune play a great role in the philosophical ethics of the West. Aristotle calls *eudaimonia* the greatest of all goods and describes it as a life that is equipped with all the goods necessary for the purpose of acting in the service of the welfare of the community. Aristotle realized, of course, that this well-endowed virtue, as he called it, is not found everywhere. The good man may lack the means to make full use of his virtue, or the means may be wrested from him by fate. In such cases, Aristotle denied the good man the title *makarios* (truly fortunate in an unlimited sense) but did not call him unfortunate because his virtue loses nothing of its absolute value.

Since the time of Kant, this doctrine of happiness, referred to as eudaimonism, has fallen into ill repute. For Kant, the well-intending will is the sole true good; and happiness, in the limited modern interpretation of the satisfaction of all wants and needs, is not a suitable end for human striving.

IKEDA: Yes, Kant holds that self-perfection and altruistic striving for the happiness of others are human duties. We must, however, keep the goals in proper order. If we strive solely for our own happiness, we are egotistical. If we attempt to make others perfect we will end up frustrated. I like to equate Kant's idea of self-perfection with Buddhist enlightenment and his striving for the happiness of others with the altruistic spirit of service of the bodhisattva.

DERBOLAV: That is an interesting parallel. Certainly one should serve the happiness of others. But, if one wishes to act in a moral way, one must not pursue one's own happiness only. Nonetheless, as a moral being worthy of happiness, man has the inalienable right to be happy.

In the face of this dilemma, Kant turns to a kind of rational belief. Just as a person may claim that his moral aspirations to perfection do not end with his coincidental death but persist into immortality, so, as a being with the gift of reason, that person is justified in claiming that the natural order corresponds with the order of virtue. In other words, a human being whose virtue has been proven will be granted the happiness he deserves.

According to this belief, God the Creator imparts happiness

since he guarantees correspondence between nature (as the basis of means to satisfy needs and wants) and man's moral performance. It is important to remember that this belief is by no means blind or capricious but thoroughly rational, stemming from man's justified claims to life on Earth. I feel that the Buddhist conviction of the validity of the law of cause and effect can be understood in the same light. It can be proven, not theoretically, but only in the form of belief. Still there are arguments for its plausibility.

If virtue contains its own value, as, with Socrates and Kant, we may suppose, we may conclude that it does not simply expire and fade into the cosmos, but leaves traces perceptible in and directly influencing the fate of a person in a positive way. Close association between the natural and moral orders of things need not necessarily be guaranteed by a supernatural god. A law encompassing both spheres, as the Buddhist Law does, fulfills the purpose, perhaps even better.

2. Sources of Guidance

IKEDA: Whether a human being lives according to a code of ethics imposed from without by some powerful exterior agent or, taking advantage of all available guidance, develops his own system of behavior from investigations of his inner self is a matter of tremendous importance to independence. Perhaps the greatest contribution Socrates and Plato made to philosophy–and the element in their thought that is most pertinent today–was making humanity itself the standard of interpretations of all things and seeking the ideal way for human beings to conduct themselves in the pursuit of the good and the just. In his *Before and after Socrates*, the English specialist on Greek philosophy C. M. Cornford has said that Socrates' greatest achievement was the replacement of ethical systems imposed as bonds from without with a system seeking the perfection of the inner soul. In his little known, but accurate book, *Kleine Weltgeschichte der Philosophie*, Hans

Joachim Störig says that Socrates' achievement is to be found less in his actual teachings than in his incomparable personality, which, as human as any we could find today, incarnates a teaching that, continuously operative and convincing from his time throughout history, posits an independent morality created within the individual human being.

But many of us find it difficult to acquire knowledge of the good and the just and have a much more difficult time putting such knowledge to use in our own practice of morality. We therefore require guidance. In medieval times, Christian theology evolved an ethical code to help human beings conduct themselves and compelled its adherents to abide by it. Though it may be an oversimplification, I think it is possible to view the Renaissance and the Reformation as reactions against the attempts of the Church to impose its ethical values on the people.

Buddhism focuses on accurately illuminating and teaching ways of eliminating obstacles making it difficult for human beings to know and practice the good and the just.

DERBOLAV: If I understand it correctly, in contrast to Christianity, Buddhism is moderate in that it conceives as its goal self-knowledge and wisdom to overcome the kind of magical practices for salvation inherent in primitive religions and demon cults. While presupposing rationality and virtue, in the Buddhist interpretation, self-knowledge penetrates surface layers to reach the depths of the soul and to empty it of externals.

Christianity does not share this demand for self-knowledge. Jesus Christ came, not to dissolve, but to fulfill the law of the Old Testament. He accepted the Decalogue, with its central command to fear God, but supplemented it with the commandment to love God and one's fellow man according to the principle of self-love. This ethic is heteronomous; autonomy has no place in Christian faith and practices. What conscience there is in Christianity is subject to the law, which it must obey. Whenever Christianity has made concessions by coming to terms with the idea of freedom, it has been nothing other than the humanistic rationality of the European spirit, which came to light for the first time in Socrates' demand for self-examination and self-fulfillment. (Luther's discovery of the interior voice of faith produced a second wave of influence.) The perspective of interiority that the humanistic requirement for self-investigation posits makes it necessary to found and to justify a set of reliable morals.

Interiority is, however, an ambiguous concept. As a comparative interiority (Kant), it may be placed inside the body, where it becomes a special category coinciding with privacy. Occasionally Freud's subconscious is understood in this way, as if its place were a layer in the structure of the psyche below the surface of the human intellect.

I do not wish to separate interiority sharply from rationality in the form of the so-called irrational, because it would then appear to be a mere logical opposite in what is actually a dialectical relationship. Perhaps *prerational* would be an appropriate term since genuine interiority always contains an element of rationality that emerges in the pursuit of enlightenment and gains independence to the point that it slightly forgets its own origins. This is why the path inward is easily misconstrued as a path downward, in other words as a spatial movement.

IKEDA: The Buddhist view is that man is hindered from self-knowledge by the so-called Three Poisons, or greed, anger, and folly. Buddhist teachings explain an essential level of pure life force on a deeper plane than the one contaminated by these poisons. The main goal of Buddhist training is to teach practical ways to evoke this pure life force.

I realize that a system of ethics based, as this one is, on religious faith instead of on the belief in the power of the intellect that is the foundation of Western tradition, might be objectionable to some people. But I believe that many Westerners today are coming to see that the power of the subconscious is far greater than anything possible to the human intellectual faculty alone and are, therefore, likely to find the Buddhist idea more compatible than they might have done some decades ago. Furthermore, Buddhist training realizes the importance of the intellect and makes full use of it in the application of faith in practice. The difference is that the Buddhist goal is to transcend the intellectual and reach a deeper level of reality.

The Christians have often taught mortification of the flesh as a way to goodness and its suitable reward. Some kinds of Buddhist thought have taught that both the flesh and the soul are sources of evil that must be destroyed to attain the ideal goal of Nirvana, which is interpreted by these people as total extinction. The approach, more consonant with the truth of Buddhism, however, is to view the body and the mind as neither intrinsically good nor evil but as good or evil according to the ways they are used. The person who trains himself to remove from his being greed, anger, and folly will evolve an independent ethical code enabling him to use his body and mind in an altruistic way. The person who does not may employ his physical and mental beings for self-aggrandizement at the sacrifice of others.

In brief, I believe that man requires help in the search of the just and good but that, instead of being forcefully imposed from without, this help must be evolved from within–by means of something like Buddhist faith and discipline, oriented toward self-knowledge and wisdom.

DERBOLAV: When man searches within himself in the right way, he cannot conceive of himself as being predominantly good or evil. Humanism and Christianity, on the one hand, and several forms of Buddhism, on the other, however, tend to see humanity as one or the other. The truth is that man contains a number of possibilities comprehending the entire spectrum of good and evil: from hell upward to Buddhahood. You believe that you have found initial access to an ethic of interiority in the Buddhist doctrine of the Three Poisons–greed, anger, and folly–which must be overcome if egoism is to be dispelled and our fellow men are to be seen, not as means, but as ends in themselves.

The relation between the ethics of antiquity–after the Socratic doctrine already mentioned–and your concept is very close. In his treatise on ethics, Aristotle repeatedly expresses the assumption that, in itself, morality is nothing but compensation of the self-centered passions or affections. He interprets virtues as nothing more than cathartics or pain-relievers of the passions and, in this respect, advocates moderation in place of pride and intemperance, calm in place of fear, justice in place of greed and acquisitiveness, and, finally, wisdom in place of folly. Only by first establishing limits to the emotions is it possible to open the way to self-perfection and to one's fellow beings, who, as partners and ends in themselves, pose additional demands. Even if the religious frameworks of their insights are completely different, do you not find certain analogies between East and West in this connection?

IKEDA: Yes, I do. The ethical codes that human beings have constructed since the dawning of awareness many millennia ago have much in common in all parts of the world, although the abstract conceptual systems developed by the higher religions differ greatly from East to West. The relative similarity of fundamental Buddhist and Aristotelian concepts comes about no doubt because both reflect ethical views handed down since the earliest phases of human philosophical evolution.

3. Suppressing or Sublimating the Passions

IKEDA: Medieval Christian theology seems to have taken two views of ethics. On the one hand, ethics was regarded as something bestowed through the affectionate will of an absolute deity. On the other hand, it was considered a field for abstract speculation. As I understand it, Christian thought claims that man, who is essentially prone to evil, is composed of physical and mental elements. Evil dwells in the flesh, which will be judged by God and can be saved only through

God's grace. For this reason, human beings must conquer the evil of the flesh and give their souls to God. Some people have, indeed, been so ardent in trying to abide by this injunction that they have indulged in fanatical kinds of physical abuse and self-abuse.

But, as I have already said, the ordinary desires of the flesh are not to be suppressed entirely. The more intense the attempts to dam them up, the greater is the rage with which they break forth when they find an opening. Perhaps it is possible to view the ribald stories of the Middle Ages and the vigorous bawdiness of such Renaissance writers as Boccaccio as examples of natural desires seeking an outlet.

The Roman papacy has taught that salvation is to be obtained only as a result of the grace of God and must be earned through service to the Church. This attitude later degenerated to the sale of indulgences as a way of making money and, arousing the indignation of Martin Luther, helped foment the Reformation.

Instead of teaching the evil of the flesh, Buddhism has insisted that it is evil to use one's mind or body for selfish advantage if doing so necessitates the sacrifice of others. Using one's mind and body altruistically is, of course, considered good.

Religions ought not–as Christianity seems to do–pertain fundamentally to a supernatural, other world, even though they establish and enforce ethical codes for this world. True Buddhism holds that both religious faith and ethics must exist within the human being, though on two levels: religion on the level of personal faith and ethics on the level of relations with other people.

DERBOLAV: You interpret Saint Paul's doctrine of the body and mind as one in which evil, in the Christian sense, is inherent in the body and, in spite of all human effort, can be overcome only through the grace of God. In doing so, you have come close to the true Pauline conception, which, without juxtaposing body and mind as two anthropological layers, sees in the body the still unawakened, natural man and, in the mind, man transformed in faith. Church tradition has constantly posed but never unambiguously solved the problem of whether man himself can effect this transformation–and even salvation–through his own efforts or whether both are possible only with God's grace.

In either case, however, man must strive to earn grace; and this is where the demand to destroy natural bodily desires (*Fleisches Lust* in the German version of the biblical term) has played a big part. You have rightly emphasized the many misconceptions and abuses arising from this attitude, for example, the medieval practice of self-torture and self-flagellation. As time has gone by, however, people have come to understand that such acts by no means open the gates to heaven. And this insight helps us see that it is better to keep at bay and sublimate natural passions instead of suppressing them, since suppression can cause great trouble, of the kind described in the literature of the Renaissance and of later times and seen in the main themes of psychoanalysis.

You describe Buddhism as a religion of interiority in connection with the inner self and as possessing a core of morality regulating man's relations to others. This brings us back to the ambiguous nature of the concept of interiority. By opposing moral interiority (in the Buddhist sense) to morality imposed from without, you approach a doctrine of moral self-autonomy developed in its classical form by Kant.

Very far from isolated innerness, private subconscious, or an irrational deep layer of the soul, this kind of self-autonomy removes the limitations imposed by such notions as an isolated ego shut up in a shell and indicates a general law of morality. In the case of Buddhism, it points toward the generality of a universal natural law. In these cases, interiority and generality stand in a dialectal relation to each other in the same sense as do rationality and irrationality.

In referring to its collective character, Jung made it quite clear to Freud that the subconscious must not be interpreted as private or solipsistic. As my studies have convinced me, the Buddhist doctrine of self-knowledge and wisdom has as its goal, not fixing the ego within itself, but allowing it to empty and to flow into the All. No specific terms, not even the technical ones of psychoanalysis, can adequately express this process. In connection with special psychological ideas, Buddhist interiority points in a quite different direction and in this way penetrates both the rational and irrational stages of consciousness. But this means that Buddhist meditative practices must be protected from both Christianizing and primitive psychologizing.

Buddhism contains a good measure of asceticism expressed in such things as the need to overcome the Three Poisons obstructing strivings for true interiority. As a rule, however, this asceticism does not strive to suppress human nature to the point where secondary outlets become necessary.

IKEDA: No doubt Shakyamuni Buddha's experiences with them and their frequent occurrences in the practices of many Buddhist sects lead you to refer to meditation and ascetic disciplines. After six years of severe asceticism, Shakyamuni himself abandons such practices as no more than physical and mental punishment hindering the attainment of enlightenment. The story of how the other ascetics with whom he had been training despised him as a failure for having broken off his disciplines is famous.

After he had made this decision, Shakyamuni refreshed himself physically with milk gruel provided by a maiden from a nearby village. He then entered a state of profound meditation, as a consequence of which he attained enlightenment.

As this should make clear, asceticism has no place in the teachings of Shakyamuni. Much more consonant with his spirit is the forbearance that has often been required of Buddhists to overcome persecutions encountered as they attempted to spread the teachings.

Meditation is widely practiced in many Mahayana Buddhist sects and, as I have said, was practiced by Shakyamuni Buddha himself. In the Buddhism of Nichiren Daishonin, however, the element of meditation is included in the chanting of Daimoku (the invocation of Nam-myoho-renge-kyo, the ultimate Law or true entity of life permeating all phenomena in the universe).

4. Child Education

IKEDA: Because a sense of ethical behavior affects all phases of life and must become a central part of a person's psychological makeup, training to acquire it should begin as early in childhood as possible. In the Japan of the past, moral and ethical training was conducted by parents and other family members in the home and started early, though it may have varied somewhat from place to place. After World War II, especially starting in the decade of the 1960s, it became increasingly common to entrust moral and ethical education to schools. A number of factors help account for this. First, increases in the number of two-generation, nuclear familes weakened the traditional family unity. In addition, during the period of rapid economic growth of the sixties, in many instances, both mothers and fathers worked and lacked time to give children moral education at home. Even more basic, after defeat in World War II, the old Japanese code of ethics either was or was believed to have been destroyed, leaving parents at a loss to know what kind of moral training to conduct. For a while after the war, the formerly held school courses in morality were discontinued, only to be reinstituted in elementary schools at a later time. When this happened, many families were relieved to be able to entrust this task to educational institutions. In some instances, they were even discouraged from attempting moral instruction at home since it might conflict with the line being taken at school. Perhaps it can be said that freedom from ethical instruction at home makes children more open-minded and cheerful. But, as I have indicated, ethical behavior must become a deeply ingrained part of the personality; and the training required to achieve this goal must start early. Children who lack such a background cannot overcome hardships later and, when they become adults, may be unable to control their own desires and impulses.

DERBOLAV: Originally, child education was a family matter. Training, which generally caused little friction, enabled younger generations to acquire the experience of older generations. Goethe once said, "I praise the way the Hydriotes (boat people) raise their children because, as inhabitants of islands and seafarers, they take their boys with them on board and let them crawl around. If they do their jobs, they have a share in the profits and that is why they soon take an active interest in trade, bargains, and booty and become the most capable coast-farers and seafarers in this way, as well as the cleverest merchants and the most daring pirates."

As soon as it is institutionalized—as soon as schools and the teaching profession are established—education all too rapidly forgets that schools must serve life. Mere transfer of knowledge assumes hypertrophic forms suppressing the function of morally orienting youth.

Not localized, this process is manifest in all cultural spheres, Eastern and Western, because it obeys a kind of development law whereby institutionalized life loses contact with general life to continue on its own way. And schools and educational reforms have had only moderate success in striving to return practicality to education; that is, to restore its life-preparatory role.

In part, what you say of ethical education in postwar Japan and its transferal from the home to the school complies with the situation in Germany, where training of this kind has assumed various forms. In the middle 1950s, it appeared as a kind of political education. In the 1970s, it was replaced by educational technology in the attempt to relocate lost practical relations in school life by reintroducing into teaching activities practical relations serving as self-control methods.

The shameful fall of the Weimar Republic and Hitler's establishment of a dictatorship were the first things to cast doubt on the German democratic disposition. In 1955, in a small book on *The Political Self-education of the German People,* Theodor Litt wrote that if postwar democracy was to survive, not only young people, but also adult generations required fundamental political education. But, because even in this field the imparting of knowledge and practical orientation seem to diverge, since he made that statement political education has become a central element in our curricula and a constant source of lamentation in our school-reform planning.

IKEDA: A similar tendency can be seen in Japanese history of the period following World War II. In reaction against militarism and military totalitarianism, after the war many people became ardent enthusiasts for political education. As part of this development, the communists, who bitterly criticized the situation prevailing in Japan before the war, gained force and increased their numbers among educators throughout the country. To counter growing communist influence, conservative authorities resorted to increasingly open and forceful interference in educational matters.

At the same time, aggravated competition for places in better schools in the hope of landing better jobs subjected Japanese young people to what has come to be called the entrance-examination hell. This, in turn, stimulated schools to strive ever more arduously to cram their students' heads with the knowledge needed to pass the examinations of that hell.

DERBOLAV: We too have repeatedly found it necessary to struggle with such cramming of surplus knowledge. So-called exemplary learning, one of the first methods used in the battle, entailed the reduction of the information acquired at school to fundamental structural insights that were supposed to have an outward-radiating effect and the compilation of learning-goal catalogues with the aid of which the conduct that was supposed to have been learned could be controlled. But this method attempted to produce practical-moral orientation technologically in the form of skills. This was a mistake resulting from the increasingly high reputation technology was gaining in all areas of life.

Yet, as you have correctly pointed out, if the individual is to live in a truly moral way, inculcation of practical morality must begin early in childhood and continue into school. As we know from Aristotle, who understood moral education not as doctrine, but essentially as the enlightenment of the moral experience, practical introduction into family morals plays a central role in child education. What is not first experienced in actual practice cannot later be replaced by theory.

IKEDA: Practice is, as you say, of the utmost importance. And family members are vital in assisting children to put moral ideas into practice. A Buddhist doctrine of interest in this connection is that of the so-called good friend, or a person who helps another in religious–and certainly conceivably moral–progress. These good friends may be of three kinds. The first is the instructor who imparts knowledge and theories. The second is the companion, or fellow seeker, who engages in the same kind of practice and serves as a model. The third is the protector who offers praise for good deeds and reprimands for bad ones.

From the child's viewpoint, fellow family members are probably either companions or protectors. No doubt companions are the most important in the inculcation of ethics and morality in the home.

DERBOLAV: Perhaps that is true. The situation is somewhat different, however, in the case of institutionalized education.

The central question that must be posed in any kind of institutionalized education is how to make knowledge practical or how to translate information into motivation. Though it is impossible to go into this difficult educational-scientific question here, I should like to make an observation that might have a clarifying effect.

Knowledge is not foreign to practice. But it can seem to be when information acquired at school is related only to distant historical and literary topics of the kind on which classical educational systems in the East and the West have tended to concentrate. The structure of knowledge based on rich experience opens technical and practical perspectives. Seen from still closer at hand, all actions have cognitive, technical, and practical-ethical aspects. And subsequent aspects are presupposed in the ones preceding them. For instance, driving along a freeway, I pass an automobile parked on a shoulder. At the time, the following possibilities present themselves: (1) I may pass the automobile without taking notice of it. (2) I may notice steam escaping from the radiator, diagnose the situation as a breakdown, realize that help is needed, and stop. (3) Having realized the need for help, however, because I have an urgent appointment I may drive on. (4) In keeping with the code of driver-solidarity, I may stop to help. (5) Having stopped, however, I may see that my technical capabilities are insufficient to provide the needed assistance.

In short, to render help, it is necessary (1) to diagnose the situation accurately, (2) be technically capable of helping, and (3) be willing to be of assistance. Realizing that a breakdown has taken place leads to the need to perform a technical function and the willingness to make the responsible decision to undertake it. In a similar way, education must move from knowledge to skill and, finally, to responsibility.

From this it is apparent that, in the extended view, moral education is casuistic enlightenment about the natures, technical potentials, and responsibilities associated with various concrete situations involving practical action. Consequently, it must not only remain open enough to orient norms, but also recognize situations analogous to those norms. Classroom educational objectives fulfill this function only when they are appropriately mentally assimilated.

Observations of this kind fall into the category of the science of education, which itself is subject to regulatory norms growing from the needs of society; that is, from educational responsibility, which by its nature must instill a sense of responsibility in its charges. In coming generations, moral training will be a central educational obligation. Obviously, succeeding in moral education demands a sound ethical order and atmosphere in both the school and the home. Violence in either of these places is a sure sign that this order and atmosphere have ben disturbed.

IKEDA: Regrettably, a pressing social problem in Japan today is violence among the young. Boys and girls from fourteen or fifteen to eighteen, who are physically as big and strong as–or bigger and stronger than–full-grown adults, beat or otherwise abuse their mothers at home or their teachers at school. Probably they impulsively resort to violence because, though physically developed, they are mentally and emotionally still children.

Another contributory factor is corporal punishment, which many parents favor and which many teachers consider acceptable. Although possibly effective when justified, such punishment invariably leaves profound, lasting psychological wounds. Moreover, when teachers resort to it carelessly, it does nothing but harm and can, I feel sure, play a part in inciting students to violence.

Judging from novels, motion pictures, and the news media, I assume that the same kind of violence is fairly common in the United States as well. What is the situation in Germany?

DERBOLAV: In the United States, such violence has become a commonplace repeatedly made the subject-matter of films. In Germany, too, there is plenty of violence on the school grounds, though mostly among pupils themselves. Acts of violence toward teachers and parents remain exceptional. But the more common instances of lamentable child-abuse, especially on the part of fathers, lead me to fear that, in German schools, the seeds of violence will someday grow into aggression against teachers.

5. Ethics and the Politician

IKEDA: Ethics, the study of standards of conduct and moral

judgment, affects all phases of human activity, including, of course, occupation, on which it exerts a tremendous influence. The lack of a sound code of ethics today seems especially pronounced in two vital human occupations: medicine and politics.

In the *Republic*, Plato, who taught the oneness of knowledge and virtue, established the Western ideal of the politician in the vision of the philosopher-king, depicted not merely as a man of learning and wisdom, but also as a person who knows himself, understands the meaning of justice, practices virtue in all his actions, and has cultivated a firm code of ethical behavior. In the East, the Confucian five moral virtues of humanity, righteousness, decorum, wisdom, and good faith have set an ethical standard demanding that the politician be a model of virtue for all other human beings. As both of these ancient systems suggest, politics is not merely an occupation, as it tends to be regarded in present society. It cannot be fitted into the narrow framework of an occupation, and the politician himself ought to realize this. Consequently, an ethical code stronger than the one required of ordinary people is demanded of the politician and of the doctor.

Operating through the existing power structure, the politician is in a position directly or indirectly to make the members of his society do as he says. On the other hand, he derives his income from money collected in the form of taxes from society members and is, therefore, in their employ. In other words, he is simultaneously a giver of orders demanding respect and a hired employee who must behave in an impartial, selfless fashion.

Of course, it may be asking too much to require all politicians to meet the ideal, which has probably never been fully realized. Nonetheless, I think we can require politicians to make more effort than the ordinary man and to strive to be worthy of the respect they command.

DERBOLAV: The question of professional ethics is increasingly widely discussed today. We have already seen that, in addition to imparting knowledge and meeting objectives, teaching must deal with its own kind of ethics. This applies to politics and medicine as well.

A number of other academic and nonacademic fields, including education, strategics, law, politics, the mass media, science, art, and religion, have their own areas of knowledge and ethical norm centers (regulative norms), all founded on the family and social-life practices that the newly developed praxiology attempts to systematize. Nothing new, the praxiological model traces its beginnings to Socrates, Plato, and Aristotle. Following the lead of his mentor Socrates, the young Plato attempted to establish a hierarchy among public functions and duties all producing different benefits but all requiring instruction from superior functions and duties in relation to their practical fulfillment. At the pinnacle of the hierarchy, he placed politics, the kingly art, so called because politics is considered innately regal in that it leads all other fields in the application of their benefits. (This is the context in which appears the passage on ruler-philosophers that you mentioned.)

IKEDA: Yes. And following the guidance of Socrates, he believed that philosophy (the love, *philos*, of wisdom, *sophia*) is the search for a correct understanding of such fundamental aspects of human life and action as justice, love, and goodness.

DERBOLAV: Plato considered philosophy singularly possessed of the insight to penetrate all the various cultural and professional areas that, each with its own functional logic and moral demands, converge in a republic. In addition, he believed that philosophy ensures the republic that these professions maintain the standards of their moral duties, or regulative ideas.

Politics, too, has its own regulative idea, which accords with the high rank Plato assigned to it and which is dual in nature. First, the politician is obliged to work for and maintain the welfare of the community. Second, he must establish justice among the citizens. *Justice* refers to apportioning prohibitions and responsibilities, benefits and burdens, and all mobile interests as regulated by law. In this context, a *just* apportionment is the one the public accepts. Community *welfare* means the standard of living politically guaranteed to the citizens and is expressed, not only in possessions and income, but also in the possibilities the community offers for the satisfaction of spiritual demands and desires.

IKEDA: Far from abstract, your interpretation of justice is firmly placed within society. The ancient Chinese, too, understood it in this way, as the legendary emperors Shao and Xun, who are said to have justly satisfied the people, illustrate. Referring to their legend, Nichiren Daishonin has called justice an attribute of the Buddha who, in the Buddha world, is as free of partiality as Shao and Xun were in the human world.

DERBOLAV: Of course, political ethics are not limited to community good and justice. As both Plato and Confucius urged, the politician must set a moral example embodying a special measure of the human virtues. That is why, though paid like all the others, the profession of politician is more than a profession. (The German language, incidentally, makes a delicate differentiation between the words *profession* and *vocation: Beruf, Berufung*.) If he is to fulfill the expectations placed on him, the politician must have a calling (vocation) to his position.

Clearly politicians fail to live up to this ideal, and the democratic system, with its open election campaigns, cannot guarantee unconditionally high-quality political ethics. It may be helpful further to enumerate, on the basis of the casuistic principle, various wrong kinds of politics. I would differentiate among politics of interest, power, perfidy, subversion, and corruption. No matter what commandment or humanistic code of virtue they violate, all of these wrong forms of politics proceed from offenses against either justice or community welfare.

Politics of interest violate justice by favoring one group

(usually that of the politician in question) over another. Without shrinking from infringing laws, power politics use such inhumane means as suppression, arrest, torture, and murder in securing dominance. Politics of perfidy defame and denounce opponents by employing morals as tactical means. Politics of subversion try to undermine existing regimes through subversive activities and revolutionary force applied to gain power for the creation of what is considered a better regime. Finally, politics of corruption oppose egoistic desires to the interests of the community.

Politicians employing political tactics of these kinds neglect their duties as a consequence of partiality and bribery and take advantage of the opportunities open only to them to acquire wealth, power, and prestige in ways contrary to what justice demands.

Of all these vices–if they may be so termed–politics of corruption enjoys the worst reputation as an expression of depravity. Politics of interest and power are more tolerated as long as they do not violate existing legal regulations and moral convictions too blatantly. Politics of perfidy reach their limits when people in power who use them lose credibility and, with it, their political credit, as a consequence of having their mendacity exposed. Politics of subversion are resisted assiduously by the existing, legitimate power but may gain recognition if they become capable of establishing a new order.

None of these abuses can be completely eliminated, on account of substantially increased chances of seducing power holders and because rigorous competition for power makes any and all means of eliminating opponents seem acceptable.

IKEDA: Sadly, as you point out, even in democratic systems, in which the populace selects the people who will exercise power, instead of approaching the ideal, politicians seem to move steadily away from it. The reason for this may be either a general lack of interest in ethics as such or a preponderance of interest, less in people who make high-sounding ethical pronouncements than in those who promise to serve the interests of the electorate.

It is desirable that all of modern society be made more aware of the importance of ethics. But how are we to bring such awareness about? The problem is difficult since it involves the innermost mind not of one or two people but of the majority of the members of society and since, transcending knowledge and logic, it delves into the deeper, subconscious levels of man's mind. In my opinion, religious movements have the key to the issue.

DERBOLAV: I see cultivating people to the point where the majority of the population can be expected to maintain a high level of political ethics as the special function of political education in schools. Once again, the kind of education needed is casuistic in that it must elucidate each specific field of endeavor and its problems, reveal the technical capacities demanded by each, and then explain the responsibilities participation in such a field entails. In this way, fields of practical action (praxiological fields) reveal themselves as frameworks that can be divided into substructures.

I should like to use economic policies to demonstrate the catalogue of political duties and responsibilities. Many aspects of the realm of economics can be politically instrumentalized: the labor market, wages, taxation, finance, currency, production, sales, and so on. All of them concern relatively limited, nonetheless interconnected, functions that can be elucidated in technical and practical ways.

Two levels may be distinguished in the path political education should take: (1) training politicians responsible for decisions and action and (2) providing each citizen with elementary instruction leading to a survey of the nature of the entire field of politics, thereby qualifying citizens to participate in political activities only by carefully observing and criticizing. (Actually most ordinary citizens are unlikely to have a chance to go any further than this.)

IKEDA: As you say, to participate, even by observing and criticizing, in politics, ordinary citizens require considerable elementary instruction. In this connection, as long as it is truly free of partisan motivation, German political education deserves praise.

DERBOLAV: In connection with the contribution of religion to political ethics, I feel a distinction must be made between what is within and what is outside the boundaries of possibility. I think it is impossible to interpret–as the great educationalist Friedrich Wilhelm Forster strove to do–politics as "organized brotherly love." Nor can politics be understood as a deliberate application of compassion. Nonetheless, with their canons of virtue, religions could restrain politicians from offending basic social norms; that is from murder, fraud, lying, and violating rights of ownership.

In addition, religion can help contain within bounds such unpleasant passions as acquisitiveness and lust for power and fame. Furthermore, as you point out, since they stem from the human spiritual nucleus, which transcends the profane conscience, religions can influence basic views of the world.

6. Ethics and the Doctor

IKEDA: From ancient times, in the East and the West alike, a strict ethical code has been prescribed for the field of medicine, which necessitates investigations of highly private matters. The Hippocratic oath, the basis of much of Western medical ethics, is reflected in the Nightingale Pledge (1894) and the Helsinki Declaration (1964) of the World Doctors' Association. In many sutras, Shakyamuni Buddha comments on basic medical ethics that, based fundamentally on the spirit of compassion, later set the standard in the Orient, especially as the Buddhist faith itself spread. The Confucian principle of humanity, too, has exerted a great influence. (Indeed, healing has been called a human art.) Both compassion and humanity continue to be models for medical ethics.

But today, astonishingly rapid developments in medical knowledge and techniques–far beyond anything conceivable in the times of Hippocrates or the Buddha–create many dilemmas not only for men of medicine and their patients, but also for specialists in the fields of law and religion.

Setting aside those religions whose dogmas reject medical therapy or who exert negative influences on development and progress in medical science, I feel that religion has an important role to play in connection with the work of doctors. As it progresses and develops, medical theory often tends to forget the human element. Nonetheless, doctors must always remember that their patients are individual human beings, and that religion can be helpful in cultivating in them the spirit of encouraging care that is important to people who are ill.

DERBOLAV: The Hippocratic oath and the responsibilities it implies established the principal orientation of the ethics of the medical world at an early time. The Buddha and Confucius contributed to the interpretation of the doctor's obligations, but Christian ethics have disregarded the connection between Jesus' preaching and his healing of the sick and, therefore, have evolved no rules or prescriptions in this field. This is true, even though Luke, author of one of the Gospels, was himself a doctor.

The early development of professional medical ethics is probably related not only to its pain-relieving functions, but also to the dilemmas–in your words–that medicine has had to face. In dealing with such dilemmas, in which each case must be thoroughly elucidated in relation to the nature of *what* is going on and with *if* and *how* something can be done about it, the casuistic method is indispensable. Even medical knowledge is unable to answer such questions clearly. If it could, there would be no dilemmas. Moreover, interconnections between the medical profession and such other professional areas as the law necessitate the consideration of the consequences and side- effects a doctor's actions may have.

(A) Euthanasia

IKEDA: Euthanasia was formerly mainly the positive act of terminating life to put an end to suffering. Recently, however, the issue has been complicated by negative considerations of whether to prolong or curtail life-supporting therapy. In addition, decisions on such matters must take into consideration both the belief that human beings ought to have the right to die in a dignified manner and the testaments that some people make expressing a wish that their own lives be terminated under certain hopeless circumstances.

DERBOLAV: Certainly every person has the right to death; that is, to die with dignity. Unfortunately, the variety and malevolence of human diseases and suffering considerably limit the possibility of a dignified death. For instance, if one accepts suicide, as did the philosophers of antiquity, at least from Aristotle to the Stoics, it is illogical to dismiss euthanasia as immoral. The Christian Church, on the other hand, has forbidden suicide and, therefore, in the light of the holiness and inviolability of human life, condemns active support of euthanasia.

This attitude is not, however, applied to passive euthanasia. To the extent to which I am familiar with their practices, as a rule, our doctors–quite a few of whom are pious Christians–are willing to comply with a patient's wish to terminate life-supporting medication or therapy when there is no real chance of returning to normal life. Whenever continuation of life means continuation of suffering, out of "Christian love"–or out of "compassion" if I were a Buddhist–I should consent to passive euthanasia.

IKEDA: It seems that many Japanese doctors too regularly carry out passive euthanasia as a way of ending suffering. Undeniably, prolongation of a life that is no more than pain violates human dignity.

The important thing is to enable the terminally ill to have a good death physically and psychologically. Passive euthanasia represents effort to eliminate suffering. I believe that, instead of resorting to terminating life, it would be better to devote attention to such ways of easing physical suffering as developing the so-called pain clinics.

In the face of the uncertainty of death, spiritual and existential suffering surging upward from the profoundest depths of life itself, aggravate physical suffering. At such times, acts of human love and compassion performed by family, loved ones, and medical personnel, too, can be extremely effective.

Moreover, a religious understanding of the nature of life and death can do a great deal to help overcome fear. In brief, developments in medical science, the compassion of people nearby, and a religious understanding of life and death can work together to make possible an end fully consonant with the dignity of life.

(B) Helping the patient face death

IKEDA: Doctors need to know how to help incurable patients wait for and confront death. How can the physician aid the patient in facing each of the five stages–denial, anger, bargaining, depression, and acceptance–into which the American psychologist Elisabeth Kübler-Ross divides the death-facing ordeal?

DERBOLAV: The answer to this question is not simple. People rooted in religion have a right to know their fate so that they may assimilate it in the light of their faith. And even such people must, no doubt, undergo the different stages of coming to terms with death that Elisabeth Kübler-Ross describes, although they may be able to reconcile themselves better than people who have no religious beliefs.

Nonetheless, a physician's frankness may seem unsuitable to people who cling to life with all their hearts and have not yet reflected on their own deaths. I endorse the view of Doctor Bernardi, a character in a play by the doctor-poet Arthur Schnitzler. Bernardi refuses to allow a young female patient, battling, in a state of euphoria, with fatal illness, to be given the last sacraments by a priest because he knows that to allow it would reveal to her the imminence of her death. I believe it is both humane and compassionate to allow such patients to have their illusions and not compel them to face tasks that are humanly impossible. Forcing them to confront it would only make death all the more difficult to bear.

IKEDA: I agree. As you say, people with religious or philosophical convictions on the matter are better able to confront death. For instance, there are many instances in which their faith has enabled Buddhists to recover from the immediate shock of the knowledge of imminent death and then to discover the meaning of their own demise and, further intensifying their own views of life and its opposite, accept death, not as suffering, but in a sense of satisfaction and fulfillment at having lived in a creative way. This is called having proper thoughts at the time of death (rinjū-shōnen in Japanese).

But, as you say, it is better to care silently and warmly for those who are unprepared to accept their own death. When the time of acceptance comes, all assistance must be afforded to assist them in conquering their dread.

(C) Abortion

IKEDA: Should the fetus be regarded as a complete human individual or is it only a part of the mother's body to a certain stage? Today at four months' pregnancy it is possible to perform amniocentesis to determine genetic defects in the embryo. Some day it will become possible to investigate fetal deoxyribonucleic acid (DNA) to make still further genetic analyses. The physician is in the dilemma of having to decide whether an abortion should be performed when evidence is found of hereditary defect.

DERBOLAV: This is actually a double question: (1) should abortions be permitted under normal circumstances? and (2) should abortions of fetuses with hereditary disorders be permitted? Without reservation, I answer yes to the second question because hereditarily defective offspring can hardly lead lives of human dignity. In Germany, in most cases, pregnant women with grave illnesses threatening the integrity of the fetus–for instance, German measles–are advised not to have the child.

As a Christian, I must answer no to the first question. I realize that my view runs counter to the juridical position of Paragraph 218 of the German Federal Republic's criminal code, which permits abortions for families in social need on the grounds that it is more humane not to bring into the world a child who, owing to material conditions, cannot be guaranteed an intact, fairly happy childhood and youth.

The argument expressed in this code is inconclusive. Indeed unfortunate social environments can stimulate young people to a productiveness far beyond their status in life. The case is similar in families afflicted with pathological conditions. As is often cited, from the eugenic standpoint, Beethoven should never have been allowed to be born: his father was an alcoholic, and his mother suffered a number of serious miscarriages. The loss the Western and Eastern cultural worlds would have suffered if he had not been born is difficult to imagine.

IKEDA: In general, I am opposed to abortions. But, when there is evidence of grave hereditary abnormality in the fetus, thorough explanations of it should be made; and, after they have been fully informed, the parents should be allowed to decide for themselves.

In the case of economic straits as grounds for abortion, I agree with you. Once again, fundamentally, parents must decide. But, before they do so, they should be instructed in the possibility of raising children with affection and love even under less-than-affluent conditions. Your example of Beethoven is an excellent one.

CHAPTER FOUR

BUDDHISM
AND CHRISTIANITY

1. Similarities

IKEDA: In my opinion, one important similarity between Buddhism and Christianity lies in the ultimate goals of the two religions. Buddhism strives for the attainment of the state called Buddhahood; Christianity is oriented toward admission into paradise. In other words, both religions concern themselves with indestructible, postmortem happiness. Assigning the ideal to an existence after death, where it is hoped eternal happiness will be found, arises from the awareness of the ephemeral nature of all happiness enjoyed in the actual world and the knowledge that all prosperity and good fortune built up now must end with death.

Pre-Christian and pre-Buddhist religions usually assumed that the postmortem good fortune of the dead could be ensured by human agents. For instance, some people believed that descendants ensured the bliss of the departed by regularly conducting memorial ceremonies of one kind or another in their names. Others felt that preservation of the corpse by such means as mummification guaranteed the happiness of the spirit of the dead. Both Christianity and Buddhism, however, introduced the idea that postmortem happiness depends not on the treatment of the remains or on ceremonies performed by descendants, but on the kinds of lives individual human beings live in this world. In other words, both religions put responsibility for happiness or suffering after life on the individual and his behavior during life.

As a consequence, the quality of life came to be judged on the transcendent plane of good and evil instead of on that of subjective criteria like pleasure. It was no longer the life of material blessing, high social position, and physical delight that was considered excellent. Instead, the life lived in accordance with either God's Law or the Buddhist Law, depending on the faith of the evaluator, was held up as exemplary. Buddhism and Christianity are considered higher religions precisely because they transcend concerns with material and social desires and lead to the fulfillment of spiritual needs.

The Japanese historical experience reinforces my conviction of a major similarity in the goals of Christianity and Buddhism. For instance, when such sixteenth-century foreigners as the Jesuit missionary Francis Xavier came to Japan and observed the ways of living and thinking of Japanese Buddhists they thought they were dealing with adherents of a variant version of Christianity. For their part, the Japanese sensed little that was intolerably alien in the Christianity preached by these early missionaries. It was solely political considerations and the fear of intervention by foreign powers, not the teachings themselves, that inspired the Japanese government later to forbid Christianity, to restrict all contacts with the Western world to a small enclave in Nagasaki harbor, and otherwise to pursue a policy of thoroughgoing isolation. When this happened, most former Christian converts either became Buddhists again or hid themselves from the world. Some inhabitants of a part of the island of Kyushu openly persisted in the Christian faith until ultimately it was necessary to fight fierce battles over the issue.

Interestingly, a kind of kindred spirit made it possible for Christians in concealment to camouflage statues of the Virgin and Child under the guise of the Buddhist bodhisattva Guanyin (Kannon in Japanese). Some of these images have been handed down from generation to generation for centuries.

Although the conflict might seem to be one between Buddhism and Christianity, in fact it was one between the Christian desire to obey only God and the government of the Tokugawa shogunate. There are virtually no instances in which Buddhists have fought bloody battles over doctrinal differences or used force to oppress believers of other religions.

I should like to hear your interpretation of the similarities between Christianity and Buddhism and the role you think their shared traits have played in elevating the human spirit.

DERBOLAV: A dialogue of this kind must begin with comparisons of the different religious systems, marking both similarities and differences and permitting limited criticism. Only if the participants move from criticism to self-criticism–with no missionizing intentions–can the dialogue be fruitful and result in bonds linking both sides. Only under such conditions can we find answers to those practical questions of a religious life-orientation that are prerequisite to the ecumenical attitude.

In spite of their ethical, liturgical, and dogmatic differences, the higher religions have many common features setting them apart from primitive religions. All religions, including the primitive ones, may be understood as ways to salvation. They differ among themselves solely in interpretations of the meaning of salvation, the ways leading to it, and the place where it is to be realized. Salvation is the opposite of the finiteness and suffering of this world. In short, it is the attainment of infinity and liberation from suffering. Believers in primitive religions trace the misery of this world to human dependence on spirits and demons whose sufferance and assistance they attempt to win by means of offerings. Similarly, as you have commented, they make offerings and perform ceremonies for the sake of the happiness and salvation of the dead.

Man takes the step to the higher religions when he believes he can attain happiness in this life and after death mainly by living an ordered life oriented toward goodness–or to use Kant's term, by following a moral course of living (*moralischer Lebenslauf*).

The question of whether man may find salvation as personal happiness in this life or may only hope for it in the form of postmortem happiness delineates the higher religions from each other. All these higher religions assume that salvation or damnation after death depends on the extent to which the individual human being has abided by or transgressed certain standards. This is believed to be especially the case when whatever divine principle the religion honors is assumed to be the standard-setter. If I understand correctly, the Buddhist believes it possible to shape earthly happiness within the bounds of the individual's karma.

In addition to this substantial center of faith in salvation, the higher religions have a number of other common features defining their inner dispositions and outer forms and making them all comparable. As has often been said, all of them have something like a moral codex. All of them have liturgical and cultural rules regulating deportment by means of articles of faith. All of them expand their practice of faith into some kind of precepts that usually contain anthropological, ontological, and theologico-cosmological convictions.

These basic requirements have consequences for all of the religions. First, is the need to establish a community of the faithful–that is, to create a church. Of course, the process of creating a church may operate on the sociopolitical structure in diverse ways.

It can remain flexible and tolerant, as in the case of Buddhism, which Karl Jaspers called the only religion that has never experienced autos-da-fe, crusades, or witch hunts. It can, however, as is especially true in the case of the Roman Catholic Church, assume a legitimate and sharply articulated organization with institutionalized salvation practices, strict admission rules, and sanctions against violations of faith.

Since such extensively ecclesiastically institutionalized religions are seldom able to usurp political power entirely or for long periods (and when they do so, theocracies result), there is always a variety of other sects, or bodies of believers, claiming to have found their own cultic and dogmatic ways to salvation and, perforce, more or less sharply contrasting with their competitors.

The formation of a community of believers gives rise to authority in matters of faith. Prerequisite to the assurance of the unity and compactness of the life and teachings of faith, such authority is essential to the ordering and regimentation of the life-rituals of members of the body of believers. It is also essential, however, to the formulation, sanctioning, and canonizing of the faith's traditions, which comprise utterances, warnings, and prophecies of the founder collected and annotated by his disciples and other believers. In the process of formulation, these traditions are homogenized, purified of corrupt elements, and made binding as the true teachings of the Master.

At a relatively early stage, the Christian Church revised wildly proliferating reports of the life and death of Jesus. Authentic material was separated from apocryphal material; and what remained became the four Gospels, the Acts of the Apostles, the Epistles, and the apocalypse of Saint John. The other higher religions have followed a similar process—the Jews with the Old Testament, the Muslims with the Koran, and the Buddhists with the doctrinal traditions of the Buddha's disciples. In short, all of them produced a tradition of belief by canonizing and further developing their articles of faith.

IKEDA: The compilation of the Buddhist scriptures was largely accomplished on four occasions spread over four centuries after the death of Shakyamuni Buddha. The First Council, attended by about 500 disciples, took place in the year of the Buddha's death, in a place called the Cave of the Seven Leaves near Rajagriha, in the Kingdom of Magadha. Seven hundred monks attended the Second Council, held in Vaisali about a century later. By the time of the Third Council, held 100 years later at Pataliputra, the three sections (or baskets as they are called) of the canon–the sutras (or teachings), the *vinaya* (or precepts), and the *abhidharma* (or commentaries)–are said to have been complete. A Fourth Council is said to have been held under the patronage of King Kanishka, in Kashmir, yet another century later.

The first two councils stressed the importance of the precepts, indicating concern with the maintenance of the Order and with setting standards for monastic behavior. The spreading of Buddhism to the laity by the times of the Third and Fourth Councils, however, made more flexible interpretations essential; and the orthodoxy of the work of these two meetings has been a target of debate.

DERBOLAV: Of course, breaks in tradition have reoriented the development of all religions. Notable examples of schisms in the religious life of the West are the breaking away of the Greek Orthodox from the Roman Church in the eighth century, their final severance in the eleventh century, and the separation between Protestantism and the Roman Catholic Church (as it was called from this stage) in the sixteenth century. And, if I am correct, a break in tradition disassociates Old from New Buddhism (Soka Gakkai, being an adherent of the new version). Old Buddhism accepts the so-called Pali Canon, whereas new Buddhism adheres to other doctrinal traditions. Soka Gakkai, for instance, reveres as it's Buddha Nichiren Daishonin, who lived in the time of Thomas Aquinas, and considers the Lotus Sutra, which he sanctioned, its binding scripture.

IKEDA: Yes. Perhaps I ought to interpolate a word or two about the relationship between Nichiren Daishonin and the general current of Japanese Buddhism. When Indian Buddhism was taken to China, its scriptures, originally given written form in Pali or Sanskrit, were translated into Chinese.

When it was introduced into Japan, however, there was no written Japanese language into which to translate the teachings. At the time of the introduction, the Japanese were borrowing the Chinese writing system. Consequently, any Japanese capable of reading at all was ostensibly capable of reading Chinese-language versions of the Buddhist scriptures.

This was beyond, or difficult for, most of the ordinary people. And, taking advantage of the general lack of information on the topic, many sects emerged to profess teachings diametrically opposed to precepts in the canonical scriptures.

On the basis of those very scriptures, however, Nichiren Daishonin castigated such sects. But since many people failed to recognize his efforts, the state of Buddhism in Japan became extremely complex.

DERBOLAV: That is very interesting. Complexity and diversity can have various influences. For example, the living energy of renewal that diversifies their forms is the wealth of religions. In addition, however, this same energy can endanger their unity. At any rate, schisms have assumed diverse characteristics that, while raising barriers of various heights among religions, have come closer to suiting the many different needs of faith.

The Greek Orthodox Church adhered more thoroughly to the traditions of Early Christianity and was more broad-minded than the Church of Rome or the Protestant Churches. For their part, the Protestants tried to break from the rigid traditions of the Roman Church and to return to the Gospels, the sources of early Christianity. By making the Gospels available to believers in their mother tongues, Protestantism opened doors to private interpretations of faith. (This explains the rich variety of Protestant sects.)

I have been told that Europeans understand the manifestations and history of Buddhism better if they distinguish between the Hinayana Buddhism of Southeast Asia and Sri Lanka, and the Mahayana Buddhism that spread from India primarily to China, Tibet, and Japan. With the relatively elitist nature of a monks' religion, Hinayana entitles only a chosen circle of the faithful to attain enlightenment and Buddhahood. As is expressly taught in the Lotus Sutra, Mahayana, on other hand, considers all humanity capable of enlightenment.

While differentiating through the formation of sects, Mahayana Buddhism has preserved a relatively unified character within those regions in which it has been accepted. Ascetic, meditative practices occupy the foreground in Chinese Buddhism, whereas Tibetan Buddhism is oriented toward magic and mysticism. Since it is primarily interested in the effects of Buddhist doctrine on life style, Japanese Buddhism can be considered more pragmatic. Is my interpretation of these characteristics correct or does it require correction?

IKEDA: Because of the system of uniting religion and politics in Tibet, Tibetan Lamaism is fairly uniformly magical and mystical in character. At one time, meditative Zenlike Buddhism, esoteric magical Buddhism, and ceremonial Buddhism mixed with Taoist elements existed side by side in China. At present, meditative Buddhism is of major importance in mainland China; and ceremonial practices form the mainstream on Taiwan and among people of Chinese descent in Southeast Asia.

In Japan, all of these kinds of Buddhism have existed side by side. But, the new religions that have gained strength among the ordinary people are characteristically, as you point out, pragmatic.

DERBOLAV: It must be remembered that each religious system contains two tendencies that influence each other mutually. First, each has a kind of productive imaginative power, that stimulates concrete explication of the practical aspects of faith and thus enriches faith in practice. Second, each has a force of critical enlightenment restraining the power of imagination and thus protecting the understanding of faith from excessively fantastic interpretations and overly powerful transformations. From critical enlightenment arise criticism and self-criticism that nourish doubts and can lead to questioning of the basis of religious conviction.

You find the similarity between Christianity and Buddhism in their both being religions of spiritual self-perfection; that is, in both, human beings are the masters of their postmortem, or even earthly, lives.

At the first encounters between the two religions in Japan, the Jesuit missionaries emphasized similarities more than differences. In this, certainly the skill of the missionaries is evident, since they wanted to build not barriers, but bridges to Buddhism and, in this way, to lead the Japanese to Christianity. And it must be said that the Buddhist-oriented population, with its proverbial tolerance, was very accommodating to the missionaries' aspirations.

Contributory to this, however, is the greater ease with which understanding and rapprochement can be effected in the living practice of religion and in the legends superimposed on them than in the area of dogma. For instance, similar to the stories of the nativity of Christ, some Buddhist legends trace the birth of the Buddha to supernatural conception. Other similarities between Buddhist and Christian traditions include a demonic temptation, the trembling of the Earth at the founders' deaths, a favorite disciple, and a traitor figure. Similarities of this kind clearly explain how it was possible for statues of Mary and the Child to be connected with certain Buddhist ideas.

But similarities of this kind are only of relative importance in comparison with the extraordinary common traits the two religions have in connection with moral beliefs. No matter whether it is called love or compassion, the inner driving force turns the hearts of Christians and Buddhists in particular ways in the direction of the poor and the weak. Both religions take account of the existential need and frailty of humanity–Buddhism extends concern even to nonhuman nature–and attempt to be of assistance.

IKEDA: Fundamentally, the Buddhist way of the bodhisattva entails both self-perfection and altruistic service for others, although, in their concentration on achieving the former goal, some Hinayana and Zen sects have neglected compassionate altruism. I suspect that some Christian sects, too, neglect the spirit of compassion and love. Obviously, however, both love and self-perfection are essential to the basic spirit of the religion.

2. Love and Compassion

IKEDA: In contrast to the spirit of love, which Christianity claims to be God's major characteristic, Buddhism emphasizes the spirit of compassion. Just as theological definitions for the love of God have been worked out, so Buddhist compassion has also been fundamentally defined as a spirit of concern for weaker beings. But this definition requires expanded explanation.

First, compassion is concern not only for beings who are weak at present, but also for those who, in the light of the karmic law of life, are acting now in ways that will result in their being weak or unhappy in the future. Such concern is made manifest in eliminating the causes of future unhappiness and providing causes leading to future happiness. This duality is the meaning of compassion, which is linguistically expressed in the Chinese two-character term *cibei* (*jihi* in Japanese) standing for two Sanskrit words: *maitri*, which means giving happiness, and *karuna*, which means removing suffering.

DERBOLAV: As I have already remarked, I am inclined to give priority to compassion—in the Buddhist sense—over love, first because compassion appears the more elemental of the two and second because it has a wider range of efficacy, extending to the nonhuman world. The Christian concept of brotherly love or charity, which is certainly different from mere affection for another person, seems to come close to the Buddhist concept of compassion.

IKEDA: Buddhist thought analyzes compassion further according to the range of beings to which it is applied. Small-scale compassion is directed only toward such intimates as family, friends, and acquaintances. Medium-scale compassion recognizes the dignity of all life and strives to protect the lives of all people, even those of no personal connection at all. Great compassion is demonstrated by people who have plumbed the full depth of the Buddhist Law and who are compassionate in all their acts, conscious and unconscious. Small-scale compassion belongs in the category of natural human love and affection. Medium-scale compassion is the product of effort and results from attempts to put into practice the Buddhist teachings the person has learned. This is the kind of compassion embodied by the bodhisattva. A Buddha, who has completely carried out the whole course of discipline of the bodhisattva, manifests great compassion.

DERBOLAV: You have convincingly shown that compassion exists on several levels. The lowest includes natural, one might say instinctive, love of the kind arising from affection and experienced among family members. Your second level of compassion must be developed until the conscience is sensitive to the claims of all humankind. Such compassion is gained through study of the Buddhist scriptures. But a human being becomes capable of the highest kind of compassion only when he reaches enlightenment, the pinnacle of self-development. At this stage, the enlightened being comprehends the sufferings and weaknesses of all living creatures, to whose assistance he is devoted, and sees completely through the apparent nature of existence. Compassion of this kind can truly be called great because, unlike second-grade compassion, it requires no conscious effort but, through practice, functions without any problem.

Even Christian charity far surpasses instinctive love and

appears to transgress the law of reciprocity, which, as we have seen, underlies all human relations. Charity does this by obliging Christian believers to be completely self-denying, even self-sacrificing. It is in this light that we must understand Christ's oft-quoted injunction, made in the Sermon on the Mount, to turn the other cheek and his command that we must all love our enemies. Deepest Christian convictions insist that even the worst sinner deserves love because he may not yet be completely lost but may be and can be redirected to the path of good.

In this teaching, though it runs counter to instinctive attitudes, evildoers and sinners are interpreted on the same plane with the poor and the weak. Other elements in Christianity, too, run counter to the ordinary sense of justice. For instance, in the parable when the Prodigal Son returns from foreign lands, the father openly prefers him to the second son, who has been true to him and has remained at home. The story of the vineyard, in which the man who has worked only the one final hour of the day receives the same reward as another worker who has labored the full day, seems equally strange. Finally, mention should be made of the shocking statement in the Gospels that God rejoices more at one repentant sinner than at 99 righteous men. (It is possible that a memory of a doctrine, still alive in early Christianity, of a complete restoration of fallen Creation is the foundation of these remarkable transgressions of the usual sense of justice. Later, the Church judged the doctrine of apokatastesis, or complete restoration of the world, to be a heretical teaching.)

IKEDA: In an earlier comment on parallel elements in Buddhism and Christianity, you mentioned a traitor figure. In Christianity, of course, the traitor is the infamous Judas Iscariot. In Buddhist stories, it is the Buddha's cousin Devadatta, who went so far as to make attempts on the Buddha's life. But the Lotus Sutra indicates the immense scope of the Buddhist power of salvation by predicting the future Buddhahood of even Devadatta. In this, perhaps there is a connection with the doctrine of a complete restoration.

DERBOLAV: Both Christian love and Buddhist compassion take as their object the poor and the weak. And in this sense, Christian love partakes of the nature of compassion. This is reflected in some Christian art. For instance, the profoundly moving chorale "O Haupt voll Blut und Wunden, . . . (O Sacred Head now wounded, . . .) from Bach's *The Passion According to Saint Matthew* can only be interpreted as an expression of compassion, of profound, unending sympathy.

I tend to consider the drive compelling people to help the needy and the suffering to be compassion rather than love, and regard this as an indication of the proximity of both attitudes in their fundamental intentions.

IKEDA: All Buddhists strive to live up to high models of compassionate behavior. The histories of India, China, and Japan offer numerous examples of rulers who have attempted to base their policies on compassion. Even the numerous political leaders who have been unable or unwilling to go this far have frequently been restrained from tyrannical acts because of the presence of models of compassionate behavior. Although it goes without saying that not all Oriental rulers have followed this course and that a large number of them have reigned with a cruelty we find inconceivable, there can be no gainsaying the good influence the ideal of Buddhist compassion has had on the monarchs of India, China, and Japan. (In the case of China, the influence of the Confucian ideal of humanity or *ren*, which preceded Buddhist influence there, has had a similar softening effect.)

I am interested in hearing your opinions on the extent to which the Christian concept of love has influenced the practical action of rulers in the West. No doubt some kings and emperors there have been moved by the spirit of love, though I must say hatred seems more conspicuous to me in most of the actions reflected in Western history. Do you concur in this opinion? If so, how do you explain why love has been less influential than hatred in Western history?

DERBOLAV: I know too little of the history of Buddhism and its influence on the political lives of its followers to make judgments or comparisons. You are certainly correct in saying that much hypocritical abuse has been committed in the West in the name of Christianity. But your thesis that Western history has been essentially determined by hatred and resentment requires examination and elucidation.

First, I doubt that such fundamental religious attitudes as love and compassion can be translated into lasting political motivations. In other words, I wonder if such a thing as Christian or Buddhist politics can exist at all. (I have already explained how an intensively humanist-Christian cultural background was unable to save the Germans from relapse into barbarism. And the same thing could be true for all other people in the future.)

In this connection, I should like to mention a few historical considerations. The Christianization of the Romans, the Celts, and the Germanic tribes–the inhabitants of the European heartland–was a process of cultural reception and cultivation that lasted centuries and can only be said to have come to some kind of a conclusion in the late Middle Ages. The moral and juridical concepts of the German peoples at the time of what is called the Great Migration of Nations were anything but specifically Christian. For instance, little squeamishness was shown in dealing with conquered and captured enemies. Clear indication of this is found in the Niebelung Saga, written by an unknown epic poet of the late Middle Ages. In this poem, Christian kings and heroes, while taking part in the ceremonial life of the Church, nonetheless murder, slay, and indulge in blood baths just like the ones that took place in the old days before the spread of Christianity.

The second, deeper, argument touches the general political ambiguity of Christian awareness. The Jews had linked their hopes for a Messiah with their longing for a mighty earthly state and kingdom. And this same attitude influenced the early Christians. Many of Jesus' contemporaries considered him to be the promised king and had difficulty comprehending his often-repeated protestation that God's kingdom is not of this world. Later the misunderstanding was cleared up. Nonetheless, the established Church continued to cultivate the pretension to dominion inherent in the Messianic philosophy and interpreted it as a claim for missionary work throughout the world.

The use and development of power in the Church realm served not only in missionizing–which, as the Crusades indicate, was carried out with great bloodshed–but in increasing the glory of God. In the name of the motto *In maiorem dei gloriam,* many cruel wars were waged; and many nonbelievers, heretics, and apostates were unscrupulously killed.

In connection with the idea of might, rulers were given–sometimes ironically–such epithets as Most Christian King and Defender of the Faith. People who made large donations to the Church were also honored in similar ways.

IKEDA: Interestingly, during what is called the Warring States period (1482-1588) of Japanese history, when the nation was split among rivaling lords struggling for political power, a prospering Buddhist sect called Jōdo Shinshū engaged in violent armed conflict in an apparent attempt to establish a religious kingdom harmonious with their own ideals–a very real kingdom on Earth. These efforts were frustrated, however, because of the traditional power of the secular authorities in Japan and because of the strength of rival Buddhist sects.

DERBOLAV: Power struggles are a source of great temptation. The extent to which this has been true for the Christian–specifically the Catholic–Church is vividly revealed in the figure of the Grand Inquisitor in *The Brothers Karamazov,* Dostoevski's most significant novel. In this story, Christ returns to Earth 1,500 years after his Crucifixion to see how his work has developed and, in Seville, encounters a group of heretics being led away to the stake. The Cardinal Grand Inquisitor, who is responsible for sentencing these people to death, energetically objects to a second (divine) intervention in the work of religious faith, which by his time had long been entrusted to the Church, and informs the returned Christ of His two unforgivable mistakes: first in giving human beings freedom instead of bread and, second, in having preached to them love instead of authority before which to bow down. Ultimately, according to the Grand Inquisitor, it is the power of the Church that makes humanity, in its weakness and immaturity, truly happy.

IKEDA: I, too, have been deeply impressed by the story of the Grand Inquisitor in *The Brothers Karamazov*. It seems to me that, though they may have been few in number, some secular rulers embodied the spirit of Christ better than the medieval Church, which often represented a kind of authoritarianism contrary to that spirit. King Louis IX–Saint Louis–of France is an excellent example of the kind of monarch I mean.

DERBOLAV: Surely the adjective pious has been applied to many Western rulers on account of the Christian virtues and the tolerance and leniency permeating all contacts with friend and foe alike. But merits of these kinds belong more properly to the private sphere of action. In the political realm, the more rulers take refuge behind such things as right and law, the more tightly their hands are bound by considerations of business and affairs–considerations that, since the time of Machiavelli, have been called reasons of state.

From the standpoint of rulers, even the power to apply Christian mercy is established by Law–as in the form of amnesty, which ordinarily only heads of state may extend.

In the realm of modern democracy, Christian or Buddhist politicians and political parties who are oriented toward one of these religions and may go so far as to include the identification of their faith in their official titles, can hardly pursue missionary work. Instead, in this connection, they must confine themselves to supporting their religious organizations or bearing witness to their Christian (or Buddhist) moral convinctions, even if this means applying legal sanctions that contravene their moral tenets. (The

German Christian parties have, as has been mentioned, attempted to gain general recognition for the Christian belief in the sanctity of human life in their struggles to determine what is and is not permitted in the area of abortion.)

In brief, each politician or party with religious affiliations must attempt to preserve personal integrity while striving to cleanse political life of corruption. Setting aside backsliding into totalitarian governmental practices or, on the other side of the coin, the activities of terrorists or so-called enemies of the state, hatred and cruelty can have but small scope for operation in the enlightened, modern democratically regulated state.

IKEDA: Certainly, as you say, cruelty should have little room for play in the daily political activities of the modern, civilized state. We must remember, however, that some such civilized states produce and stockpile vast arsenals of weapons powerful enough to destroy millions of people and perhaps all humanity. I consider dealing with this problem, and thus eliminating the danger of annihilation, and contributing to the creation of true peace the best way for people of faith to manifest love and compassion.

3. Buddhist Influences on Christianity

IKEDA: The idea that Buddhist teachings and philosophy may, at one time or another, have influenced the development of Christianity is entertained by many scholars and offers a fascinating source of speculation. Of course, since religions are generally based on the writings or words of their own founders or other special authorities or on divine revelations, it is impossible to prove or, often, to find so much as a trace of outside influence. Consequently, the influences that Buddhism may have exerted on Christianity, or that Christianity may have exerted on Buddhism, must remain a matter of hypothesis.

But, bearing in mind the truth of this statement, I think that

Jesus Christ could have known of Buddhist teachings for the following reasons. In the time when he lived, though the Roman Empire was pushing in from the west, the area that is now Iraq and Iran was under the dominion of the sprawling Parthian kingdom, which formed a bridge between Rome in the west and the kingdom of Kushana–where Mahayana Buddhism flourished–in the east. This contact and the lively exchanges that took place in cultural and trade terms along the ancient Silk Road make it seem unlikely that Mahayana priests and scriptures could not have reached the West, and especially such an international center as Alexandria. Consequently, it is perfectly conceivable that, as he was growing up, Jesus could have come into contact with Buddhist priests and scriptures. Is it not, therefore, possible that the Christian doctrine of love could be a variant of Buddhist compassion?

DERBOLAV: Christian love and Buddhist compassion resemble each other in fundamental purposes. Christian sympathy for the sufferings of others–especially for Christ's passion–represents nothing other than deep, unending compassion. For its part, Buddhist compassion includes the self-denial, even self-sacrifice, characteristic of Christian love.

Apparently, the junior Mahayana adopted from Hinayana the bodhisattva–later more frequently bodhisattvas in the plural–as a numinous figure of salvation to which believers could turn for help. As has been pointed out, bodhisattvas are beings destined for ultimate enlightenment–Buddhahood–who have abandoned this goal to dedicate themselves to fellow human beings. But such similarities as these between Christian love and Buddhist compassion need not necessarily arise from historical dependence.

IKEDA: Of course certainty on such matters cannot be achieved. King Ashoka, who is thought to have reigned in the third century B.C., sent out emissaries urging ideals of compassion and peace to distant lands. Among the destinations of his emissaries are mentioned the names of cities in Greece and Egypt. Furthermore, the Indian campaigns of Alexander the Great no doubt opened up frequent avenues of intercourse with the Western world.

Geographically and culturally, India is cut off in the north and northeast by the Himalayas, the Pamir Highland, and the Taklamakan Desert. For this reason, contacts have usually been easier and more intimate between India and the West than between India and China. Nonetheless, Buddhism passed into China and Southeast Asia. If this is the case, it is by no means inconceivable that it might have passed westward as well.

Obviously, even if it did move in that direction, it would have found surviving difficult because of the violently exclusive nature of the monotheistic religions prevailing there–Judaism, Christianity, and Islam. Rejection reactions on the part of the adherents of these faiths may account for the total lack of evidence to substantiate early Buddhist influence in that part of the world. Still I do not think we should rule out the possibility.

DERBOLAV: I have delved into these questions, examined what has been written on the subject and asked experts their opinions. These are the results of my investigation. We may certainly assume contact between King Ashoka and Hellenistic rulers from names mentioned in his thirteenth rock edict that most probably refer to Antiochus of Syria and to other rulers of Diadochian times. Evidence suggests that the early Christian Church and the Church fathers came into contact with Buddhism. The *Stromata* of Clemens of Alexandria, who lived about 200 years after Christ, mentions a *Butta* venerated as a god by the Indians for his exceptional piousness. Other passages speak of Indian saints described as living the way Buddhist arhats lived.

The Roman Church's Father Hieronymus (fourth century A.D.) reports that followers of the Buddha believed the founder of their faith to have been born of a virgin–which, indeed, might suggest Christian influence on Buddhism. Other elements of Buddhist influence are found among the

Manicaeans. It is quite possible that these traces indicate only the tip of a still-submerged iceberg of a mutual exchange of ideas. (The missions of the Thomas-Christians in India and the Nestorians in China also deserve mention.)

One indication of the extent of our ignorance of these matters lies in the remarkable fact that the legend of the Buddha–perhaps through the mediation of the Thomas-Christians–was adopted in the widely read story of Barlaan and Josaphat in the Middle Ages and even found reception in the Holy Calendar of the Church. Paradoxically, at a later time, without its Buddhist origins' being detected, it returned in Christian guise in the missionary stories to the converted in China and Japan. The name *Josaphat* is nothing other than *bodisat*, a popular shortening of *boddhisattva*. *Barlaan* derives from *vilaubar* and from *baghavan*, which means something like the illustrious one.

IKEDA: The names of Barlaan and Josaphat, which are Persian, are said to have entered the stories of Christian saints through medieval Persian translations into Pahlavi of such stories of the life of the Buddha Shakyamuni as the Lalitavistara. Then, through still further translations into Arabic, Greek, and Latin and then into the various Western European languages, Saint Barlaan and King Josaphat came to be regarded as actual historical personages. Japanese Christians, too, recognize a scripture called *The Deeds of Saints Barlaan and Josaphat*.

DERBOLAV: Hermann Beckh, the eminent expert on Buddhism, insists that the adoption of later forgotten elements of the Buddhist tradition into Christian legends was not intended to sponsor recognition of Buddhism in the Occident. Quite on the contrary, it tried to furnish evidence of the way Christianity can assimilate outside messages of salvation, for instance, Indian ones, and transfigure them into Christian allegories. In any case, this has certainly been the case in the Middle Ages and early modern times.

IKEDA: Of course, most other religions and philosophies have the ability to assimilate alien elements, too. Indeed, such assimilation must be interpreted as surprising in Christianity, which in most instances gives a strong appearance of being exclusivist.

DERBOLAV: When, at the beginning of the nineteenth century, Europeans started realizing the significance of Buddhism as a dominant Asian religious community, it was first philosophy–Hegel, Schopenhauer, and Nietzsche–then Indiology and comparative research in languages and cultures that stimulated interest in Buddhist thought by evaluating the meaning of its sources on a text-critical basis. From such study, astounding similarities between Buddhist texts and the texts of canonized or apocryphal Christian Gospels became apparent and seemed to point to Buddhist influence on Christianity.

The community of the Essenes is thought to be the place where Jesus–during his early encounter with John the Baptist and his Essenian followers–could have come into contact with Indian thought. (This already somewhat bold presumption makes superfluous the even riskier one that, in the dark years of his life between the time of John's death and his own short career as a wandering preacher, Jesus embarked upon journeys to the Orient and possibly made contact with Buddhism.)

IKEDA: In the Gospel according to Saint Matthew (Chapter 4, Verses 12-16), the following is said of this period in the life of Christ: "Now when Jesus had heard that John was cast into prison, he departed into Galilee; And leaving Nazareth, he came and dwelt in Capernaum, which is upon the sea coast, in the borders of Zabulon and Nephthalim: That it might be fulfilled which was spoken by Isaias the prophet, saying, The land of Zabulon, and the land of Nephthalim, by the way of the sea, beyond Jordan, Galilee of the Gentiles; The people which sat in darkness saw a great light; . . ."

None of the other gospels has any comment to make on this

period in Christ's life, until the time he was thirty years of age. Though bold, the assumption that he might have traveled to the Orient and might there have come into contact with Buddhism ought not to be flatly rejected. Some people who are unwilling to subscribe to this theory nonetheless recognize the possibility that he might have made similar contact in Alexandria.

DERBOLAV: In the early 1880s, Rudolf Seidel believed he could show more than 50 parallel passages between the Pali Canon and the New Testament. Although Seidel's method was critically contested, later Albert Edmunds supported and Richard Garbe upheld four parallels. The first was a parallel between two prophecies: Simeon's prophecy, made in the Temple, of Christ's mission and the saintly Ashita's presage of the Buddhahood of the infant Gautama. The second was a parallel between the demonic temptations both Christ and the Buddha underwent. And the third and fourth pertain to walking on water and multiplying bread to feed the masses.

Recently, the influence of Buddhist tradition on Christianity has been more concretely substantiated. Starting with the often-stated relation between the *Dhammapada* (the first part of the Pali Canon) and the Sermon on the Mount, Roy C. Amore has attempted to put the various parallels between Buddhism and Early Christianity into historical context. He advances the hypothesis that textual source Q, which (along with the Gospel according to Mark) served the evangelists Matthew and Luke as a model for their own conception, was strongly influenced by Buddhism. He claims that the later the Christian texts, the stronger the Buddhist influence exerted on them, because the missionary movements instigated by Buddhists and Christians must have encountered each other repeatedly.

IKEDA: Would it not seem that if the source on which Matthew and Luke relied was strongly influenced by Buddhism that the fountain head of the influence should be traced farther back than mere contacts between the missionary movements of the two religions? I believe the influence of Buddhism should probably be pursued to the very starting point of Christianity.

DERBOLAV: Perhaps. And it should be noted that Amore himself traces even the central message of Jesus to not Hebrew-Judaic, but to Indian-Buddhist sources. This would come close to your interpretation of Christian love as a variation of Buddhist compassion.

I find this interpretation interesting but am reluctant to endorse it for the following reasons. First of all, the decisive passages in the New Testament where Jesus introduces his commandment of love, point back to statements in the Old Testament calling out for charity (of course, only in reference to the Jews themselves). Both derive their standard from self-love.

Secondly, the sublimation of charity into complete self-denial and self-sacrifice on the one hand, and love for enemies on the other, must be understood as opposition to the religion of divine law as set forth in the Old Testament. Christ's teaching of unconditional love sweeps away the severe principle of reciprocity–in the sense of an eye for an eye and a tooth for a tooth. I gladly concede that this interpretation could have been supported by the Buddhist doctrine of compassion. One could go even further and assert that the principle harmony could significantly intensify mutual influence in other areas, too. We are, however, concerned only with Buddhist influence on Christianity.

IKEDA: As another example, might not the Buddhist concept of hell have influenced Christian concepts of postmortem punishment? The vigorous way in which the horrors of hell are described in Buddhism and Christianity have more in common with each other than either has with the tamer Greek concept of Hades and the similar indigenous Japanese idea of *Yomi*, the realm of the dead. In both the Greek and Japanese versions, the condition of the dead is unrelated to the good or evil of performances during life. In Christian and Buddhist versions, however, a strong cause-and-effect relation determines whether the dead enjoy bliss or suffer torment.

DERBOLAV: Connections between the Christian ideas of hell and its punishments and Buddhism seem historically probable. Witness is borne to the relation in the well-developed portrayals of hell in the Byzantine Church in the East and in Dante's *Inferno* in the West, in the mountains of hell depicted in Giotto's Renaissance frescoes in Padua, and in the rich inventory of hell's torments drolly and fantastically painted by Hieronymous Bosch.

True the Western idea of hell as an abyss or cave with many compartments arranged in a downward spiral recalls Buddhist analogies. But Buddhism rarely depicts hell apart from, but usually together with, the entirety of fate, in which all living creatures find themselves included; that is, in samsara, or the cycle of transmigrations.

IKEDA: The sufferings depicted in Dante's Inferno seem to include the Buddhist worlds of hell, ravenous demons, and belligerent asuras. The correlation between evil during life and punishment after death is illustrated in the Buddhist compartmentalization of hell, which has eight infernos and eight icy places of torment. The kinds of evil leading to punishment in each kind of hell is set forth in detail and in a highly imaginative fashion.

DERBOLAV: Lamaist Buddhism depicts the cycle as a wheel held by a ferocious demon gripping fast, with teeth and claws, an inner cycle of existence, which is the world of gods, demons, human beings, beasts, and beings cast into the fires of hell and purgatory. In the outer circle of the wheel are depicted the twelve links of the chain of causation resulting in transmigration. The Buddha, however, who has found liberation from samsara, sits on a lotus throne in peaceful meditation, either in the center of both circles or outside them. Portrayed in many different forms, because of its connection with fate, this wheel is sometimes referred to as hell. Incidentally, it is a representation of the wheel that I own that first stimulated my interest in this subject.

A variation of the Christian version of hell as a mountain is the idea of hell as a city, which is conceived of as the opposite of the city of heaven. According to the Christian understanding, the individual existence ends in heaven or hell. It may be thought of as continuing in one of these conditions but is never reborn again. And in Christian artistic representations, the Buddhist fields of existence are replaced with pictures of the various kinds of sins and transgressions and punishments corresponding to them. The paintings of Hieronymous Bosch show how the fantasy of horror can be rendered in lovingly detailed painting.

4. Law or an Anthropomorphic God?

IKEDA: The most salient difference between Christianity and Buddhism has to do with interpretation of ultimate reality: Christians consider it to be an anthropomorphic god, whereas Buddhism considers it to be a law. Catholics, Protestants, Greek Orthodox, and other branches of Christianity and their various subsects differ on many points. But, since they all recognize the Bible as the basic scripture, they all accept the unique anthropomorphic deity called God as the creator and source of all things and recognize in Him very humanlike and violent emotions of love and hate. On these points, the numerous divisions of Christianity differ very little.

In contrast, Buddhism postulates the possibility of countless worlds throughout the past, present, and future in the whole universe and assumes that there are countless Buddhas in those realms. Furthermore, since a Buddha is one who has been enlightened to the truth and since the truth is an ubiquitous absolute transcending time and space, it is possible that unlimited numbers of beings have been enlightened to it and will be enlightened to it. It is further possible that, if they discipline themselves to think with increasing clarity and profundity, all the unenlightened people now in existence will someday become Buddhas.

Buddhas are enlightened to the truth. Consequently, the truth is the source from which Buddhas come into being. Buddhism teaches that the truth, or the universal law, is the parent, teacher, and master of the Buddhas. Whether human beings live in accordance with, or fall away from and turn their backs on, this law determines whether they will be happy or unhappy in this life.

Obviously, by the word *law* Buddhist teachings do not mean the legal restrictions established by mankind to regulate society. Instead, the universal law might be compared to the natural laws controlling the operations of all phenomena. Human beings must obey such laws for their own good. For instance, a person who knows and understands the law of gravity will not leap off a 50-meter cliff thinking he has only 50 centimeters to go. And, if he is foolish enough to take such a leap, it will be much the worse for him. Furthermore, the happiness and unhappiness derived from living in accordance or at odds with the universal law are not limited to the material pleasures and distresses of this world, but persist after death.

In my opinion, the Christian doctrine of an anthropomorphic god with human will, emotions, and intellect is possibly an effective way of teaching people who are incapable of high-level, abstract thought. But people who can think this way will no doubt find it not only unsatisfying, but dubious in many respects as well. To give only a simple illustration, the existence of large numbers of wicked people apparently enjoying the blessings of God, who is supposed to determine happiness and unhappiness, casts doubt on God's impartiality and wisdom.

DERBOLAV: During the 2,000 years of its theology, all possible objections to Christianity have been entertained, each of them releasing vehement controversies. Among them is the objection against an anthropomorphic god. In thinking about this problem, I should like to limit my discussion to three trains of thought. The first is an attempt to justify Christianity against your objection. I shall bear in mind, however, the many blows that enlightened criticism has dealt the idea of a personal god within the Christian tradition itself. In the course of the discussion, it will be essential to deal with the interpretations of relations between religion and philosophy, or scientific research, in both East and West.

The second line of thought will entail a deepening of the difference you have mentioned between Christianity and Buddhism in connection with the Christian interpretation of history as God's acting with humanity and the Buddhist interpretation of it as a cycle of reincarnations of universal life, within which the individual integrity is retained.

The third will deal with the obstacles to understanding and sources of thought the Christian tradition holds for the believer and ways in which the believer may cope with them. All three will stay within the confines of a comparison of Christianity and Buddhism and will try to answer your objections.

In his *Antichrist*, Nietzsche resolutely pointed out the superiority of Buddhism over Christianity—a superiority that you too assert. While calling both religions nihilistic and decadent—in that, as has already been said, they concern themselves with the poor and the weak—in the same breath, he pronounces Buddhism to be a hundred times more realistic than Christianity because it inherited an objective, cool approach to posing problems and evolved from a philosophical movement, hundreds of years old, that had already done away with the concept of God. Buddhism, therefore, struggles, not against sin, but against suffering and thus stands beyond both good and evil.

For this discussion, whether Nietzsche is correct in these last two assertions or in his own nihilism is beside the point. In making these comments, however, he characterizes Buddhism as a spiritually mature and virile religion and thereby touches on another point of difference with Christianity.

Without doubt, the Christian faith contains childlike features. Christians see themselves as children of God who, in their self-development, must become as little children again. Jesus invites the little children to come unto him and threatens with severe punishment anyone who harms or causes any of them pain. Certainly there is no reason why Christ should not speak to human beings as if they were children and use the mythology and imagery of the Divine Father and of his own nature as the Only Son sent to Earth to fulfill the task of saving humanity. Nor is speech of this kind foreign to the Buddhist, who, as you have pointed out, warms to the idea of the universal law first when it is perceived in the role of Father, Teacher, and Master.

IKEDA: Yes, as you say, the Buddha is enlightened to the law but is endowed with the three virtues of Teacher, Master, and Parent. More than a teacher who instructs in the law, he is a master who protects and a parent who loves compassionately. The Buddha does not create and impose the law, since it predates him in existence. Instead, he is the mediator who reveals the law to human beings. If the Buddha were its creator, the law would stand in the mediating relation between him and humanity. The mediator is essential because the law cannot speak for itself.

In the Judaic, Christian, and Islamic traditions, prophets perform a similar mediating role. And the authority of the prophets has been passed on to churches and caliphates, which have preserved absolute sway over their followers.

In Buddhism, however, the Buddha is the mediator; and the law is the absolute. By studying and training themselves in the law under a Buddha's guidance, human beings themselves are capable of attaining Buddhahood.

In contrast, in the monotheistic religions, the absolute is an anthropomorphic deity whose will governs all things. In brief, while regarding them as children, Buddhism expects people to attain adulthood. For their part, however, the monotheistic religions seem to consider human beings eternally to be children who must always obey and be loved by God.

DERBOLAV: As has often been the case in the history of the Catholic faith, the fantasy of devoted faith can be enlivened and made more concrete by a mythological presentation. I might cite this example from the not-very-distant past. A person who takes a graphic view of his religious faith will probably be offended by the teaching that, whereas God the Father and Christ the Son are enthroned in Heaven, Mary the Mother of God died an earthly death and thus shared the fate of other mortals. In 1951, with the establishment of the dogma of Mary's ascension, the Church fulfilled the need for balance in this connection by uniting the Holy Family in Heaven.

On the other hand, working against the swelling of the elements of fantasy in faith is the reflective power of an enlightenment attempting to demythologize images of this kind, which it regards as provisional. (Rudolf Bultmann's celebrated demythologizing campaign had venerable precursors in centuries of attempts to view faith from an enlightened view in philosophy, science, and the humanities.)

Assuredly, Christian explanations of faith have had their mystical and their rational sides. For instance, among the early Protestants, circles of theosophists relocated the divine process of God-made-man, the Crucifixion, and Redemption from historical fact into the individual soul. In another theosophist version, God was thought to be capable of recognizing himself in man. As a consequence of the rational components of this explanation of faith, the Christian doctrines of the Creation and of Salvation were reduced to an abstract god, who, after creating the world, left it to its own natural-historical dynamics. This Christian conception is called Deism. The God behind Creation became superfluous when philosophy and science found explanations of the formation of the world that were more effective than accepted Christian ones. Out of such a course of development could evolve the idea of a rational world order very closely approximating the Buddhist Law. (This is reminiscent of the explanation formulated in Antiquity and developed into the Stoic idea of unvarying natural laws.)

IKEDA: As the individual human being grows, acquires knowledge, and attains self-cognizance, it is only natural for him to become dissatisfied with still having to do only what his father–even a divine father–says. Instinctively, the mature individual wishes to make his own interpretations of the world and to walk his own path. The Buddhist method of teaching the way to all people agrees with this human desire for independence. The modern attempts at enlightened views that you mention also seem to be motivated by a similar desire for independence.

DERBOLAV: In another sense, rational explanations of faith were able to mollify the strife for superior rank that frequently arose among the religions of the world. The parable of the rings in Lessing's *Nathan* illustrates this.

On his death bed, a certain man gives to his three sons three rings, all of which the owner values equally highly. The rings stand for three religions: Judaism, Christianity, and Islam. Two of the rings are perfect copies of the other–the true–ring, which has the power of making the person who wears it pleasing to God and man. In the dispute over which is the true ring that naturally arises among them, the three sons apply to a wise judge in the hope of discovering which ring best fulfills the purpose of making the wearer pleasing to God and man.

The parable suggests that a religious system can substantiate its claim to truth (and preeminence), not through historical and dogmatic proof, but through practical performance. Identification of the true ring–that is, demonstration of preeminence among religions–will probably remain an open issue until the end of time.

A solution of the kind set forth in the parable of the rings is close to the explanation offered by Deism in that it replaces the love the Gospels require us to demonstrate toward God and man with a desire merely to be pleasing in their eyes. This in turn makes disputes for preeminence among the higher religions anachronistic–an opinion with which I feel certain you concur.

Incidentally, I have heard of a Buddhist parable that expresses a similar intention. A father attempts to draw his children from a burning house by promising each of them a special wagon but, once they are out, gives them only one–but the finest–wagon.

IKEDA: The parable you mention is the *Parable of the Three Carts and the Burning House,* found in Chapter Three of the *Sutra of the Lotus of the Mystic Law.* The fundamental teaching of the parable is that the enlightenment of the Buddha transcends ordinary mortal powers of comprehension. Although the children request only carts pulled by deer, goats, and bullocks, the father has prepared for them a great, splendid cart drawn by a pure white bullock. This wonderful vehicle stands for the law leading to Buddhahood. Since it is something of which they have no experience, ordinary people find it difficult even to want to attain the supreme state of happiness that is the Buddha condition.

DERBOLAV: We must not overlook the importance of Hegel, the most influential and significant German philosopher of religion, because he made an interesting attempt to synthesize dialectically the mystical and rational branches of faith. According to Hegel, God, as the universal spirit, reconciles himself with the individual spirit of man so that, no longer separate, the two combine in the holy spirit of love that emanates from Christian community life.

But speculation about the nature of God can help us no further in this discussion because the scientific and humanistic interpretation of faith, which replaced the philosophical one in the middle of the nineteenth century, has, one by one, dismantled such elements of Christian belief as the idea that God and His Son are enthroned in Heaven, that man is God's creation, that all men may hope for a life after death, and that Christianity–like all the other higher religions claiming to reveal absolute truth–is unique and without historical analogue.

IKEDA: A religion claiming to have no historical analogue might seem at a glance to be one based on faith, but the faith on which it rests can be blind.

Nichiren Daishonin taught the necessity of the principle of religious criticism and, on the basis of comparative relativity, demonstrated the superiority of his Buddhist Law. In the present age, which is dominated by a spirit of scientific criticism, a religion that attempts to divert the eye of relative comparison from itself, will have difficulty winning faith and support. Of course, people who are basically uncritical might embrace such a faith warmly.

DERBOLAV: The disciplines that have brought about the stripping down of Christianity may be ordered into a spectrum leading from physics through biology and psychology and as far as history (comparative study of religions).

According to the interpretation of the world–to which we all long ago subscribed–evolved by physics, there is no longer an above or a below and, therefore, no heaven in which God abides and no hell for the Devil. Darwin's theory of biological evolution connects human life with animal life, from which the former is said to have evolved genetically. This makes the idea that God created man untenable.

Nor has psychology stood by idle in this process. First Feuerbach and after him Marx, Nietzsche, and Freud sought to prove that the eternal life in paradise is a projection of human hopes and yearnings and, once seen for what it truly is, is exposed as false and empty. When this happens, humanity's concern is redirected to the here and now.

Comparative research has shown that no one element or feature is exclusive to any one religion and that, therefore, no religion can claim to be absolute. Some decades ago, in

Leningrad, I was astounded to see the way the so-called Museum of Atheism strives to support its convictions by showing that all the things the Christian Church claims as its own doctrines–the virgin birth, the teaching of the incarnation of God, salvation by the Messiah, and even the Last Judgment–are also integral elements in other religions.

IKEDA: That is interesting. The Soviet Union and other socialist nations have adopted a strong antireligious stance, perhaps for practical reasons. In the East-European countries where socialism now holds sway, the roots of religious (Christian) faith among the people are so deep that, in the face of government disapproval, the churches continue to be regularly full. No doubt, the authorities in these lands have felt compelled to rely on vigorous antireligious campaigns to destroy the roots of faith.

DERBOLAV: Perhaps that is true. But even more revealing in connection with the process of stripping Christian teachings of a claim for absolutism is the discrepancy between the historical facts of the life of Jesus Christ and what church teachings later made of them. Indeed, the idea of Jesus as the Son of God, Mary's perpetual virginity, and her part in the divine nativity can all be rather convincingly shown to have been taken over from Hellenistic sources.

In the light of the destructive effects science and learning have had on faith, it is scarcely surprising that theology, too, should adopt the same line as did Rudolf Bultmann, following the lead of Martin Heidegger, when he reduced the traditional substance of religious faith to the naked facts of the fall of humanity to sinful man and his subsequent ascension to a higher self.

IKEDA: It would seem that in the modern world, science and its positivistic attitudes have had an oppressive and constricting influence on Christian dogma in the West. Modernization has had a similar effect on some branches of religion in the East as well, although Buddhism is much less affected than some religions since, understood correctly, its teachings do not conflict with science.

DERBOLAV: As you suggest, for a good 150 years, Christianity appears to have been retreating in the face of philosophy and scientific learning. Of course, one asks oneself whether the abstract God of the philosophers, on the one hand, and the atheism of scientific learning on the other actually represent the final word on the subject. For the sake of making a convincing counterargument, it must be realized that there are various kinds of meaning that fall outside the objective grasp of scientific learning. Since the meaning of religion is certainly the most complex of all, the acts of salvation represented in it go substantially beyond all the aspects of the fields of scientific learning I mentioned earlier.

There are scientific problems in the interpretation and substantiation of the Christian faith: criticism of sources, textual research, and historical research. Nonetheless, none of the scientific disciplines, including physics, biology, psychology, and history, reveals exactly what Christianity means by "the divine." The impossibility of finding this meaning in the first three disciplines is self-evident. But even the empirical historian can do no more than register the existence of such men as Jesus and the Buddha, the destinies they experienced, the convictions they pronounced, and the effects of their teachings. The historian cannot substantiate alleged miracles or establish the truth of convictions and teachings.

The situation for a historian concerned with Christian salvation is quite different. It is with his work that an approach to new, religious realms of meaning begins. The God of Abraham and Isaac reveals himself, not as the god of the philosophers, who stands for the rational world order, but as the Lord of History at three of its most salient points: the Creation and the first prophecies, God's incarnation as Christ the Savior, and the Final Judgment at the end of time (the eschaton, or end of history). It will be noticed that this series of events necessitates the fusion of Judaism and Christianity, which claims to be the fulfillment of its predecessor.

The convinced Christian believes and puts his hopes in the salvation God offers mankind in these acts, for all of which the personality of God is an indispensable prerequisite. Nor is it possible to detract from its credibility in the eyes of believers by asserting that it is only a fiction that human beings themselves have created.

IKEDA: Perhaps. Nonetheless, I think it is going too far to attempt to attribute both creation and salvation to God. Most religions, including the indigenous Japanese one, have myths of creator divinities. But creation and salvation must be mutually contradictory. Salvation implies the commission of some sin that needs to be forgiven. If God is omnipotent, why did he create humanity to sin? His doing so looks like a mistake in creation itself. This is why I feel attributing both creation and salvation to him within the historical current is unreasonable.

DERBOLAV: I see the actual gulf separating Christianity from Buddhism, not in an objection to anthropomorphism, but in the historical theory that I briefly outlined. In spite of a lack of progress in its temporal aspects, for the Christian, history is goal-oriented. For the Buddhist, on the other hand, history is a chain, or cycle, of reincarnations leading into infinity. Its end, or eschaton, lies in later reincarnations, especially those that allow the human being to avoid hell and attain heavenly regions, and in his ultimate extinction (nirvana) at the time when he has purified and perfected himself to the extent that karma makes further rebirths unnecessary.

IKEDA: You are speaking of the teachings of Hinayana Buddhism, which, popular in Sri Lanka, Thailand, and Burma, was the first kind of Buddhism with which Europeans came into contact. The teachings of Mahayana Buddhism, which passed through Central Asia and China to reach Korea and Japan, are somewhat different.

Although its ultimate goal, too, is the attainment of Buddhahood, the teachings of Mahayana–and especially of the Lotus Sutra–interpret this Buddhahood as a state of the joyful contemplation of both life and death, experienced, as part of the repeated cycle of transmigrations, without sinking into suffering. The individual life that undergoes the cycle of transmigrations is one with the eternally abiding, universal force of life.

DERBOLAV: The doctrine of reincarnations of the individual life from the universal life poses no more problems for understanding than does the Christian dogma of the resurrection of the flesh, since both are elements of the kind of rational belief that I have already mentioned. But, for the Christian, the concept of an eternal recurrence of similar life forms–that is, the self repeated in changing forms–as the Buddhist view of history implies it, is alien. It must be remembered that Nietzsche evolved his theory only after he had declared God to be dead and had asserted the meaninglessness of history. The person who believes himself to be included in a divine plan of salvation no doubt finds this perspective nihilistic.

It may be, however, that the Buddhist doctrine of reincarnation is interwined with human horizons of meaning in the way in which it complies with human reason on two points. First, by linking the teaching of karma with the cosmic law, the Buddhist doctrine satisfies the human sense of justice: in a new, or perhaps even in this, life, good deeds return in the form of good fortune. Second, the final goal of Buddhism represents a typical human approach in that it conceives of ultimate enlightenment of the individual as a confluence with the universal law, a harmony with everything in nature and the cosmos.

Without doubt, these two points reveal the greatness and dignity of Buddhism. But, it seems possible to find in them a trace of anthropomorphism, at least to the extent that the Buddhist law in effect complies with human standards. With the exception of the analogy between it and a human father, teacher, and master, the law constitutes for the Buddhist a final guarantee for the prevailing of justice in this and all other worlds. And justice is, indisputably, a singularly human principle of dividing and ordering.

IKEDA: Buddhism is, as you say, founded on law. Just before his death, Shakyamuni told his followers that they should make the law their teacher. The religion later spread among many peoples; and objects of faith–later in the form of carved images of the Buddha, who was to an extent deified–became increasingly important. As time passed, this tendency gained impetus with the result that statues of a great variety of Buddhas other than Shakyamuni and of bodhisattvas and of Shakyamuni's major disciples, including Shariputra and Mahakashyapa, came to be produced and venerated.

Furthermore, sects uninterested in the pursuit of and training in the teachings of Buddhism and concerned solely with personal salvation through the compassion of the Buddha came into being and grew influential. The principal images employed by such sects were usually Amitabha-buddha or Mahavairochana-tathagata, who never actually existed and are only touched on in the scriptures.

Shakyamuni Buddha emphasized the law and attempted to lead people to it. Therefore, any Buddhism based on his teachings requires study and discipline in that law. Never having existed, Amitabha-buddha and Mahavairochana-tathagata can never have taught the law. Consequently, they themselves became the object of faith of their followers.

In sects in which this occurred, the law was supplanted from its position of central importance; and anthropomorphic figures became religious nuclei.

DERBOLAV: I now come to my third reflection, which deals with the distressing difficulties involved in understanding the Christian faith. You have already touched on one of these by sharply contrasting the supposed benevolence of the Christian God with the obviously unjust allotment among human beings of the good things of life.

The ineradicable evils of life have frequently challenged Christian theologians to invent, in a process called theodicy, any and all possible arguments to free God of responsibilities for them. No convincing vindication has been forthcoming, and all attempts at finding one have remained tentative. Such explanations that suffering is a trial, a means of education, or a heavenly decree that mortals, with their finite reasoning faculties, cannot comprehend are insufficient and only provoke further questioning.

Not only Christianity, but also Buddhism, to the extent that it considers maintaining a balance between moral deeds and happiness in life possible, is confronted with a similar difficulty because the abundant examples of disparity between evil and allotment of good fortune in life are indisputable.

IKEDA: Yes, and the founder of the faith I embrace, Nichiren Daishonin, entertained doubts on this point. The Lotus Sutra says that people who believe and practice its teachings may be tranquil in this world, but the life of Nichiren Daishonin himself was far from tranquil. One of his major writings, *Kaimoku-sho* (The Opening of the Eyes) deals with this issue from various angles and arrives at conclusions that we find convincing.

DERBOLAV: On at least one point, the Christian understanding of faith has been more difficult than the Buddhist. Saint Paul and after him Saint Augustine, Calvin, and many others have linked salvation with the idea of predestination, according to which many are called by God, few are chosen, and the remainder fall by the wayside. The doctrine, of course, runs counter to the idea of the equality of all human beings before God.

As we have seen, in relation to the possibility of enlightenment, Buddhism escaped this kind of elitism by abandoning its monastic nature at a relatively early stage. Today, in keeping with the teachings of the Lotus Sutra, Buddhism speaks impartially to all people.

This issue posits a second complication that has sharply divided minds throughout the history of Christianity. The question is whether we owe our good deeds (and the happy life in heaven resulting from them) to ourselves or to the grace of God. I believe that some Buddhist sects–notably the Pure Land Sect–consider grace a precondition for salvation, without, however, assuming the existence of a god. (For this reason, Nathan Söderblom has called enlightenment a gift of grace without a giver.) Other Buddhist sects, however, reject the concept of grace. Nichiren, for instance, went so far as to call the idea a way to hell.

IKEDA: Perhaps I should explain why Nichiren Daishonin took this attitude toward grace in connection with the Pure Land Sect and Amitabha-buddha. First it must be pointed out that the Pure Land desire for the grace of Amitabha-buddha, who is thought to reside in a paradise many millions of realms to the west, fundamentally resembles the salvationist attitudes of Christianity and Islam. The difference between them is, however, salient. Amitabha-buddha became a Buddha through study and discipline in the Law, which therefore takes precedence over all other things. Furthermore, Amitabha-buddha is only one of the innumerable Buddhas thought to inhabit the universe.

Nichiren Daishonin considered the Pure Land sect the way to hell because its founder Hōnen (1133-1212) attempted to turn people toward his own sect and away from faith in the Lotus Sutra, the teachings of which Hōnen called profitless. Nichiren Daishonin insisted that, no matter how much grace might be forthcoming from Amitabha-buddha, it could exert no saving influence on people who sullied and turned their backs on the Mystic Law, which takes precedent over all and is, therefore, supreme. The attitude of people seeking salvation from Amitabha-buddha can be compared to a child standing on a cliff and longing to reach his mother, who stands across the crevice on the opposite cliff. Though inspired by the purest motivation, if the child attempts to leap across to his mother, the force of gravity will inevitably pull him to his death at the foot of the cliff.

DERBOLAV: A universal doctrine of grace probably deprives humanity of freedom and, at the same time, of responsibility. In this connection, the Christian faces a dilemma. Obviously human beings can will nothing that is not willed by the omnipotent God. Otherwise, man himself would be a small god in his own realm. But if human beings desire to preserve their freedom, how is it possible to reconcile free will with divine decree? No plans for combining the two offer any further assistance.

Perhaps the issue must be stated dialectically. Within his own freedom, the human being must decide and achieve while realizing that his innate abilities are a gift of divine grace. Saint Augustine said that what he had deserved (*merita*) are at the same times gifts of God (*munera dei*). And Karl Jaspers, whose philosophical faith was certainly not that of a dogmatic Christian, considered the idea of the individual's conceiving of himself as something that has been bestowed or given (*Sich-Geschenkt-Sein*) to be the fundamental religious experience in general.

IKEDA: In other words, the lowly self becomes ultimately worthy of respect. In the monotheistic religions, the self achieves awareness of itself by considering its existence to be a gift of God. Buddhism, on the other hand, teaches self-awareness achieved as a result of perception of one's own inherent Buddha nature.

DERBOLAV: Still more problematical in the Christian practice of faith is what I call the *do-ut-des* (I give in order to receive) attitude toward God; that is, the attitude of serving God solely in the hope of reward.

It is true that the principle of reciprocity forms the functional basis of communal living. Order and justice can prevail only when each intention meets a corresponding answer, in cases of both good and evil.

Human beings are centrally inspired by a need for balance and see inevitable connections between the gift and a return gift, between love and gratitude, and between crime and punishment. But can this principle, which runs through and determines all human intercourse, be applied to relations between God and man? In other words, can God be constrained by sacrifices and good deeds? Can God be bought? Since Kant, who did not view merit and reward as consequences of moral acts but saw reward and morals as coincidental with each other, the idea of doing good for the sake of rewards has come to be an unbearably distressing difficulty in the area of ethics and morals. The religious articulation of the relation between man and God cannot be allowed to fall behind the refined ethical standards set by such secular philosophers as Kant. This is why I believe the inability to eliminate this attitude of doing good for the sake of reward only will put Christianity–and all other religions believing in the possibility of gaining postmortem happiness by striving to achieve moral aims–in mortal danger.

A god who can be bought is certainly a greater challenge to religious feeling than one conceived in purely human terms as being inspired by hate and love. Buddhism is free of this dilemma because it considers the ethical performance of the individual to be directed solely toward the self or other human beings. It seems to me, however, that the Christian can find freedom from this dilemma only in adopting, not an active, but a reactive attitude toward God. The Christian can ask God for grace or help but can never evaluate his own merits as deserving of either. (The Buddhists of Soka Gakkai turn to their Gohonzon, as objects of veneration, for help in accomplishing things.) Inspired by Christ's message, the Christian must approach God under the inspiration of love and gratitude only–gratitude for the unrepayable advance redemption God offers all humanity.

IKEDA: What you say about a god who can be bought is highly

important and demands comment in connection with a point related to prayer that, I think, sets the Buddhist and Christian attitudes apart from each other. You are correct to say that members of Soka Gakkai turn to the Gohonzon for assistance. Nichiren Daishonin himself vigorously exhorted us to pray to the Gohonzon in earnest faith so that nothing will remain to be attained. On the other hand, he cautioned against having faith solely in the hope of attaining reward in this world and told us not to doubt, though we lack the protection of heavenly beings, and not to lament, though human life is turbulent.

The apparent contradiction in these two teachings is resolved when it is remembered that, in Buddhism, the ultimate reward is the attainment of Buddhahood, which is the establishment of a self strong enough to overcome all the hardships of life. A person with this kind of strength experiences a state of complete satisfaction in which nothing remains to be attained.

As you say, it is conceivable that an anthropomorphic god can be "bought." A law, however, like the Buddhist law, cannot. In other words, for the Buddhist, prayer is not designed to produce a desired end. Instead, it must be accompanied by effort and the performance of reasonable acts. As a fundamental principle, we turn to the Gohonzon in prayer in order to strengthen ourselves and our willingness to make the necessary effort.

DERBOLAV: The God of the Old Testament is one of wrath and punishment. And the Jews are accustomed to interpreting the sufferings of both individuals and entire peoples as God's punishment for committed sins. But Jesus revised this conception by replacing the wrathful with a loving and merciful God. He regarded it as Pharasaic to brand unfortunate people as sinful or guilty. He could not, however, completely eradicate from his followers' minds the self-interested approach to God that simulated doing good with an eye to reward. Had he been able to eliminate this attitude, the Middle Ages would probably not have witnessed the

Inquisition or witch hunts. The philosophy represented by the heresy trials and witch persecutions of the period interprets conspicuous physical or psychological deformities as divinely conferred stigmas and regards human pronouncements of judgement and condemnation as ways of carrying out sentences already handed down by God.

Things of this kind lead me to regard as especially dubious the desire to find literal traces of God's workings in all the events of an individual life and, in so doing, to fail to take into account one's own limited understanding. Similarly, it would seem to me that Buddhism, too, must attempt to determine the extent to which it is capable of proving historically the operation of either individual or social karma.

But the hardest nut to crack in connection with Christian belief is the doctrine of the resurrection of the flesh; that is, resurrection of the dead in the forms they had when they were living. Even seen from a vantage point removed from commonplace, mundane standards of happiness and even when so-called eternal life is equated with pure contemplation of God–which would coincide with Buddhist enlightenment and concord with the universal law–the death of the individual human being seems too final and irrevocable not to awaken doubt about life after death.

Perhaps, as Cardinal Newman once formulated it, faith is in its ultimate sense the ability to tolerate religious doubts. Religion's highest achievement for human beings is to give them the strength to overcome death. Of course, religions are helpful in many of the issues of life as well–for instance, in helping formulate the kind of moral orientation we have already discussed. They do not, however, provide anything that secular reason cannot give–at least to mature and cultivated people. Reason, however, offers no convincing consolation in connection with death. From the Buddhist standpoint, would you agree with this interpretation?

IKEDA: From the Buddhist's standpoint too, the highest achievement of religion can be called giving human beings the strength to triumph over death. We are told by Nichiren

Daishonin to devote attention to other matters only after having learned how to face our final moment. And, as is recorded in the sutras, death was one of the four sufferings–the other three being birth, aging, illness–that motivated Shakyamuni to abandon the secular life for a life of religious endeavor.

Buddhists overcome death through enlightenment to the nature of life as something eternal, not terminated by death, but continuing forever, while manifesting alterations of phase from life to death. In other words, death is only a change. Such enlightenment not only eliminates fear and insecurity over death, but also provides a basis for thinking about actual life and its goals.

It is in this sense that true Buddhism can offer us something that secular reason is incapable of providing. Knowing that we will not become nothing when the present day ends– knowing that there will be a tomorrow–compels us to choose a way of life that takes into consideration plans for that tomorrow and for years into the future.

DERBOLAV: It appears to me that Christian thinking comes closest to the Buddhist concept of the law in the Deistic form of the god of the philosophers and a rational world order. Christianity still has not recovered from the blow delivered to it by scientific criticism. But, I believe this dilemma can be avoided as long as one understands clearly that the basic sense of faith always precedes its theoretical interpretation. In other words, the assertions of faith must remain incomprehensive within the abstract horizons of science because religion seeks something different and more concrete than science is willing to contemplate. As Hegel says in his philosophy of religion, the scientific enlightenment must first be enlightened about itself and its own limitations. For their part, however, the defenders of religious faith must abandon the currently popular practice of attempting to justify religious content by means of scientific arguments.

Must believers in Buddhism struggle with similar questions? You have said that the first Europeans to be converted to

Buddhism were most fascinated by its rationalism. And it is often asserted that faithful Buddhists have no difficulty reconciling their beliefs with the results of modern science–especially the natural sciences. Indeed, since he has no miracles to justify and since his kind of self-perfection is a spiritual process comprehensible in psychological terms, the Buddhist may well have less difficulty on this point than the Christian.

The situation is more troublesome, however, in connection with the Buddhist ontological foundation; that is, with the doctrine of the eternity of the world, the plurality of worlds (as long as this does not mean simply other galactic systems in the universe), and the force of universal life continually reproducing and reincarnating.

I should be interested to know whether Buddhism engages in a struggle to resist scientific investigation similar to the one Christianity wages. If such is the case, I should like to know the method the Buddhist employs to reconcile divergences in the interpretations made by faith on the one hand and science on the other.

IKEDA: The fundamental field of Buddhist thought is the law governing the force of life and the clarification of principles for the elevation of the human personality. This no doubt overlaps in many zones with modern psychology. Indeed, insofar as I can tell, developments in psychology seem to endorse the correctness of Buddhist teachings.

It is true that, in his sermons, Shakyamuni made use of the views of the world and the universe widely held in the India of his time and that many of those views have been discredited. None of this material, however, concerns the fundamentals of Buddhism. Therefore, conceding to modern science in connection with it in no way shakes the foundations on which Buddhism rests.

The Buddha is the Enlightened One, who accurately perceives the true nature of the Three Worlds. These worlds, however, are not the physical worlds. Instead, they represent the desire and anger of human life and the suffering that invites such emotions. The Buddha, therefore, knows how human beings can find liberation from suffering. Buddhism is always willing to concede on points connected with fields that are the proper study of the sciences and never feels the need to engage in combat with them when they indicate a truth that is out of harmony with material found in the scriptures.

5. The Essential Dialogue

IKEDA: At the conclusion of a famous series of lectures, the late Arnold J. Toynbee said that, when future historians come to write about our times, they will probably be little interested in the fates of democracy and communism but will concentrate their attention on what happened when Christianity and Buddhism reached a profound level of mutual understanding and exchange. I suspect that this statement, which is as grand in scale as we have come to expect of Mr. Toynbee, is an accurate prophecy.

Nineteenth-century Europeans demonstrated considerable interest in Buddhist studies. But in general, disillusioned with Christianity, they were attracted by the atheistic and, in their interpretations, rationalistic nature of the primitive Buddhist teachings found in the Pali canon. This often led to misinterpretations. It is true that Buddhism has no need of—indeed, rejects—such doctrines as that of the absolute creator God or of such miracles as the Immaculate Conception and the Virgin Birth. But this is not to say that Buddhism is in any way equivalent to modern rationalism or positivism. Buddhism actually transcends the world of reason to become what might be called antirational. In spite of this, basing their thinking on the Pali canon only and overlooking such other major currents as later Sectarian Buddhism, Esoteric Buddhism, and Mahayana Buddhism, many late-nineteenth-century European scholars and philosophers became infatuated with Buddhist philosophy for the rationalism and positivism they imagined they found in it.

But in his monumental *Buddhismus–Buddha und Seine Lehre–*

which incidentally has been translated into Japanese–Hermann Beckh made a much more accurate appraisal. He said that Buddhism is neither what Westerners call atheistic nor philosophical rationalism. He went on to say that the goal of his work was to help people realize the true nature of Buddhism and, by reflecting on it, to acquire a deeper comprehension of the meaning of religion in general and of religion in daily life. In Beckh's opinion, true scholarly research in Buddhism is useful in promoting a deeper understanding of all religions, including Christianity.

Beckh rejected as useless all attempts at establishing the superiority of one of the two religions over the other since he felt total impartiality is impossible, even to people with the highest motivations. He insisted that Christianity and Buddhism are not two opposed teachings struggling for supremacy, but two variant currents of life. In saying this, he touched on the keypoint in making possible the kind of true dialogue between Christianity and Buddhism that is more essential to the world today than ever before.

DERBOLAV: I do not believe that the German approach to Buddhism was as one-sided and limited as you assume, especially in the light of openness to areas other than early Hinayana. In recent decades, indeed, Germans have directed more and more interest to Chinese, Tibetan, and Japanese Buddhism.

A dialogue of the kind both you and I envision is possible only with the participation of representatives of both sides of the issue. I believe that today such a thing is coming to pass. In the past, textual matters were preeminent. Today, however, people are mainly concerned with the way the Christian and Buddhist systems elucidate such subjects as suffering, love, life, belief, and even such complex themes as the mystical.

The influences between Japanese and German thinkers have been reciprocal. For instance, such Japanese experts as Daisetsu Suzuki and Satoshi Ueda took the treatises of Rudolf Otto and Heinrich Dumoulin as models. Bunyu Masutani, Keiji Nishitani, and Hideo Mineshima, too, participated in the exchange. On the other side of the coin, step by step, European Protestant and Catholic theologians–like Henri de Lubac, Paul Tillich, and Karl Rahner–advanced sufficiently to make it possible for the German specialist in Buddhism Hans Waldenfels to hold far-reaching discussions with philosophers of the Kyoto school. Without being limited to single subjects and particular phenomena, these talks dealt with central perspectives of the ways in which Christianity and Buddhism can contribute to solving fundamental problems related to God, the good, the future of mankind, the total significance of existence, and so on.

On the methodological side, encounters of this kind have involved common effort in the direction of a hermeneutic approach or even to a kind of logic of interreligious understanding advancing critically toward the tasks and possibilities of positive compromise. Instead of comparing texts, as was once common practice, participants in exchanges today compare whole systems. Sympathetic objectivity is taking the place once occupied by ethnocentric prejudice. And the description and acceptance of existing differences leads first to self-reflection, and then to self-criticism and the possibility of substantially closer mutual approach. Especially noteworthy in this connection are Hans Waldenfels' acknowledgement of what he calls the "fascination of Buddhism," his cautious efforts to eliminate "widespread Christian intolerance," and his penetrating analysis of religious tolerance in general.

Furthermore, as I have already pointed out, comparison and criticism are essential to fruitful dialogue. In addition, they must be conducive to self-criticism making both transparent and permeable the barriers that formerly have separated the Christian and the Buddhist viewpoints.

Before leaving this topic, I should like to mention the tendency to otherworldliness inherent in both Christianity and Buddhism, a characteristic we have not yet touched on. Together with aspirations for self-perfection, both religions evolve from an altruistic ethic of service to others. In religious terms, this ethic takes the form of enlightenment in Buddhism and devotion to God in Christianity. In the final analysis, service to others naturally entails helping people to triumph over the fate and suffering to which existence in the world binds them. In both religions, the way to enlightenment of devotion to God intensifies the tendency to flee from the world and existence.

Intuitively Plato used the world of ideas as a way of finding detachment from the body and in this way virtually equated philosophical striving with a death yearning. Christianity took over much of the Platonic attitude, which precedes Christ's exhortation to repent because the kingdom of God is at hand. Schopenhauer and his followers have shown that the Buddhist tradition, too, manifests pessimistic interpretations of existence and life.

IKEDA: As I have indicated, Hinayana Buddhists, concerned with their own individual enlightenment solely, tend to turn their backs on the practical world. Mahayana teachings set out to change this but sometimes manifested tendencies to escape from reality. One of the goals of Mahayana Buddhism is saving others. But the enlightenment of the individual, too, remains a goal. And a fairly large number of Mahayanists have turned from reality in their strivings to attain enlightenment. True practitioners of Buddhism must always keep the possibility of encountering this problem in mind.

DERBOLAV: It would be a mistake to reject or diminish the transcendental elements in both religions in order to root them better in the reality of life. As I have said, the final, decisive problem of existence–death–can hardly be solved without the help of religion. Nonetheless, I should like to plead for an attitude in both that might be called either Christian or Buddhist realism, by which I mean imbuing daily human life with love and compassion. This is the greatest task of all. The spirit of the bodhisattva, who postpones his own enlightenment in the name of the altruistic service of others, indicates the presence of this attitude in Buddhism. For the Christian, union with God should inspire willingness to sacrifice happiness for the sake of others. It is in this kind of realism that I see the basis on which our two religions may overcome all of their admitted differences and enter into fruitful encounters.

IKEDA: Exactly. The Mahayana scriptures repeatedly insist that altruistic service for others is the true essence of Buddhism and tell those who follow the Hinayana path of seeking only their own enlightenments that they will never attain Buddhahood. In the *Vimalakirti Sutra*, the wealthy lay believer Vimalakirti, for whom the sutra is named, says to the bodhisattva Manjushri, "I am in pain because other sentient beings are in pain." The Mahayana spirit of altruism expressed in this remark is not only a point on which Buddhism and Christianity can come together, but also a fundamental precept that all human beings must constantly bear in mind to help them live up to the best of which they are capable.

6. Buddhism in Germany

IKEDA: More recent contacts between Christianity and Buddhism in the West than the ones mentioned in the preceding question are equally interesting. In the early days of the nineteenth century, most of the great European powers regarded India and her surrounding nations as places to be colonized. Aside from political and economical phenomena, however, a group of devoted scholars, inspired solely by intellectual curiosity and enthusiasm, undertook the serious study of Indian culture and, of course, Buddhism. The University of Berlin became one of the world's leading centers of such study.

People other than scholars, too, turned their attention toward Buddhism. Disillusioned with the Church of Rome, which had been the center of Western-European Christian life since the Middle Ages, and with the Protestant faiths that had arisen in reaction against Catholicism, many philosophers and men of letters of the early nineteenth century began looking hopefully for spiritual sustenance to the religions of the Orient.

DERBOLAV: People turn to Buddhism for various reasons. The English were lead to it through their colonial ties with India. In the case of the Germans, probably more reasons were at work: literary ambition; interest, nurtured by German idealistic premises, in Indian-Buddhist philosophy; and inclination toward cultural and linguistic research, which, with the emergence into the light of ancient Buddhist traditions, appeared to be highly rewarding fields of study; and finally, as you point out, strong religious need that, having been thoroughly disappointed by all forms of Christianity, sought a better kind of satisfaction in Buddhism.

IKEDA: As the Protestant faiths born as a result of the Reformation settled into more or less fixed patterns, the European mind found itself compelled to seek new ideals. And, as I have said, this stimulated expectations in the religions of the Orient. Perhaps the Germans were more attracted to these religions–among them Buddhism more strongly–than most other Europeans.

Under the influence of the Romantic movement, which gained great impetus in the early nineteenth century, German writers and philosophers were quick to demonstrate interest in the religions of the East. Goethe, Hegel, and Schopenhauer had a certain amount of knowledge about India as early as the first part of the nineteenth century. Later, however, the introduction of large numbers of Indian texts provided people like Nietzsche with a wealth of much more detailed information. In his criticisms of Christianity, Nietzsche refers to Brahman and Buddhist teachings.

In the twentieth century, Karl Jaspers, who was profoundly interested in Buddhism, conducted highly influential research on the great Buddhist philosopher Nagarjuna. And the novelist Hermann Hesse wrote on the topic of Gautama Siddhartha.

DERBOLAV: Yes that is true, but it is interesting to notice that the philosophical impetus for the German Buddhist movement did not come from either Hegel or Nietzsche, for both of whom Buddhism had a purely provisional significance. Hegel thought of it as only a moment in the self-development of the absolute spirit, or as only a preliminary stage to Christianity. Nietzsche, on the other hand, while considering it a later, more mature religion, used it only as a weapon against Christianity.

The only German philosopher who was able to make a philosophical commitment to Buddhism was Arthur Schopenhauer, who combined traditional elements of Brahmaism and Buddhaism (as they were then called) in the formation of his own pessimistic metaphysics of the will. In indication of his own shift from theoretical interest to actual profession of the religion–and perhaps a little in snobism–Schopenhauer had a statue of the Buddha gilded and placed in his own home. He was the first German to do so.

After Schopenhauer, the Buddha was elevated to the level of a literary theme. In 1869, Josef V. Widman wrote his *Buddha-Epos* (The Buddha Epic). Philipp Mailänder wrote his poetical *Philosophie der Erlösung* (Philosophy of Salvation) in 1874, and his *Buddha-Fragment* appeared in 1875. In 1899, Ferdinand von Hornstein published his *Buddhalegende*. And Fritz Mauthner's *Der letzte Tod des Gautama Buddha* (The last death of Gautama Buddha) caused a sensation when it appeared in 1919, at the time when Hermann Hesse was working on his short story *Siddhartha*.

IKEDA: I see. First the life of Shakyamuni caught the attention of literary artists. At this stage, possibly stimulated by a certain fascination with the exotic, Germans were more interested in actual biography than in Buddhist teachings.

DERBOLAV: Not entirely. To put the matter in a clearer frame of reference, it will be useful to point out the principal characteristics and development of the German Buddhist movement, which has existed since the 1880s. Initial impetus for the movement came from the Pali Text Society, founded by Thomas William Rhys Davids, and by a translation into German of Sir Edwin Arnold's famous poetic work *The Light of Asia*. From this it is clear that, in the acquisition of Buddhism by the Germans, neither purely philosophical-scientific nor missionary purposes assumed preeminence. In fact, both went hand in hand in all the activities of the movement.

Outstanding spokesmen for the movement were such renowned Indologists as Karl Seidenstücker and Karl Eugen Neumann, both of whom earned great respect by translating the Pali Canon. For Neumann's special eloquence as a translator, his work in translating Buddhist texts has been compared with Luther's labors in rendering the Bible into German. Another scholar, Friedrich Zimmermann amplified Seidenstücker's handbook of the Pali language with his own *Buddhistischen Katechismus* (Buddhist catechism) and in this way contributed significantly to the institutionalization of the German Buddhist movement.

This movement indeed demonstrates an overlapping of theory and practical faith since both Indologists and lawyers, doctors, scientists and so on who had converted to Buddhism as a consequence of personal encounters in East Asia with different indigenous forms of the religion participated in missionary and adult-educational activities in the support of missions and organizations expounding the meanings of Buddhist texts.

IKEDA: I am well aware of the combined respect for both theory and practice in the approach to religion of, not just Germans, but also of Europeans in general. This is very important. People remained unconvinced by practice forced on them without sufficient theoretical explanation. But, once basic principles are understood, Europeans tend to be willing to put them into practice. Failure to understand this aspect of their personality can lead to the mistaken idea that Europeans are concerned solely with theories and principles.

It is because they respect both theory and practice that I believe Europeans can find compatible the teachings of Nichiren Daishonin, who said that without both practice and learning there can be no Buddhism.

DERBOLAV: Characteristically, the German Buddhist movement centered on certain individuals. Its initiators first took such large cities as Berlin, Leipzig, Munich, Frankfurt, Hamburg, Dresden, Hanover, Bremen, and Wiesbaden as their centers. And, up to the present time, these places have been nuclei for associations, groups, unions, and assemblies engaged in missionary work and education and frequently publishing periodicals and magazines. It was only at a relatively late time that these local organizations advanced on the all-German, European, and international scenes. The German Buddhist Society, founded in 1955, was renamed the German Buddhist Union in 1958; and then, in 1961, joined the World Fellowship of Buddhism. The Buddhist Union of Europe, which held its first congress in 1977 at the House of Tranquility in Rosenburg, was not founded until 1975. The same apparently irrepressible tendency to schism into sects clinging to various interpretations of the teachings that plagued Buddhism in the land of its origin has worked against efforts for union among all these organizations.

IKEDA: It is possible that the tendency to factions in Buddhism in the Orient inspired the tendency to schism you mention in connection with European scholars and men of religion.

All religions demonstrate such a tendency, which I believe can be traced ultimately to what Shakyamuni Buddha called the Three Poisons of greed, anger, and folly. In the case of Buddhism, schism and opposition have usually arisen over differences in choice of a scripture to regard as fundamental or in interpretation of the same scripture. Nichiren Daishonin shows that, if we trace these issues back to the original teachings of Shakyamuni Buddha himself, all such differences resolve themselves. Nonetheless, dissension continues today because some people persist in being more attached to their own authority and advantage than to the truth.

DERBOLAV: Another characteristic of German Buddhism has been the tendency to unite with Hinayana and its monastic tradition. This explains the German preference for the Pali Canon. With his *Buddhist Catechism*, Zimmermann gave this tendency its first impetus by making the teachings of the World-honored One guiding moral principles for individual human life.

With his entrance into a Burmese monastery in 1901, Allen Bennet McGregor set off a chain of ordainments of German Buddhists. Plans to establish Buddhist monasteries in Switzerland, on the isle of Sylte, and in Berlin-Frohnau fell through. Nonetheless, German Buddhist monks did manage to found a retreat, consisting of five wooden huts, on the island of Polgasaduwa (in southern Sri Lanka) in 1911. Called the Island Hermitage, the retreat accommodated seven ordained monks and three monastery laymen until the beginning of World War I. The island was sold in 1914; and the two world wars interrupted but could not entirely obliterate the monastery's way of life. Three waves of similar activities, involving about a thousand European Buddhists, took place between 1903 and 1914, between 1924 and 1939, and then after 1953. But the activity subsided in the late 1950s.

I should now like to turn to some of those differences that I have already said separated various German groups from each other. First, practical Buddhist believers separated themselves from scholarly Buddhist researchers, who, so their critics said, were hindered in understanding the inner meaning of Buddhism by their predilection for the Vedanta (ancient Indian sources of Buddhism). But, since, as has been said, most German heads of Buddhist schools and associations tended to unite research, missionary work, and instruction in a practical way of life, the tension arising from this difference remained a phenomenon of only peripheral importance.

IKEDA: This is an important point. The correct Buddhist way is, as you say, to unite research, missionary work, and instruction in a practical way of life. All individuals have distinctive talents and abilities. Some are good at research and poor at missionary work. Some are good at missionary work but find putting faith into practice on their own difficult. Ideally the Buddhist should strive to unite all three of these things within himself and certainly should respect people who are good at the things in which he himself is deficient.

DERBOLAV: Much more troublesome for the unity of the German Buddhist movement was the struggle between representatives of what may be called old and new Buddhism—not to be confused with what is today called the New Buddhism in Japan.

In 1906, Karl Seidenstücker founded the Buddhist Society, a kind of missionary association that had fifty members and sponsored a journal called *Der Buddhist*. In addition, with Walter Markgraf, Seidenstücker founded the German Pali Society. Then, in 1921, together with Georg Grimm he formed the Buddhist Community for Germany, which put out the journal *Buddhistischer Weltspiegel* (Buddhist World Mirror), which for the first time attempted to make Buddhism attractive to ordinary laymen.

Grimm himself acquired great influence as a publicist, his works being translated into English and French and even into Vietnamese. In sharp contrast to Schopenhauer's poetical-mystical interpretation, Grimm saw Buddhism as a standard for orienting life and as a thoroughly realistic rationale whose teachings could be supported by syllogistic proof.

Grimm's most ardent opponent was the Berlin doctor Paul Dahlke, who, with a new theoretical interpretation on the one hand and attempts at founding monasteries on the other, ushered in the second period of German Buddhist learning:

new Buddhism. Although both were drawn to Buddhism by a criticism of their times for its regrettable lack of religious attitude and decline of fundamental moral values, Grimm and Dahlke sharply opposed each other in connection with the interpretation of the self.

Grimm allied himself with a fundamental teaching–predating both Hinayana and Mahayana–of the Buddha, who denied the existence of an everlasting, eternal, essential, self in the impressions, sensations, emotions, and other elements of the personality. At the outset, both Dahlke and Grimm shared this opinion and rejected the empirical reality of the self (atman). Grimm, however, went a step farther by interpreting the nonexistence of the individual self (anatman) to mean the nonexistence of everything: the whole world is anatman. But, according to Dahlke, in stating this, Grimm was actually returning to the point at which he accepted a transcendental self or atman. Dahlke himself, however, viewed the self as nothing more than a conceptual abstraction.

IKEDA: It seems to me that the difference between Grimm and Dahlke reflects a long-standing dispute between Hinayana and Mahayana Buddhism. In its attempts to crush the worldly Epicureanism prevailing in India in its time, Hinayana insisted that everything was ephemeral, composed of suffering, impure, and devoid of a persisting identity or self. While agreeing about the ephemeral nature of the phenomenal world and the individual self, Mahayana Buddhism perceives a greater, lasting self in the world of the law, which is a pure realm filled with joy. While manifesting the changes called life and death, this universal self is immutable and persists through transmigrations.

DERBOLAV: Dahlke succeeded in turning younger generations of German Buddhists from Grimm's position and in attracting them to his own sober, positivist view of the problem of the self. It must be added, however, that both men gave attention to only one aspect of a latent dialectic.

The controversy between the two men is today almost

forgotten. But for the sake of understanding it better, I should like to make two remarks. You yourself have commented that the constancy and identity of the self represent a decisive prerequisite for the cycle of transmigrations (samsara). You have further said, however, that this constancy and identity is inexplicable on the basis of empirical evidence of man's existence in this world. This contradiction explains both why the question is important and why German Buddhists of the old and new persuasions persistently posed it.

But this discussion is eclipsed by the dialectic developed by Nagarjuna (second century of the Christian Era) and made known in the West in the interpretation evolved in the 1950s by Karl Jaspers (who, while accepting the so-called new Buddhist view, remained a philosopher without being converted to the Buddhist religion).

Nagarjuna's dialectic is close to the double-negation method first set forth by Plato in his *Parmenides,* rounded out by the negative theology of the Middle Ages, and finally elevated to a systematic principle by Hegel. Nagarjuna's version may, however, be more subtle and radical than these other dialectic models.

If I see it correctly, following a path of consistent philosophical criticism, Nagarjuna attempts to establish a position beyond metaphysical realism and pure phenomenalism—which he described as detachment from the world (and from detachment itself). In Buddhist terms, this is called an emptying. By declaring the evidence of appearances and the terms and differentiations of language to be both being and nonbeing (in other words, to be insubstantial illusion) he intended to balance all of the phenomena of the universe. Truth as truth in the highest sense manifests itself only in the void of illusion. In other words, the Buddha exists because there is void.

I should be interested to hear how this issue of illusion, metaphysical realism, and phenomenalism is dealt with in the tradition of Nichiren Buddhism.

IKEDA: As I have said, the conflict in opinions is one between

Hinayana and Mahayana Buddhism. As part of the Mahayana tradition, Nichiren Buddhism accepts the Mahayana resolution of the issue as conclusive. The teachings of Nichiren Daishonin are concerned with the permanent, immutable Law–the greater self–and with its nature and ways of perceiving it.

DERBOLAV: Later the German Buddhist movement moved away from Hinayana in the direction of Mahayana, opening itself to other Buddhist doctrines and thus contributing to further division and splitting. In the course of these developments, Tibetan Buddhism–especially after the exile of the Dalai Lama, in 1959–and Japanese Buddhism gained increasing influence in Germany. Schools (or sects) that, partly traditional, have rivalled each other in Germany include the Karma-Kagyü school, known as the sect of virtue, which is housed in a famous monastery called Tsurpu and is directly subordinate to the Dalai Lama himself, and the Sakyapa school, which springs from the circle of Atisa's followers. These sects entered Germany either directly or by way of Switzerland and attracted many new believers because of the practical aspects of their religion, based mainly on meditation and sutra recitation.

In this connection, its special forms of meditation made Japanese Zen very attractive to the Jesuits. Laymen, too, were drawn to it, but more for the wide range of its practical aspects, including breath-control methods, archery, kendo fencing, ikebana floral arranging, the tea ceremony, ink painting, and calligraphy, all of which are intended to lead toward satori, or enlightenment.

Although the first works on these subjects, introduced to Germany by such Japanese authors as Shuei Ohasama and Daisetsu Suzuki and such Germans as August Faust, met with little popularity, a later boom in publications on Buddhist subjects inspired the famous Protestant theologian Ernst Benz to remark sarcastically that Zen had become so widespread that it was hard to demarcate Zen Buddhism from Zen snobism.

In Austria, Fritz Hungerleider, one of the most outstanding experts on Chinese Buddhism, worked with conviction to propagate Buddhism and, in Rosenburg, conducted Zen seminars that were eagerly attended by Germans and Japanese alike. Kishi Nagaya was so stimulated by attending these meetings that he formed other Zen groups, for instance the so-called Community without a Door, which came into being in Berlin in 1971.

In the middle of the 1950s, in addition to Zen, Pure Land Buddhism (Jôdo and Jôdo Shinshû) Buddhism, which springs from the tradition initiated by the priest Shinran (1173-1262) stimulated considerable reaction not only in Germany, but also in England, Belgium, the Netherlands, and Luxembourg.

Finally, through the missionary work of Soka Gakkai, especially in its center in Frankfurt, Nichiren Buddhism is becoming increasingly well known in Germany.

In 1962, the five largest Buddhist associations in Germany had a total permanent membership of 620. In addition, from 2,000 to 4,000 people–mainly academics, writers, intellectuals, scientists, and doctors–sympathized with Buddhist thought. In 1984, Karl Josef Notz made a thorough investigation of the German Buddhist movement and came to the conclusion that Buddhism can develop in Germany though it probably will not attain the status of a mass movement.

IKEDA: You mention the popularity of Zen in Germany and France. I suspect that the similarities between it and the kind of meditation practiced in Christian monasteries–similarities that may account for the large number of Zen practitioners in this part of the world–will lead to the ultimate absorption of Zen into Christianity.

Though still small, with only a few hundred members, Soka Gakkai Internationale Deutschland e.V. has the faith and the firmly established, distinctive doctrines to ensure its slow, but steady expansion. It is to be hoped that each member of the organization will strive to study and master the teachings of Nichiren Daishonin. When our German members have acquired a correct understanding of the principles of Buddhism they will be able to breathe new life into the tradition of culture and learning evolved throughout European history and in this way to contribute to its further development. When this happens, I am certain it will attain the status of a great mass movement.

CHAPTER FIVE

EDUCATION

1. Learning of Primary and Secondary Significance

IKEDA: The ultimate purpose of education is the formation of the individual human being, not only by sharpening and improving his intellectual potentials and providing him with a rich store of information, but also by inculcating in him ethical and moral standards. In this sense, I agree with the remark once made by a certain philosopher to the effect that education consists of what is left over after the person forgets all the data imparted to him in school.

But throughout history, people everywhere have tended to overemphasize the acquisition of knowledge at the expense of moral and ethical training. Everyone knows the trivia on which the medieval Scholasticists lavished attention. In more modern times, Montaigne was able to complain that both students and teachers in the system under which he was educated would have been rendered no more able even if they had possessed more extensive knowledge. He went on to remark that his father devoted all his care to stuffing his son's head with learning almost entirely without touching on judgment and virtue.

Nor has the situation been much better in the Orient, where the Chinese system of examinations for advancement in the civil service has set the example. This system was limited to the mastery of vast amounts of knowledge about the classics

157

and minute debates on the same subjects. Do you agree with me that moral and ethical training ought to take first precedence in education?

DERBOLAV: The educational ill you mention is to be found all over the world, wherever there are schools. In the German-speaking world, we use the term *Verkopfung* to indicate the kind of one-sided school education that encompasses, not the entire human being, but only the one small part called the intellect. The term means what you, and Montaigne, indicate when you speak of stuffing the brain with learning and leaving completely untouched capacities of judgment and the moral disposition, or conscience. I should like to add to the complaints of Montaigne, which you cite, those of the Moravian educational reformer and theologian Comenius (1592-1670), who, in his *General Didactics*, polemicized against the fruitless erudition propounded in the schools of his time.

IKEDA: As I know from reading the Japanese translation of *General Didactics*, Comenius has many acute comments to make. He warns against attempting to force recalcitrant pupils to learn and says that a teacher who does so is not thinking of the well-being of his charges. He further says that it is the teacher's responsibility to find some way to kindle in pupils' breasts the desire to know and to study and to avoid causing young people so much hardship that they lose the will to learn.

DERBOLAV: Seen clearly, stuffing of the head is no more than a continuation of the process whereby, from the casual pedagogic influence of adults on children, schools grew into well-organized, independent organizations. And, as might be expected, hypertrophy of mere classroom knowledge has been troublesome throughout all the centuries during which schools have evolved. As you point out, in the tradition of European education the so-called Liberal Arts, and in the Orient the Chinese classics, have represented a constant, time-tested canon apparently including everything worth knowing.

But the canon expanded by accretions of additional knowledge and, therefore, constituted an increasing challenge to student memories.

To explain how empty knowledge has come to dominate education, it is necessary to examine the anthropologico-philosophical background. Human beings require education and cultivation insofar as they are open to the outside world. The positive expression of this openness is the ability to exhibit reflexive actions in connection with the outside world; that is, to demonstrate reflectivity. It is possible to write an entire treatise on human reflectivity. Here, however, I shall limit myself to two factors, which are highly significant to our problem.

Human reflectivity manifests itself in speech and thought. In other words, on the one hand, it is responsible for the verbalization of our behavior and, on the other, it includes a tendency to elucidation and a critical element, which, in turn, leads to scientific investigation. Sooner or later, verbalization of conscious knowledge leads to the development of some kind of written script. Plato has a profoundly meaningful myth that sheds light on the ambivalence of the discovery of writing, which simultaneously reduces the labor required of the unaided memory and makes possible the perpetuation of our spiritual experiences in the form of ideas and conceptions. Both of these are prerequisite to the formation of culture and tradition and to the creation of schools for their transmission to posterity. With their appearance, thought and, later, intellect come to the forefront. In Goethe's anecdote about the Hydriotes, we have already seen that such things are largely wanting in primitive culture. No doubt, schools in cultures lacking written languages would be no less intellectually oriented than those in cultures with their own written scripts; but the limits of the memories of both teachers and students must necessarily restrict their didactic ranges.

Removing even the oral element and thereby limiting pedagogic contact to what sociologists called analogue communication causes the range of objects with which dealings are possible to the "closest environment" (Nächste

Verhältnisse), in the words of the Swiss educational reformer Johann Heinrich Pestalozzi (1746-1827). The laboriousness of conversations among deaf-mutes clearly illustrates my meaning and reveals how important the communicative function of language is.

But communication relevant to affairs can degenerate to chatter and does so whenever the impulse merely to talk gains the upper hand. This brings us to an important difference encounterable in two forms.

The famous eighteenth-century English satirist Jonathan Swift has an amusing comment to make on the attempt to avoid drifting off into mere chattiness. Lemuel Gulliver, the hero of Swift's *Gulliver's Travels*, visits an institution known as the Academy of Lagado. Among the many foolish research projects of the famous and infamous academy is one with a philosophical background. Since words stand for things, the Lagado proposal–advanced on the ludicrous grounds of sparing the lungs–is that people should carry around with them all the material things that are the topics of their conversation. When they encounter someone with whom they wish to communicate, saying nothing, they merely present their partner with the object in question. This system no doubt would have the advantage of rendering superfluous any need to go into differentiations of individual languages. On the other hand, it would compel speakers to hire servants to haul about all the things that were likely to play a part in conversation or to limit communications to topics involving only things near at hand.

Obviously, however, except in a fictitious realm like Gulliver's, our world is no longer and never again can be without written language and speech. Furthermore, the human capacity for reflective thought enables us to transcend all levels of linguistic utterance–nomenclature and composition–and to build new semantic relations. The possibilities for expanding the developing realms of linguistic meaning are so wide that levels of abstraction are boundless. In dealing with both phenomena and texts, it is of course essential that the thread of our reflective intervention remain firmly attached to reality. In both cases, reflective thought can either degenerate into trivial chatter or elevate itself to the level of scientific abstraction.

IKEDA: Human beings have been able to evolve philosophy and religion because of the ability to employ oral and written language in expressing abstract concepts. In addition, language enables us to bring into being things that do not exist yet. But the power of creativity is lost when language is abandoned and communication is forced to rely on physically present objects. Such totally abstract thought as occurs in mathematics, for example, can only exist if free of bondage to concrete things. It is true that spoken language can sometimes be mere chatter, but we must remember that chatter itself can result in creativity.

DERBOLAV: From its origin, the fruit of enlightenment, science has been destined to elevate the prescientific, anthropomorphic-mythological conception of the world to the level of controlled understanding and elucidation. The philosophy of antique-medieval times resulted from an enlightenment of this kind. The term The Enlightenment, as it applies to Europe was, however, essentially coined to indicate the turning away of the European spirit from Church doctrine, which, from the viewpoint of the new critical spirit, represented immaturity. (Kant called The Enlightenment an awakening from a state of self-imposed immaturity.)

Modern individual disciplines, which have to a great extent parted with philosophy, resulted from a further critical thrust generally called the second, scientific enlightenment. The antique-medieval philosophy was of a hermeneutic-speculative kind. The elements of its construction were the Aristotelian principles and categories–primarily the Platonic idea, or the principle of purpose and form. In spite of the sober style of Aristotelian writings–evolved by later schools–the form of expression of this philosophy was the metrical speech of a didactic poem or dialogue, as is witnessed by the pre-Socratic philosophers and Plato.

The *Artes liberales* of late antiquity considered themselves to be a compendium of speculative-hermeneutic world knowledge, including knowledge of a mathematical and natural-scientific variety (arithmetic, geometry, astronomy, and musical theory) and of the language-oriented disciplines (grammar, rhetoric and dialectics). For centuries, these contents, often in modified forms, were presented to generation after generation of young people as the material that had to be mastered.

IKEDA: Before the modernization program launched in the late nineteenth century, Japanese education had centered on venerable Chinese classical texts like the Confucian Analects, Mencius, the Neo-Confucians, and Sima Qian's celebrated *Records of the Historian*, all of which had been read by many generations of students. In the modern period, however, there is so much to be learned in connection with modern science, that these works have been relegated to courses on Chinese literature or history. No doubt the case is similar in Europe with the formerly central study of the Greek and Roman Classics–Homer, Plato, Aristotle, Caesar, Cicero, and so on.

DERBOLAV: As we have already seen, under these circumstances, even in the case of the so-called *studia humaniora* of the old humanism, materials studied were less of an empirical-scientific sort and more texts of classical authors considered educationally valuable for their specifically human substance. It is in this connection that the second important difference between significant communication and mere chatter arises.

Great masses of pedantic lumber can accrue to the fundamental knowledge structure of the texts being studied. And, unfortunately, this lumber puts as great a burden of urgency on student memories as does the legitimate object of communication contained in the texts. The extravagant amount of erudite labor devoted to philological research on Homer or Plato bears witness to this.

In this connection, it is important to draw a distinction

between what may be called learning of primary and learning of secondary significance. I will use Kant's philosophy as an example, although the thought of Plato or Aristotle would serve as well. A person who understands Kant's categorical imperative as, first, the need to examine all moral maxims that may be generally applied as obligatory to all human beings and, second, as a final ethical criterion has at his disposal knowledge of primary significance. He who knows the historical stimuli Kant dealt with in this doctrine, his psychological state during its formulation, the examples he employed to demonstrate his meaning, and the proximity between the Golden Rule of daily life and Kant's doctrine possesses knowledge of secondary importance—knowledge he can forget readily as soon as he has mastered the task of the moment. Such knowledge is what Comenius called fruitless. It is, furthermore, the kind of learning that the philosopher you mentioned had in mind when he said that education is what remains when you have forgotten all you have learned.

IKEDA: Goethe is commenting keenly on this same kind of thing when he has a student in *Faust* say that one may safely take home anything written down in black letters on white paper. This attitude reflects the kind of mistaken thinking to which both students and teachers are susceptible. Students frantically take down notes; teachers test them to see how much of the material they have memorized. On the eve of examinations, students burn the midnight oil cramming information only to forget it all promptly the moment the test is over. Increasing quantities of information to be mastered only aggravate this unfortunate educational error.

DERBOLAV: In the wake of the second, scientific enlightenment, the differences between meaningful communication and chatter take on a new character. In contrast to the older speculative-hermeneutic one, the modern theory seems to be constructive-hypothetical and to have passed through a series of methodical progressions.

Its evolution began by replacing old categories of purpose

with the idea of causality. It then moved on to quantify all qualitative scientific findings, which, once quantified, may be formalized mathematically. It ends with the technicalization of experimental research means (the stage to which the use of the computer belongs). The individual modern disciplines (increasingly, the humanities and social sciences as well as the natural sciences) constantly produce experimental, mostly statistically worked-out data that the sciences attempt to connect systematically on the theoretical basis of constructive-hypothetical fantasy.

In its most modern stamp, the difference between meaningful communication and empty chatter (or between structural knowledge and mere pedantry) assumes the form of the discrepancy between basic constructive-hypothetical knowledge and knowledge of data alone. And, it is clear that the school, as the transmitter of tradition, of which science, too, is a part, cannot remain unaffected by such developments.

School curricula and their educational elements incorporate all three areas of knowledge. And the monstrous expansion of the amounts of material that they must cover can be explained simply: it is the result of an inability on the part of teachers–and more basically of curricula structuring–to hold within bounds those fruitless aspects of learning that I have called chatter, pedantry, and data-knowledge in their instructional planning and realization.

IKEDA: In the present age of rapid scientific advance and electronics communications, the tendency to overstress acquisition of knowledge has gained new impetus. I have heard that the amount of material Japanese school children are supposed to master in a given period is even greater than what is required of students in some other countries. I know that a large number of Japanese instructors are so hard put to cover everything set forth in their curricula that they have no time to pay attention to the needs of less-gifted children, who, therefore, often become bored and disillusioned and turn to outside, not always wholesome, interests. This is one cause of delinquency. Given the Japanese pressure to place children in the best possible schools in order to ensure better future job opportunities, a large number of children are forced to attend extracurricular preparatory schools to acquire the knowledge needed to pass difficult entrance examinations. Such preparatory schools are currently among the most prosperous of Japanese business undertakings.

I can understand that modern living makes tremendous intellectual demands on people. Nonetheless, I feel that schools, in Japan at any rate, teach a great deal of superfluous material. Young people should be thoroughly instructed in the basics, with less attention paid to their ramifications. In the present age of rapid change and development, a great deal that seems highly important today is outdated tomorrow. Consequently, children need to know fundamentals that will enable them to master refinements and advances at the time when they are pertinent and needed.

For life in the world today, as for all other times, places, and races, ethical standards and what Montaigne calls *virtue* are more important than any other item in a school-child's curriculum. As I have noted earlier, the training required to inculcate such standards in young minds must begin at home, but school too must bear part of the responsibility. It is in school that children can see ethics and morality at work on a scale larger than they can experience in the home.

DERBOLAV: I understand what you mean when you say that Japanese elementary schoolchildren are required to know as much as many university students in other countries. The situation in Germany is similar except that the system of entrance examinations, which have made getting through Japanese schools a true hell, has been moderated in Germany by a method of determining admission to the next educational level at the preceding level through appropriate final examinations and evaluations.

Nonetheless, it has been shown that almost all of the educational reforms intended to make our schools more effective and up-to-date (for instance, the 1972 reform for the advanced level of our gymnasia) have indirectly lead to excessive curricula overloading. The result is that, in Germany too, less talented children are left by the wayside. The function performed by preparatory schools (*juku*) in Japan is fulfilled by tutors who must drum into the heads of the sons and daughters of solid-middle-class families the information the schools failed to impart.

Criticism does not imply that reforms are in vain. Appropriate reforms must be introduced and must extend beyond mere organizational and method procedures. Both of the improvements you suggest seem highly noteworthy. You suggest concentrating the curriculum on a fundamental kind of knowledge enabling students to apply basics to factual problems in various fields. In doing this, you touch not only on my doctrine of differences in kinds of school learning as a way of explaining the origins of the excessive material in modern curricula, but also on the nature of the remedy for the situation; that is, a basic, general education characterizable as you have described it.

In other words, first basic elements and fundamental structures for each field of study must be arranged in a way in which factual elements may be understood and clarified in systematic context. Information acquired subsequently will not remain isolated and rootless but will be firmly fixed in a matrix.

IKEDA: Just as we human beings function successfully because all parts of our bodies are articulated, so information learned can only function meaningfully when integrated with other knowledge and experience. Furthermore, when related in this way to other knowledge, information is easier to retain. I call the framework in which information can be integrated and interrelated fundamental general education.

DERBOLAV: Your demand that education be based on the inculcation of moral standards seems equally as important as your idea of a general education. I agree with you in general, although I select a different way of attaining the goal.

Certainly transmission of knowledge differs from the

inculcation of moral standards in that it depends on the memory to reproduce information either for the purpose of an examination or as working material for the acquisition of further knowledge. Establishing moral standards, on the other hand, is a personal address to the student with the aim of orienting actions in future situations toward desirable goals and functions. This is possible only if the attempt to establish such standards is practically consonant with the situations the individual must face. (We have already seen that Aristotle's interpretation of education was as a kind of elucidation of the concrete ethical experiences of action. And Hegel's opinion that early moral instruction is useful probably arose from valid hopes that human beings put to practical use in adult life things they learn from verbal instruction during childhood.)

But at this point your opinion and mine diverge. I prefer to connect the two ideas that you suggest separately into one fruitful insight. You consider ethical education at school more effective than similar education in the home because you see morality on a larger scale in the scholastic setting. Your opinion is correct but requires further explication.

I do not consider transmission of basic knowledge in school courses and inculcation of moral standards as separate tasks. As I have already remarked, I interpret moral education as casuistic clarification analyzing given behavioral situations, which are structurally implied in all truly significant school subjects. I refer to this as the praxis-relevance of school instruction.

IKEDA: As you say, the two are not separate tasks. Imbalance between transmission of knowledge and ethical ability has resulted in a situation in which startling advances in physics, biology, and nuclear physics have put horrendous means of destruction into human hands. Inculcation of moral standards from the earliest childhood and integrating them with the rest of the child's knowledge and experience are of the utmost importance. Actually I think we probably agree on this point. I merely mention the scholastic situation separately because I think ethical education establishes the direction in which the organic intellectual whole moves.

DERBOLAV: Of course, some learning situations will always entail mere drilling of information.   There will always be fields of behavior in which good morals will be modestly inculcated.   No doubt, the family is responsible for transmitting such virtues as truthfulness, loyalty, tolerance, love of peace, and camaraderie.   And in most instances cultivation of this kind is structured so simply that few problems arise.

Much more important are those complex areas of vocational, political, and social behavior that students must encounter in later life and in which cultivation is far from simple.   The person who wishes to deal with such fields successfully must both reveal their meanings and then, using what Hegel called the "effort of concept," translate the meaning into the often highly divergent circumstances of given situations.   And this demands sound instruction.

2. Education and the Political Authorities

IKEDA: The kind of voice political authority can have in the management of a nation's educational system deserves the strictest scrutiny.   In Japan, as probably in Germany, in the years preceding World War II, the government was able to intervene decisively in matters of education.   Basing their policies on the idea that Japan is a divine nation, the government at the time demanded service to the state and absolute obedience to official orders.   The aggressive militarists made use of this situation to drag the nation into war.   And it was education that made possible the nationwide dissemination of the idea of the divinity of the Japanese.

After the war, all this changed.   As the constitution clearly states, Japan became a pacifist nation.   And once again, it was education that helped alter the state of mind of the population at large. Now that the security-treaty system between Japan and the United States has been strengthened, it is still education, supervised by political authority, that is trying to guide public opinion in the direction of rearmament.

DERBOLAV: Certainly the question of the extent and legitimacy of political influence on educational life is a trouble spot. A range of problems arises in this connection in all political orders in which the educational system–as was formerly the case in Britain–lacks extensive autonomy. With outrageous ease politics can make education an expedient instrument when it attempts to force educational life not only to follow the changes and fashions of political consciousness, but also to help bring such changes about and anchor them in the minds of the younger generations.

As you point out, within the last fifty years, education has forced Japanese youth to embrace first imperialism then pacifism and, finally, to accept the necessity of reintegration into the established system of national blocs. In Germany, since 1945, it has been attempted to entrust to education the task of democratizing the German people–in two ways since East and West Germany interpret democracy differently.

Because political-party, not impartial, considerations are often their motivation, the influence and intervention of politics in education ought not to be condoned. Nonetheless, a sharp articulation of their systematic connections makes the relationship between education and politics appear sober, if complex.

Politics must fulfill for education the kind of regional competence that it fulfills for economy, law, health services, and military (strategic) security.

IKEDA: Certainly for politics to assume a leading part in matters of welfare and of social aid in time of disaster works toward the general happiness and is, therefore, desirable. Furthermore, it is probably inevitable for politics to make adjustments to protect society from the complications of vast scientific and industrial structures.

But, reflecting the boundless expansion of human greed, political authority, like other kinds of authority, strives to bring everything under its control. Training and forming the young people who will be responsible for the future is a task worthy of the greatest respect. Allowing political authority to interfere in it seems to me to trample on human dignity.

DERBOLAV: Regional competence consists of three elements. The first includes both educational policy and pedagogy, for which it is responsible. The other two, economic and political, go beyond pedagogy and open up wider horizons of motivation.

As we have seen, the goal of the pedagogic responsibility is to use appropriate means–education and instruction–to guide young people to maturity and independence. Educational policy must dedicate itself to the attainment of this goal. Its specific task is to complete its contents and–since it is relatively formal and abstract–give it qualification consonant with the political and social character of the time. Most often national constitutions lay down standards for this.

Like the Japanese, the people of the Federal Republic of Germany consider themselves a peace-loving nation that, while siding with the West in the East-West conflict, wishes to cultivate good relations with all nations. But, a few decades ago, German educational policy was ruled by Hitler's national imperialism (as that of the Japanese was controlled by a different kind of imperialism). Still earlier, the Weimar Republic made a fruitless effort to publicize its understanding of democracy through educational means. No pedagogic efforts of this kind can succeed because–and this makes matters all the worse–they contravene educational responsibility. Nazi policy certainly did this by forcing German youth to be absolutely obedient to Hitler, instead of helping it make its own independent judgments.

In short, wherever possible, we must sharply resist political manipulation of education but must, at the same time, accept legitimate political influence on education as necessary and unavoidable because of the interrelation between the two.

IKEDA: The sharp reduction of illiteracy that has taken place since the establishment of a modern system in which education is a national concern is certainly laudable. As I have said, no task is more important than training and forming people who will be responsible for society in twenty or thirty years. And I cannot help believing that attempts on the part of people in political power to control education for the sake of guaranteeing their own positions must inevitably lead to grave trouble. As you no doubt know, supervision of school textbooks by the Japanese government (in the form of the Ministry of Education) recently caused a furor, that reached international scale, by tampering with accounts of the history of World War II. In textbooks' descriptions of Japanese actions in Korea, China, and Southeast Asia, the ministry forced authors to replace the word invasion (*shinryaku*) with the word advance (*shinshutsu*), and, when this was reported abroad by the news media, several nations loudly announced their distrust and distress.

DERBOLAV: Educational policy is responsible for both curricula and textbooks. Ministerial committees, including both educators and politicians, generally make plans for both. And, in this connection, it is unwise to assign too much importance to particular persons in analyzing political influence on education. In reality, political concepts and doctrines play a larger part in forming education-system guidelines than do individual human beings. Within committees responsible for these matters, however, small groups can dominate and support obsolete ideas. This is how I interpret the attempt of the Japanese Ministry of Education to veil semantically and thus to extenuate the aggressive, imperialistic policies pursued by the Japanese Army in Korea and Southeast Asia during World War II.

Indeed, some subjects, like history and languages, are especially susceptible to such politico-ideological reworking.

A number of history texts written in the Federal Republic of Germany have also been repeatedly criticized for their accounts of World War II and have been reproached for prettifying even though the works themselves were done in good faith with no intention on the authors' parts of playing down the question of guilt.

To prevent such developments, a standing committee composed of both Germans and Poles checks all textbooks for possibly inappropriate expressions.

IKEDA: In Japan, virtually all textbook authors are keen anti-militarists and address the severest criticism to the actions of the Japanese government during World War II. The Ministry of Education, however, reviews their work and demands revisions that arouse the wrath of peoples in other Asian nations.

DERBOLAV: In addition to its pedagogic aspects, the competence of educational policy includes, as has been said, economic and political elements. *Economy* in this case means provision of all material things necessary for the execution of all educational functions. These economic necessities encompass not only space and buildings, but also teachers, whose recruiting and training are economic tasks. Even when parents bear the major financial burden of their children's education, an economic power is needed to administer and employ funds properly.

Ultimately, education may be considered a kind of commodity, which like all the other commodities in a society, should be justly distributed. It is the political aspect of educational policy that carries out this function by distributing justly opportunities for education (and, along with them, opportunities for employment). In this context, *justly* does not mean *equally* in the egalitarian sense. If it did, the task of distributing educational opportunities justly would be easy to fulfill.

Diverse standards may determine proportions on the basis of which distribution of educational opportunities is made.

Furthermore these standards are guided by divergent interpretations of the nature of a just social order. The liberal model–as the case with us–values achievement and, therefore, tends to given preferential treatment to gifted children, in accordance with their desire to learn. A socialist interpretation tends to show preference to the needy and weak in order to grant them human assistance to compensate for the things nature denied them. Finally, a conservative attitude supports hierarchical structures within society and recommends a mixed system of education-opportunity distribution according to the various natures of the component social strata.

IKEDA: Everyone will agree that distribution of education opportunities must be just, though opinions no doubt diverge on the actual nature of the term just. Of the three that you mention, I am inclined to favor the socialist concept of showing preference to the needy and weak, although I think that, in addition, it is essential that gifted children should be provided with opportunities according to their desire to learn.

DERBOLAV: I have made this differentiating analysis of the plexus of roles in the field of educational politics not to underrate their tremendous responsibility (as you rightly point out, the fate of the next two or three decades is in their hands), but to correct the preconceived notion that all interventions of politics in education are violent, capricious, or even destructive. Quite to the contrary, most political measures in the field (apart from obvious mistakes, of course) are rather sensible and well-reasoned, although they are frequently planned and implemented in so one-sided a way that they contravene other equally valid claims.

For example, in the 1970s, the social-liberal coalition in West Germany set up what were called comprehensive schools (*Gesamtschulen*) under the motto "Better education chances for the needy and weak," and went so far as to make schools of this kind obligatory for all children. In doing so, they endangered the continued existence of the German *Gymnasium* (a secondary school preparing students intending to go on to university), which has a long tradition and enjoys the support of the majority of parents in our country. Today, however, a certain balance has returned to secondary-schooling in Germany.

The necessity to make plans to a large extent on the basis of uncertain future prospects has brought perhaps unjust discredit to educational policies. For instance, during the period of German economic boom and euphoria (in the 1970s) many new kinds of universities were created by authorities who failed to take into consideration the lowering effect of contraceptive medicines on the birth rate. And, while at the present moment growing numbers of young people are still applying for admission, by the 1990s, many of these new schools may be without student bodies.

IKEDA: For the past decade, I have been insisting that education should be totally independent of the control of political authorities. My view–and I should like to have your opinion of it–is that education ought to be made the fourth branch of our parliamentary democratic system to stand on an equal footing with the legislative, executive, and judiciary branches. Though I realize that many serious problems would have to be resolved–for instance, selection of the people who would determine top educational policies–I nonetheless insist that a system of this kind ought to be instituted, at least in the industrialized nations.

In the past, education has occupied too weak a position, especially in relation to the executive branch; and I make this proposal in the hope of rectifying the situation. As the fourth branch, education should fit into the present system, in which all branches cooperate and mutually influence each other without allowing any one to gain sway.

Education must move with the times and with society. In the system I envisage, it would carry out the work of training the leaders of tomorrow without being dominated by the opinions of people currently in political authority, just as the legislative branch, without external interference, preserves and implements nationally established justice.

Politicians must not be allowed to influence education to the extent that young people, who will be the first sacrificed in time of belligerence, are conditioned to regard war as good and to go to battle at the call of old officials who will never have to face danger on the field or to divert a people's attention from domestic problems by stirring up conflict with an outside nation.

DERBOLAV: Your idea of ranking education as the fourth branch of the parliamentary democratic system reveals welcome respect for both democracy and education. From this, I would not, however, infer a special position of power–either inherent or man-granted–for the cultural area known as education. Instead, I prefer to interpret what you say as expressive of the need to treat this extraordinarily sensitive, spiritual emporium–to use the word in the sense of a place of exchanges of knowledge and information–with utmost care without attempting to force or constrain it in any way. In education, as Hegel said, everything more or less takes care of itself.

Education is most truly important when left intact and unmanipulated. It is said that education is mankind's second nature, behind which the first nature remains very elusive. Human beings owe ultimately to the education they were given or denied everything they are and have, what they have done and left undone, and their successes and failures. The effects of instruction are far-reaching and difficult to foresee. For instance, even in rectifying errors–which are likely to occur in the field of education since they occur in human life in general–one must not resort to brutal correction and interference, which can have unwanted side-effects too pernicious to justify the achievement of the desired goal. In such instances, correction is tantamount to what might be called un-correction.

Our educational system would not be a human institution if

it needed no reform of any kind. But all reforms should proceed to greater effectiveness step by step over a long period, throughout which effects and side-effects should be observed and controlled.

Since the end of World War II, on the international level, education has been represented by an important authority in the form of UNESCO. And, although you may disagree, it seems to me that granting this organization increasing weight in the play of political power might help us approach the ideal you have developed.

You must remember, however, that what you wish to elevate to the position of a fourth governmental branch is not so much education itself as education in a politically reworked form, or an authority of educational policy, which is indispensable as the spokesman of education.

If this premise is granted, it becomes necessary to select people qualified to fulfill the tasks of such an authority. Of course, they must have the same qualifications as any responsible politician. In addition, however, they must be competent in pedagogical and political matters. Consequently, in their selection, preference should go to people from the teaching profession over persons of other callings. People of political responsibility today have easy access to and indeed cannot do without technical counsel. But the final decision on given political matters is in their hands. And, for this reason, they must have the competence to make sound judgments in many fields.

Perhaps a world in which education was actually a fourth governmental branch would be, "The best of all possible worlds." In actual fact, however, we live in what might be called the "second best of all possible worlds," in which the position of this fourth branch is already filled by journalism and the other media.

My diagnosis must seem deplorable to a person who objects to journalism because of its tendency to triviality, its often inadmissible research practices, and its irresponsible way of hunting good stories. It is perhaps some consolation to realize that, in the final analysis, gathering information, reporting it, and commenting on–even basically criticizing–it are related to education–particularly adult education–even when the media themselves only present the material and leave the task of digesting it up to the individual.

IKEDA: The mass media, which undeniably present much that is questionable and perverted, address themselves to adults who can, or ought to be able to, discern and select for themselves. Education deals with children who lack such powers of judgment. Furthermore, adults do not need to accept what the media present at face value; and no one coerces them to accept it at all. School children, however, must accept what is presented to them in textbooks and by their teachers; and examinations are a kind of coercion requiring them to retain it. Consequently, biased emphasis in textbook contents can produce the gravest results. This is why I insist that maximum effort must be exerted to minimize such biases.

3. Absenteeism

IKEDA: Among the juvenile-related problems afflicting Japanese society–notably violence in the home and at school–class absenteeism is especially interesting since it has a strong bearing on general attitudes toward education. On the increase since the 1960s, absenteeism is not the mere truancy, or playing hooky, as the Americans say, that has been with us since time immemorial. In its graver forms, absenteeism becomes a pathological fear of going to school that does not seem to have been common in the past.

DERBOLAV: We have already seen two causes for uneasiness about education. One is the school organizations' loss of contact with social life. The other is the stuffing of students' heads with classroom information (concentration on mere knowledge). Now we turn to students (and teachers) and attempt to see how these causes for uneasiness reflect in pupil behavior. These reflections may take the passive form of absenteeism for shorter or longer periods or the active form of such aggression as protests against school discipline and drill. An examination of these factors will bring to light the contribution of teachers as well.

Absenteeism and violence are only two symptoms of the flaws in contemporary school life. Confronted with all of these faults, parents and teachers find themselves unable to cope. The mass media pounce on stories dealing with such problems and present them to the public eye blatantly and nakedly but soon drop them again. The problems become objects of scientific research only when they prove capable of attracting attention for long periods. And, even then, it takes years before reliable, durable insights are forthcoming from the inevitably ensuing controversies.

IKEDA: I agree that absenteeism and violence are only symptoms of a general malaise. In addition, you are correct to point out the way the mass-communications media pounce on stories about such things and give them sensational treatment. The important thing is for us to persevere coolly and with determination to attempt to treat the whole sickness, not merely its surface manifestations.

In Japan, specialists divide absenteeism into two categories: acute and chronic. When, at the outset of puberty, a child who has always been a good, regular student in the past suddenly refuses to go to school, the condition is acute. The condition is described as chronic when it starts early in school life and persists for years. Often such children are overprotected and seek asylum in the home when they find they cannot tolerate the tensions of outside life. In such instances, responsibility rests largely on the home, and not on the school at all.

Acute absenteeism, however, reveals a flaw in the educational system, particularly the overemphasis on information and the severe competition in tests for school advancement that characterize schooling in Japan today. The high hopes parents and relatives have for a child who has always been good can become a burdensome pressure; and when, at puberty, the young person begins to see things in the first light of physical maturity, questions arise as to the significance of all the information he is supposed to master. He wonders why he must try to study for promotion in school, as his parents and teachers urge. Sometimes his quandary becomes so serious that he refuses to attend class. Parents then further irritate him by insisting that he study and go to school. The young person resists all such urgings and, shunning his family, locks himself up in his room.

The outcome of this process is not always bad. Some strong young people, who formerly relied too much on their families and relatives, gain a degree of independence from this temporary period of self-isolation and may even work out a tentative program for their futures. When this happens, they finally reestablish contacts with their family surroundings and resume attendance at school, stronger, better, and more considerate than they were before. Sometimes, indeed, children who have undergone this ordeal grow into much finer, more self-reliant adults than do the perpetually good children who remain reliant, self-centered, and immature for never having undergone such psychological tempering.

Unfortunately, however, the outcome is sometimes much less satisfactory. Not all children have the psychological strength and insight to survive this period of isolation and to work out their own independent ways of living.

I think that we as adults are responsible for the creation of an education system that will enable children to develop independence and create their own futures without undergoing the ordeal of even a temporary period of isolation from school and loved ones.

DERBOLAV: Conspicuous in Germany are stress suffered by children because of their apparently unusually heavy study loads and the efforts of many parents to keep their offspring up to the mark by giving them physical stimulants that sometimes resemble drugs in their effects. It is not, of course, suitable for parents to have no interest in their children's school work (as sometimes happens in broken families or in families of the lowest social levels). But, in some instances, parents are so desperately concerned about their children's marks that the children react negatively. And, if their marks are poor, when they bring–or are supposed to bring–their report cards home after the quarter or half year, thousands of them are unwilling to show them to their parents and either run away or slip out of sight to evade dreaded punishments. Some even kill themselves.

Those children who find the courage to go home with bad report cards are sometimes met with beatings in which parental power triumphs barbarously. It is important to note, however, that the brutality parents display in such instances is not a sign of malice but an expression of embarrassment, even despair, over a situation they cannot understand and begin to regard as a kind of doom. In these cases, neither parents nor children are wanting in good intentions. But good intentions alone cannot ensure success in school. It is, therefore, to an extent understandable that students are little attracted by schools where even the best intentions soon wane.

IKEDA: In Japan, parents rarely beat their children for getting bad marks in school. Nonetheless, children are frequently subjected to cruel psychological pressures. A number of years ago a case resulting from a boy's reaction to such pressure shocked the entire nation. The father of the family was of the business elite, and the oldest son had been accepted by one of the best universities in the country. No matter how he tried, however, the younger son could not pass university entrance examinations. Although the immediate cause was apparently discovery of his having pilfered and spent his parents' money, it was actually psychological stress that ultimately drove the boy to beat father and mother to death with a baseball bat.

DERBOLAV: When asked, teachers paint a different picture. They complain about steadily decreasing student performance combined with lack of interest, discipline, and obedience and about uncontrolled rowdiness. Their complaints are seldom exaggerated. Rowdiness–and the kind of vandalism you mention–are more likely in schools that have been created specifically for the advancement of the weakest.

A certain report on the atmosphere in German schools spoke of "... broken chairs with three legs, smashed windows, half-destroyed coat racks, shredded wallpaper, electrical wires sticking out of light sockets, masses of chewing gum stamped into cracks in tile floors, cigarette stubs in halls and corridors, tossed-away paper lying around waste-paper baskets, and intolerable noise during class. During breaks, students sit on the ground, smoke, drink Coke, and play skat."

Under such circumstances, it is scarcely to be wondered that teachers are not displeased by the absenteeism–short or protracted–of students who tend to be the causes of disturbance.

IKEDA: Although it is understandable that teachers should be relieved by the absence of troublemakers who set a bad example for the others, the mission of an educator is to try to put such problem students back on the right path.

DERBOLAV: Sadly enough, it is not only rowdies or even teenagers going through puberty-related crises who become truants. Often it is innocent rural students who have farm chores to perform either before or during class and either arrive at school exhausted or fail to come at all.

School is, of course, obligatory. And there are ways of controlling attendance. But there are just as many sneaky ways of duping teachers and justifying one's absence from class. For many habitual truants, what is supposed to be nine or ten years of compulsory education actually amounts to no more than four or five. And this abbreviation has evil consequences. For example, some such children never master the fundamentals of the German language. They cannot read and often cannot write their own names. In other words, they are in a condition known as secondary illiteracy that, without doubt, is surprisingly widespread in civilized nations today.

Though actual figures are probably higher, records claim that there are about 300,000 such functionally illiterate people in West Germany, 500,000 in the Netherlands, 2 million in Britain, and from 20 million to 30 million in the United States. Schools are not without responsibility for this state of affairs since, somehow, their failure results in students' rejecting them.

IKEDA: Aside from a small number of very old people who never had the chance to attend school and, therefore, cannot so much as write their own names, the illiteracy rate in Japan is nearly zero. This is especially remarkable given the complexity of the Japanese writing system. It can be said, however, that many young people make mistakes in the use of Chinese characters and use incorrect spoken language.

DERBOLAV: Is it correct to agree with those critics of more than a decade ago who insisted that our school civilization–or more precisely the scholastification of our society–has reached a dead end? Over ten years ago, the writer Ivan Illich, who is famous in Japan too, loudly demanded descholastification and the elimination of schools as malignant growths on society. He proposed doing this by substituting for the traditional school less grievous ways of leading children and adolescents to the functions of adulthood. But, in Germany, history passed his proposals by, making it impossible to prove the extent to which they represented empty Utopianism and the extent to which they contained fruitful possibilities of improvement. UNESCO compiled an essentially moderate reform plan called "Permanent Education," that proposed a life-long cycle in which periods of instruction alternated with periods of free activity and verification with the aim of liberating children, adolescents, and young adults from the stress of school. But the program met with very little response.

IKEDA: Tsunesaburo Makiguchi, the first president of Soka Gakkai who, as an elementary-school principal, devoted his life to educating children, advocated a half-day school system that seems to have something in common with the Ivan Illich and UNESCO proposals. Makiguchi would have had children spend half of each day learning by working in actual society and the home and the other half acquiring intellectual knowledge in the classroom.

4. Violence at School

IKEDA: As I mentioned in the preceding question, violence in school is a major social problem in Japan now, as it has been in the United States for a number of years. (At present, American schools seem unable to do anything to curb vandalism, or violence to school property, as opposed to violence perpetrated against another human being.)

Violence among students is nothing new in Japan. But for a student to attack a teacher or to vandalize (especially through arson) school property is a recent development.

Does Germany face a school-violence problem similar in nature and dimension to that of Japan and the United States? How do you think we can best deal with this issue?

DERBOLAV: In addition to various other factors, aggression and school violence can arise from the behavioral insecurity that, as we know from studies by Helmut Schelsky, is characteristic of adolescence. This plus the phenomenon called acceleration, which, recognized twenty years ago, leads even to intensified physical growth, makes it understandable for adolescents and even younger children to treat teachers as peers and, without accurately evaluating what they are doing, react brutally to educational discipline.

IKEDA: Statistics show that three-quarters of the offenders in such cases are between 13 and 15 years old, or junior-high schoolchildren. The remaining one-quarter falls between 15 and 17 or 18; that is, senior-high-school age. A number of factors help to account for this age spread. First of all, in

Japan, school attendance is legally compulsory only through junior-high school. As time comes either to move on to senior-high school or go out into the world to work, young people are often disturbed by the decision to take or decline the tests required for advancement or by the need to find a job. Physiologically and psychologically, theirs is an age of resistance and insecurity that can easily degenerate into aggressiveness.

Nonetheless, most young people sublimate these pressures by discovering other goal orientations. In other words, there must be some other factor stimulating young people to resort to violence. The Soka Gakkai Educational Division Human Research Association conducted a survey among students at Tokyo public schools in the hope of discovering this factor and produced some very interesting results.

To the question "Have you ever wanted to do the following things?" 60 percent said yes to violent action at home; 26 percent said yes to violence against teachers; 20 percent said yes to vandalism of school property; 22 percent said yes to shoplifting; 5 percent said yes to sniffing paint thinner for the intoxicating effects. A quarter of the students interviewed admitted to having entertained the wish to beat their instructors. When asked their opinions of students who struck their teachers, 40 percent of the children interviewed said such actions are probably unavoidable. When asked their reasons, 55 percent said it was because their teachers do not understand them; 32 percent said it was because they disliked their teachers' attitudes or how they speak.

DERBOLAV: The Soka Gakkai investigation makes it clear that, to some extent at least, teachers in Japan are implicated in a causal way in these phenomenon and stimulates an inquiry into the ways teachers cause such mischief in school life.

First, instruction, like all routine work, is based on a psychological mechanism that, though easily seen through, is difficult to transcend. In school work, this mechanism is such that teachers show greater sympathy to quick, good learners than to weaker students, whom they consider impediments to goal achievement. As a further ramification of this mechanism, teachers tend to brand such students as indolent. This stigmatization clearly establishes a vicious circle leading the stigmatized student deeper and deeper into failure and depression.

IKEDA: You are quite right. Once a student has been branded as indolent because of a single failing, the stigma is extremely difficult to erase. Since too few teachers are willing to make the effort to attempt to erase it by taking into consideration the various potentialities and characteristics inherent in each individual, students frequently react against this–from their viewpoint–lack of understanding.

DERBOLAV: In addition, the good or bad nature of the learning atmosphere must be taken into consideration. The prestige of a given kind of school affects quality of learning. In the society of poor students, the individual is unmotivated to rival his peers and, therefore, lapses into indifference and apathy. In Germany, this occurs frequently in the kind of school known as *Hauptschule*, which has a bad reputation, and no doubt takes place in schools at various levels in Japan, too.

Under such circumstances, it is scarcely surprising that, not only teachers, but also education in general falls into discredit. In this connection, Illich's urgent plea for the de-scholastification of society has stimulated two exaggerated reactions in Germany: antiauthoritarian education and, more recently, antipedagogics. The first approach interprets the authority–or as is said, the authoritative attitude–of teachers as the cancer causing the misery in our schools and proposes establishing a kind of partnership relation between teachers and students. Antipedagogics goes a step further to consider all educational actions in connection with young people, from infants through adolescents, badly manipulative and, therefore, wrong. Advocates of this position propose, not a partnership, but a "friendship with children" and add to an inadmissible total equality between expounder and learner a sentimental kind of love that is supposed to be more than traditional "pedagogic Eros."

Both programs clearly reveal what sad fruits can be borne of critiques of schools and educational purposes made by adults who consider what they are doing to be absolutely right. It is perfectly obvious that a certain authority is indispensable in education and that, consequently, liberation of children into autonomy cannot begin in infancy.

IKEDA: Obviously total equality between teacher and pupil is inadmissible. It must be remembered, however, that teachers' attitudes are one cause of school violence. Patently, faculty members must strive to deepen their understanding of their pupils and learn to respect each as an individual human being. The tendency to overstress acquisition of knowledge prevalent in education today pushes teachers to be partial toward students who learn fast and well and makes it difficult for them to preserve a balanced view. No doubt, for this reason, the whole education system needs revising. But, no matter what the system, a teacher must be a person of sound ideals, self-aware, proud of his role, responsible, and worthy of the respect of his students. In my opinion, these are precisely the characteristics most lacking in too many teachers today.

DERBOLAV: Your interest in assisting school education to overcome its difficulties and cease presenting itself to pupils as an alien, unattractive power and thus to win their cooperation is naturally directed ultimately toward teachers. Quite consistently, you consider revamping the role and position of teachers more important than the rectification of the deficiencies we have mentioned as existing in the schools themselves.

IKEDA: Of course, rectifying deficiencies in the schools themselves is important. But the most essential issue is human contact between teacher and student. If such relations are distorted in any way, all revisions become meaningless.

DERBOLAV: Traditionally, German teaching too has dealt specifically with the problem of the teacher and has shifted from an idealistic research of models to a critical analysis of the teacher's role. In the 1920s, Georg Kerschensteiner considered it possible to apply Eduard Spranger's typology to teachers, whom he categorized as of the so-called Social Type. In doing this, he failed to take into consideration the specific social form the teacher-pupil relation constitutes.

Questionnaires have shown that nothing defames a teacher so much in students' eyes as unjust behavior toward them. But this evaluation seems beside the point when one analyzes all of the tasks teachers must perform in school. They are not merely instructors and educators. (Work in this capacity, too, entails not only a full range of social contacts–not merely encounters with students between classes–but also an understanding that instruction itself as a means of educating emanates a certain style.) Beyond this, however, the teacher must fulfill a series of bureaucratic tasks and, in giving students grades, performs a kind of political function. How can the teacher deal impartially and competently with all these diverse tasks?

IKEDA: In Japan, owing to strict controls exercised by officials of the Ministry of Education, teachers are required to make a great number of reports on administrative matters. This imposes a heavy burden of office work, which they must perform in addition to their major task of instructing children. Troublesome phenomena of this kind are common to all bureaucratic organizations.

DERBOLAV: Attempting to discover how teachers can carry out all of the diverse tasks imposed upon them brings us to the topic of their training. Earlier, we discussed the well-intentioned but ultimately unsuccessful course along which

German education reforms progressed. The course was especially mistaken in matters of teacher training.

There can be no doubt that schools and education must provide the younger generations with a key to the intensely scientific world in which we now live. For this reason, attempts have been made to orient school education scientifically, not only in the German gymnasia, but also at all other educational levels extending down to preschool. This, in turn, has compelled teachers at all strata to adopt science as their model. Students, therefore, must leap over learning connected with everyday, prescientific matters and, without special assistance in making the transition, enter the realm of scientific abstraction.

To this must be added the constant change taking place in both the theory and the practice of teacher training and the influence exerted on that training by the various existing forms of school organization–comprehensive high school, differentiated special schools (gymnasia), and so on–and the systems of examinations associated with them.

A student may, with trouble and difficulty fulfill all the requirements by going through all the formalities, passing all the examinations, and in a more or less dilettante fashion acquire a further infusion of scientifically oriented thought by attending seminars on teaching method. But such a course of training does not and cannot make that person a good teacher, if, when it is over, he merely puts it pleasantly behind him.

In Germany, as in all other fields, in teaching too, professionalism has been so all-permeating that the old idea of a pedagogic calling has been eliminated, leaving behind nothing more than the official, formal, academic, teaching trade.

To end this comment on the negative aspects of German schools and education on a less pessimistic note, I should like to add the following point. You say teachers today lack traits that can win respect in students' eyes. In addition, I find wanting the confidence that the work of teaching–no matter how defectively or ambiguously imparted–is not merely a function to be fulfilled by means of educational technology, but also a profoundly, humanly significant work enabling the teacher to rediscover himself in the people he trains and educates. Inspiring in teachers confidence of this kind may be the way to restore a part of the faith in teaching as a special vocation that was once common to both European and Asian teaching traditions.

IKEDA: The question of whether teaching is just another job or a true vocation is significant. In Japan, after World War II, teachers began participating in labor movements in order to better their working conditions. As this happened, they came to consider themselves more or less ordinary workers. There is certainly nothing wrong in their struggling to improve the conditions under which they work. But, when doing this causes them to abandon awareness of education as a vocation, their self esteem and dignity diminish. This point deserves consideration as one of the causes of the current desolation of the teaching field.

I do not imply that teachers must tolerate poor working conditions because theirs is a vocation and not a mere job. But any person doing any kind of work that contributes to the good of society should take pride in his labor as a calling. We can expect nothing fruitful from educational activities conducted by people who have lost enthusiasm and an awareness of the tremendous importance of their vocation as the personality-formers of people who bear the responsibility for the future.

Education today must discover a new starting point in inspiring–not compelling–teachers to develop self-awareness of the high nature of their calling.

5. Juvenile Delinquency

IKEDA: Though juvenile deliquency has been a problem in Japan for a long time, the social status of delinquents today is higher than that of such offenders in the past. Once most juvenile criminals came from impoverished, ill-educated, or broken homes. Today the offspring of families in good financial condition with both parents living account for the majority of juvenile offenses, which range from theft (the most frequent) to extortion, violence, and sex-related crime. Most of the stealing is done not out of necessity, but for thrills. Something similar can be said of the motivation behind the other kinds of offenses mentioned. Sociologists refer to this phenomena as amusement-oriented delinquency.

Its major cause seems to be a general lowering of awareness of standards and rules extending throughout the family, the school, and all society. Furthermore, the hedonism prevailing in modern society and a plethora of pleasure-directed advertisements and other information easily influence susceptible young people to forget social rules in their eager pursuit of fleeting delight.

DERBOLAV: Today, as juvenile delinquency has become especially notorious, it is the trend to think of youth predominately in a negative light as protesting, restless, disturbed, dropouts. In ancient times, it was said that women were best when not spoken of. The same thing is assumed to be true of youth today. Under these circumstances, the period between childhood and adulthood–the time for imparting discipline, cultivation, and civilization (stages Kant traced in human history, but also stages in the course of individual human development)–should pass by as eventlessly and as inconspicuously as possible. To people who feel this way, the best answer to give when asked how their children are is "All right."

People are always ready to see something ill in children who step out of the shadows of normalcy and demonstrate symptoms of deviation. Moreover, the press has a special liking for picking up the shocking things young people do and showing them in a sensational light.

IKEDA: Young people often start out merely deviating and gradually, in reaction against criticism and nagging from adults, sink into delinquency. Journalism aggravates the situation by, as you say, picking up every untoward thing young people do and treating it in a sensational manner. Children ought to be protected from such unfeeling adult behavior. Unfortunately, however, a surprisingly small number of adults have the conscientious understanding to offer the needed protection.

DERBOLAV: Objectively analyzed, public attitudes on this topic run in three directions: 1. the quantitative expansion of juvenile delinquency; 2. the increasing depravity of juvenile offenses; and 3. a growing inclusion of younger and younger age levels in the critical zone of liability. (A certain report on trends in Japan comments that, in your country, juvenile delinquency is growing at a rate double that of the increase in adult crime. Although I make no judgments on Japanese society, from this study I have learned the interesting fact that crime in Japan is generally much lower than it is in Europe.)

To determine how typical such trends are under the circumstances prevailing in Germany, it is necessary to compile a list of all variables making possible a qualitative and, to an extent, quantitative analysis of the problem of juvenile delinquency. Next a systematic study of the numbers and gravity of crimes–presupposing a loose correlation between the two–would be necessary. Then it would be essential to examine the age levels, social backgrounds, and motivations of all people considered suspects.

Most common among young criminals are petty crimes involving damage or loss of property. Next in frequency are theft, robbery, embezzlement, and forgery. These crimes constitute the transition between petty offenses and acts of brutality usually ending in bodily injury. Sexual offenses and attempts against life are rare among juveniles. Of course, a number of other criminal acts fall outside this list.

IKEDA: Juvenile criminal acts that you mention as most prevalent–damage and loss of property–may well be committed with an attitude no more serious than the one that leads children to scribble on the living-room wall or appropriate for their own use things that are by right common family property and may, therefore, arise from mere ignorance or lack of awareness of social rules. Delinquency of this kind might well be prevented through education. Adults are too severe when, judging on the basis of their own criteria and assuming that children understand social rules that are in fact unknown to them, they brand such misdemeanors as crimes.

DERBOLAV: In the affluent society of Germany, as you say is the case in Japan as well, motivations for juvenile crime can hardly be said to stem from hunger or actual material need and are essentially pleasure-oriented. Indeed such crime frequently arises from a passion for gambling or adventure. Young people of a higher degree of schooling are rarely involved in serious crimes like robbery and breaking and entering, whereas as much as 10 percent of such crimes are committed by students from the special schools for academically weak children (called *Sonderschulen* in Germany). On the other hand, students from schools for higher achievers (the gymnasia, for instance) are excessively highly represented in cases of shoplifting, misappropriation, and forgery.

Though it might seem likely, it has not yet been proven that such conditions as unemployment as well as alcohol and drug abuse play important roles in juvenile criminality. It is true that in 1977, in the environs of Munich, 50 percent of the unemployed young people were involved in crimes; and the figure rose to 66 percent in the case of such serious crimes as theft and robbery. In contrast, only 10 percent of the young criminals were shown to be under the influence of alcohol. And, in only one-third of one percent of all cases was there evidence of drug use. As a rule, crimes committed by people under the influence of alcohol were violent, usually involving bodily injury.

IKEDA: This is understandable since nonviolent crimes require a modicum of self-control, which alcohol and drugs reduce.

DERBOLAV: As is indicated by the negative results of an inquiry into the matter conducted recently at the European Court at The Hague, the assumption that the rapidly rising unemployment rate leads to more juvenile crime is no more than a legend. Within my own sphere of observation–Munich and environs in the late 1970s–the rates of increase in juvenile and adult crime are approximately the same. And some studies claim that the supposed greater increase in crime among the young is a statistically created myth.

These facts mean that we must be cautious in dealing with quantitative data and, all the more so, with qualitative analyses. For instance, it is impossible to prove the existence of a trend for crimes to be perpetrated by increasingly younger individuals. Furthermore, it is reasonable to assume that the majority of juvenile crimes–especially pleasure-oriented ones–occur episodically and are developmentally conditioned. Moreover, acts of juvenile criminality serve as the beginnings of criminal careers only in the presence of pathological tendencies and a combination of unfortunate social conditions.

It must be recalled that juvenile criminality is dominated by petty acts, causing little damage–50 percent of such crimes in Munich involved losses of less than 10 marks. Caution is needed, too, in speaking of the intensified brutality–often hawked on by the media–of juvenile crimes. Such an assumption depends on how statistical research is conducted and interpreted.

IKEDA: Clearly the task facing us is to create an overall social mood in which standards and rules are respected in the home and at school and to educate young people in such a way that these standards and rules become deeply rooted in their awareness. As I have already had occasion to say, such education and training must begin in preschool years in the home; and, without concentrating exclusively on the acquisition of knowledge, schools must train their young charges in the practical application of social standards.

Some people believe that governmental intervention in the form of legislation is justified for the sake of improving lax public morality. Certainly the blatant sexual portrayals of many of the books, photographs, and motion-picture posters surrounding young people is undesirable, as is the excess violence portrayed in some television programs. But legislatively interfering with such things is equally undesirable, since it can infringe on artistic liberty and the freedom of expression. The course adults must follow is not to try and remove all offensive elements from the environment–an impossible task at any rate–but to instill in children the judgment and self-control to remain unstained by unwholesome factors. Resistance to contamination must be cultivated, since children bred in a hothouse atmosphere of overprotection are unlikely to be strong.

DERBOLAV: In dealing with this whole problem it must be remembered that the point is not what happens or has happened, but what the police have registered as crime or suspect of being criminal. Not every adult who has been the victim of juvenile delinquency goes straight to the police. Many settle the matter with the young offender himself to spare themselves trouble and then use the occasion as motivation to make their property more secure. In general, it can be said that the more serious the crime, the more accurate the statistics.

Indisputably, juvenile crime is a regrettable ill, the minimizing of which is the responsibility of adults. But it must be conceded that prison does less to promote the development of children and the young than any other place. Although prison may have a rectifying influence on adults, wardens can be expected to exert no educational influence on children and young people under their charge, even when the much-vaunted opportunities for further education and training are provided. All that young people acquire in prison is, at best, further motives for new punishable offenses and tricks whereby to pursue them successfully. Consequently, juvenile prisons are as a general rule the first stage in a professional career of crime.

IKEDA: Juvenile correctional institutions publicize the methods of dangerous criminals, who are held up as heroes, and in this way often supply young people with an education in iniquity. What then is to be done to reduce juvenile crime?

DERBOLAV: We are in agreement that, in our hedonistically oriented civilization, which commercializes all kinds of entertainment, from pornographic excitement to excessive violence, a readjustment of our environment promises little hope of success. Sadly, the seductions of our environment can poison traditional family moral standards. In our circumstances, on the one hand the media illustrate how quickly it is possible to become rich and famous by means of crime and corruption, while Marxist-bred sociocritical ideologies, on the other hand, despise the established respect for personal property, which they brand as legalized theft.

Hoping to immunize children and young people against undesirable influences might appear mere wishful thinking. Nonetheless, I feel that hope can be found early in the family, which you have repeatedly described as the nucleus of moral education.

I regard the family as having a double task. Young children need loving care if they are to accept their parents' life standards without reservation. Providing that care is one of the family's tasks. At a later time, when they are about to become integrated in their own peer groups, children need help in dissolving family bonds and initiating self-development.

The possible good and bad significances of youthful self-development are clearly indicated by certain social phenomena. For instance, criminal offenses committed by bands of juveniles, dropout groups, and certain sects that appeal to young people who lack guidance or a home by pretending to offer them true group life reveal how the impulse to develop independence can go astray. On the other side of the coin, certain youth organizations commit themselves to fruitful work and, in this way, help others in an altruistic fashion.

We must, therefore, welcome and approve all political, social, and private support for the integrity of the family and all control and rehabilitation of youth organizations by supporting their productive activities. Although they may not eliminate juvenile crime, without doubt a serious social problem, such measures may at least keep it within bounds.

6. Fairy Tales

IKEDA: The educational value of the folk story or fairy tale is a question of great interest. In recent times, parents, in Japan at any rate, seem to veer away from old-fashioned children's stories in favor of gentler ones that contribute to the cultivation of well-rounded, considerate personalities.

The older stories, in both the East and West, are, however, often quite grisly and frightening. The tales told by the brothers Grimm, for instance, are full of horrors. No matter how poor they were, judged by ordinary standards, their parents deserve little praise for leaving Hansel and Gretel alone in the forest merely because they had no more food to give them. The witch in the house of cakes is fearsome indeed in the way she fattens children to eat them. And Hansel and Gretel themselves demonstrate scarcely laudable sides of human nature when they gleefully shove the old witch into the hot oven.

As fierce and bloody as such tales are, however, they are usually passed on to children by kind and loving mothers or grandmothers. I cannot help wondering what their purpose is. I realize that psychologists and other scholars have extensively analyzed and interpreted folk tales; but I should be very interested to hear your views on them and the educational effects they produce.

DERBOLAV: The subject matter that their creators' imaginations have employed in this literary genre–especially the many gruesome and horrifying experiences the stories relate–can hardly be conducive to the fundamental trust that psychologists like Eric H. Erikson hold as a prerequisite of a healthy, untroubled way of life.

But the horrible element is predominant only in some folk tales, like those collected by the brothers Grimm and, of course, *Hänsel und Gretel*, which you mention as an example. (It is true, however, that some tales, though specifically educational in nature, fall into this category. E. T. A. Hoffmann's notorious *Struwwelpeter* is a case in point.)

In contrast to the folk tales, a genre of literarily composed fairy stories (*Kunstmärchen*), which has been purged of horror and refined, appeals not only to children, but to adults (parents and teachers) as well.

For their part, true folk tales bear traces of the era in which they came into being and reflect the bitter social needs of the peasant and artisan populations. In addition, they brim with the superstitions that Christianity proved unable to eradicate.

A striking indication of the signs of the times embodied in these tales is the malicious, often witchlike role assigned to stepmothers in many of them. At the hands of these women, innocent children seem to be fated to undergo terrible things. Behind this portrayal of stepmothers is an indication of the high mortality rate of women in childbirth before the discovery of the nature of puerperal fever. Widowers left with numerous children to look after had to find replacement-mothers as quickly as they could; and, as might be expected, hastily selected stepmothers did not always live up to expectations.

Without doubt, the power of evil, horror, and the gruesome in folk tales does not fit into the sentimentally purified world of childhood experience as we should like it to be. The discussion of the remarkably unchildlike nature of many of these tales began with the Grimm brothers themselves–the very fathers of the genre–who addressed their contemporaries in a defensive and apologetic way. Nor have great educators remained silent on this topic. Differences of opinion about fairy tales can be traced as far back as Plato; and to Rousseau, Kant, Jean Paul, and Friedrich Schleiermacher; and up to Ellen Key and such psychologists and psycho-analysts as Charlotte Buhler, Anna Freud, Bruno Bettelheim, and Erich Fromm.

The purists among these people–surprisingly, Plato, Kant, and Rousseau the so-called child-discoverer are in their number–interpret children on the basis of the tabula-rasa model and consider folk and fairy tales lies and deceptions that must be kept away from children at all costs.

People with a deeper, more open understanding, who accept the difference between children and adults–Jean Paul, Friedrich Schleiermacher, Ellen Key, and most of the psychologists and psychoanalysts fall into this category–view folk tales as reality on a scale suited to children and consider the wealth of their content a great help in juvenile development. These people speak in terms of what they call childhood's magic phase, which has its own special structure and precedes distinction between the worlds of fantasy and real experience. With its egocentric stamp, this phase gives plenty of scope to the anthropomorphic way of thinking. Life in it knows only extremes of big and little, beautiful and ugly, good and evil but does not recognize intermediate shadings between opposites. And, as was once said, it liberates the heritage of fantasy and myth inherent in every child.

IKEDA: Fairy tales teach children of the existence in the world of good and evil and inculcate fear of evil. As you say, the wicked stepmothers appearing in them reflect the conditions of the times in which the stories came into being. I believe that, in addition to this, they teach children gratitude for the loving mother and father who protect and make them happy.

DERBOLAV: Modern psychoanalysts are less naive than the older moral purists in their evaluations and criticisms of folk stories and trace the cruelty in these tales to the sadistic tendency of human nature. As an example of the approach, the newer kind of interpretation sees the very name *Little Red Riding Hood* as a symbol of menstruation and the story as a version of a girl's first encounter with sex. The wolf, who represents the male, carries out the sexual ceremony in a cannibalistic fashion (Erich Fromm).

IKEDA: Fromm's interpretation strikes me as a little farfetched. The moral appended to the story by the Frenchman Charles Perrault seems more to the point.

Perrault says that it is a grave error for children, especially pretty, gentle little girls, to lend an ear to strangers, for, if they do, they can expect to be gobbled up by the wolf. He then goes on to say that not all wolves are alike and that the kind to be most on guard against is the shrewd, quiet, smooth, unruffled, friendly, kindly, soft-spoken wolf who follows girls home and right to the bedside. As everyone knows, he adds, the gentle wolf is the most dangerous. In other words, Perrault points to sexual experience as a wolf about which little girls should be wary.

DERBOLAV: Clearly, interpretations of the kind mentioned earlier further lower the estimation of fairy tales as reading material for children. And they lose their final credit as juvenile literature when they are interpreted in the Marxist-oriented ideological critical fashion, according to which folk and fairy tales reproduce the feudal and bourgeois social structure of the times in which they are set and uncritically perpetrate to generations of childish auditors the idea of obsequious women, regimented children, and the either violent or good-natured fathers.

IKEDA: However, I think it should be pointed out that, as is illustrated by Hansel and Gretel when they push the witch into the oven, not all fairy-tale children are completely submissive to authority and some could have provided young Marxist readers with splendid revolutionary examples.

DERBOLAV: The dispute over the pros and cons of these tales

can be rounded out with a consideration of the convincing, moderate interpretation of depth psychology in such works as Bruno Bettelheim's *The Uses of Enchantment: The Meaning and Use of Fairy Tales*. Bettelheim insists that still another element must be taken into consideration in interpreting folk tales. That element is the mortal fear of death that all children experience and with which they must somehow come to terms in early childhood. The fear may have a number of things as its cause: the trauma of birth, traumatic experiences during early infancy, or the loneliness of separation from others that can terrify children. In the eyes of the psychoanalytic interpreters, in their very horror and cruelty, folk tales bring cathartic liberation from this fear. Or, as Bettelheim puts it in connection with *Hänsel und Gretel*, "If our fear of being eaten takes the form of a witch, we are freed since we can burn the witch in the oven."

A child does not push away the terrifying elements encountered in fairly tales, nor does he pass them by because his naive mind is incapable of understanding evil. Instead, he relates them all to himself and passes through all of them with the intensity of his own purification. It is prerequisite, however, that ultimately everything be put in order in a way that does not violate the impression of a safe and sound, childish world. Children are not like readers of detective fiction, who presuppose that good triumphs and evil is punished. Still, they are capable of understanding death and tragedy, as is clearly indicated by Antoine de Saint-Exupery's *Le Petit Prince*.

In agreement with all the defenders of the educational fruitfulness of the childish world they represent, I favor retaining folk and fairly tales as juvenile literature. In addition, I consider it erroneous to wish to purge that world of all its horrid, fearsome, and gruesome elements, although modern story tellers might tone things down a bit or adapt them to the times.

IKEDA: In Japan, witches and goblins are replaced by red and green demons, usually, but not always, male; possessed of horrendous strength; sporting one or two horns on their heads; wearing tiger skins around their waists; and bearing long, heavy, iron rods. Popular belief sometimes sees the work of demons in artifacts from the Stone Age or in natural features that look as if they might have been artificially produced. (Such creatures have influenced vernacular speech in most parts of the world. For instance, the word *oni*, or demon, is used in Japanese to mean cruel, unscrupulous human beings, just as such people are described as devilish and fiendish in English.)

Demons and goblins might be interpreted as representations of the bad aspects of human nature and might, therefore, serve the purpose of the instructive negative example.

DERBOLAV: Popular myth and imagery prevailing in their land of origin determine whether such characters take the form of witches and goblins or red and green devils. Furthermore, it would be strange if our present-day technologically oriented world failed to influence children. Recently, in the West, technical fantasy has produced the Muppets of television fame and has been concentrated in Mickey Mouse and in Donald Duck, who not long ago celebrated his fiftieth birthday.

Probably no literary creations remain alive longer in the consciousness of generations or appeal more strongly to the needs of fantasy than fairy tales and children's stories. The Grimm brothers and their contemporaries from the German Romantic period collected, or created, an invaluable treasure of such stories, which was internationally enriched by other European nations throughout the nineteenth century.

I should like to cite four works in this field that have left an especially strong impression on the childish imagination in the West. One is *Le Petit Prince*, by the French aviator Antoine de Saint-Exupery, which I have already mentioned. The second is *Alice's Adventures in Wonderland* by the Oxonian mathematician Charles Dodgson, whose pen name is Lewis Carroll. The third is *Die unendliche Geschichte* (The Neverending Story), and the fourth is *Momo*, by the German author

Michael Ende. These books are appealing for the way in which they break with established stereotypes and introduce new elements of fantasy.

One can only be completely captivated by the Little Prince, who falls to earth from his tiny planet; requests the narrator to draw pictures of animals and animal pens for him; has remarkable adventures on travels to other planets; and finally, after a sad and moving farewell, returns to his own planet. Lewis Carroll is unsurpassed in the kind of thing he does when he shows Alice and the encounters made possible by her changing physical size with a whole world of personified animals. And Michael Ende's art of peopling his fairy-tale land, called *Phantasien*, with surprises thought out to the last detail is difficult to equal. His inspired idea of weaving the little boy who is reading the "never-ending story" into the narrative itself, putting the reins into his hands, and then allowing him narrowly to escape from the compromising world of reality is unexpected and original enough to amaze the most jaded reader. (The device does, of course, have forerunners in the folk-tale poetry of the German Romantic period.)

The little girl Momo, the heroine of the book of the same name, fascinates the reader with her readiness to listen patiently, a readiness that gains her new friends, reconciles squabblers, and even conquers the time-saving association of the little gray men, who, if I am correct, represent the deluded context of modern commercialism.

These stories appeal not only to children but also to all adults who have a longing to return to the land of childhood, even if for only a brief and limited period. Brahms convincingly expresses this longing in this well-known song *Sehnsucht*.

IKEDA: The things that recall childhood differ from individual to individual. The aroma of a piece of madeleine infused with tea vividly recalls the past for the hero of Marcel Proust's *A la recherche de temps perdu*. But changes occurring with the passing of time make the world we experience very different from the one experienced by our children. Having been brought up on the same fairy stories preserves a common foundation at the personality level where spiritual ties transcending generations may be formed. This is why today, when alterations in society and life styles take place at a more violent pace than ever before, protecting this foundation by carrying on the venerable tradition of telling the old fairy stories is immensely important.

CHAPTER SIX

FOR THE FUTURE

1. Bulging Cities and Vanishing Forests

IKEDA: Though the planet Earth must accommodate many future generations, driven by desires or acting under foolish impulses, people today threaten to make the globe uninhabitable for those who will follow us. When man first appeared on Earth some hundreds of thousands of years ago, his comparatively small numbers and relative lack of technical skill prevented his doing too much harm to the natural environment and its power and rhythms. Human beings came to take so optimistic a view of the inexhaustible blessings nature offers that, in our modern period of tremendous technical sophistication, many still believe destruction of a part of the environment can make no great difference to the total scheme of things.

But, though undeniably mighty, the natural world is delicate too; and the complex actions of all its parts are densely and intimately interwoven and interdependent. The destruction or alteration of one small region extends to neighboring regions and ultimately affects the entire globe, as a stone cast into a still pond makes rippling circles that soon disturb the entire surface. Since human activities depend on its subtle harmony, any alteration in the world of nature could make continued survival of our species impossible. Our situation is like that of some fragile, delicate substance on the shore of a pond. A stone thrown into the water even at a great distance can cause waves that, extending to the bank, can wash that substance away.

We are able to live because of an ecological system slowly and painstakingly evolved on our planet over thousands of millions of years and because of the essential elements stored in that system. Oxygen in the atmosphere is only one of them. But human action frequently destroys the very elements on which we depend. For instance, by consuming such fuels as wood, coal, and petroleum in too great a quantity, we are reducing the amount of oxygen in the atmosphere. We further aggravate the situation by polluting the seas in which dwell vegetable plankton that replenish oxygen and by cutting away the Earth's forest cover, which serves a similar purpose.

DERBOLAV: Our dialogue would fail to complete its task if it did not deal with the future of mankind and of life in general–on Earth, if life is actually limited to our planet. You mentioned first destruction of our forests and pollution of our environment.

Before going into them in detail, I should like to discuss the background from which the imminent catastrophes you mention–signs of our times–have arisen.

IKEDA: The problem has broad ramifications, but arises from one source: so-called progress in human civilization. I consider it correct to go into the background of this syndrome of problems.

DERBOLAV: The branch of study known as stratobiology, or exobiology, which has developed from a combination of natural sciences and has been in existence for about 60 years, deals with the question of life and intelligence on other planets in other stellar systems. There are two general opinions about the possibility of extraterrestrial life. One considers the assumption that the existence of our own species on Earth is unique to be human arrogance, and insists that astrophysical conditions permitting the existence of life (even higher, intelligent forms) must prevail elsewhere in the infinite expanse and plenitude of galactic stellar systems. The other opinion holds that the appearance of humanity and of intelligent life is a unique historical occurrence that, because of the extraordinary complexity of the required conditions, is virtually impossible to repeat.

Each opinion excludes the other, and at the present time it appears impossible to settle upon either. Nonetheless, both locate the specific characteristic of human civilization in its technical efficiency and not in cultural productivity as reflected in such philosophical and spiritual aspects as art or religion.

The human life situation has been altered to both our advantage and our deadly peril in our animal relationships. But the change has not been brought about by the legacy of our written literature, the products of philosophical reflection, or self-orientation in the world as evolved by philosophy. Nor have such things as architecture or sculpture (the preservation of which you quite rightly consider the obligation of all humankind) brought about the change. The source of the alteration has been solely and exclusively the technical reworking of nature and the things human beings, owing to their constructive inventiveness, have been able to generate from its wealth of productive possibilities.

It is interesting to note that, in questioning and probing the possibilities of technical civilization on other planets or in other stellar systems, the exobiologists either forget or soft-pedal two essential stimuli for humanity's technical productivity: the stimulus for industrial production arising from profit interests and the stimulus provided by the power-drive inherent in the defense establishments of the great powers.

Certainly, whereas Christians of an earlier time considered themselves divinely decreed from the cradle to be subjected to nature, the technical efficiency of civilization has made human beings masters over nature and has provided food, dwelling, and all of the amenities we could desire.

IKEDA: Many ethnic mythologies include elements of justification claiming technological powers to be divine gifts.

For instance, Chinese tradition says that a legendary monarch named Buxi initially instructed the Chinese people in hunting and fishing, another similar figure named Shennong taught them agriculture and medicine, and the fabled Yellow Emperor (Huangdi) taught them metallurgy. In Greek mythology the titan Prometheus, who stole fire from the heavens for the good of humankind, was severely punished by Zeus, the monarch of the gods.

Believing themselves commissioned by God to have providence over all other creatures, Christians have never interpreted technical skills and powers as evil.

DERBOLAV: The relatively primitive agricultural techniques of preindustrial times took from nature what she was ready to give. In other words, it allowed nature to remain in full possession of her own powers. Industrial-technical reworking of nature, however, has resulted in the kind of continually growing, virtually uncontrolled exploitation that Marx myopically perceived only in connection with the working classes. (In the period that has passed since Marx, workers have learned how to deal with such exploitation.) Nature, which Marx overlooked, cannot defend herself. She must accept what human beings, a thousandfold more than her match, do to her and must be what they make of her.

IKEDA: Marx no doubt overlooked nature because he was unable to break from the Judaeo-Christian tradition according to which nature is to be exploited by human beings.

DERBOLAV: In relation to an interplanetary consideration of the context of this problem, nothing brings the full extent of the economic and strategic stimuli for technical progress more clearly to light than the destruction human beings are wreaking on their own natural environment.

The steady increase of our population, which has long gone unchecked and which is now becoming a grave threat, patently reveals the negative and positive elements that, intricately intertwined in technical and industrial effects on world civilization, have, if not caused, at least made possible these symptoms of catastrophe. Let us assume that world population stood at about 250 million at the time of Christ's birth. In the next 1,600 years, it reached 500 million. It took only two centuries more to bring the population count to a billion and only another century to double that. Since 1930, when two billion people inhabited the Earth, the count has risen to four billion. And by 2000–15 years hence–we will have to reckon with about six billion.

IKEDA: In other words, in the mere fifty-some years since 1930, the world population has more than doubled. Plotted graphically, population increases in the past century or so can only be called explosive.

DERBOLAV: The greatest future increases will take place in developing regions in India, South Asia, Africa, and South America. According to statistics presented at the World Population Conference in Mexico City in 1984, every minute, 234 babies are born–136 in Asia, 41 in Africa, 23 in Latin America, and 34 in all the industrialized nations. At present, the world population is increasing at a rate of 80 million a year.

Parallel with this growth is the trend to urbanization, which can only lead to increased environmental pollution. Cities with extensive industrial enterprises are growing on a gigantic scale. For instance, the region between Washington D.C. and Boston is one completely urbanized sprawl in which live 40 million people, or about as many as live in Spain and Portugal together.

At the beginning of the nineteenth century, the percentage of the world's population living in cities of more than 20,000 was 2.4 percent of the total population of the globe. By 1951, city dwellers had come to account for 21 percent of the population of the world; and, by the year 2000, their number will increase sixfold. Capital cities, bursting at the seams, already indicate this trend especially dramatically. By the end of the century, the urban population will have come to outnumber today's world population, since, as a rule, owing to the steady concentration of populations in cities, the urban population grows five times as rapidly as the rural population.

The progressive escalation of human population is a natural expression of human biological vitality. In preceding centuries, Malthus's simple laws of self-regulation–starvation, infant mortality, short adult life-expectancy, epidemics, and plagues–maintained a relative balance and kept the number of human beings down. But advances in medical science and the development of such things as penicillin, pesticides, and inoculations, which have eliminated diseases like smallpox, and care–though still incomplete–of the peoples of the Third World, have eliminated the effects of self-regulation by increasing life-expectancy and decreasing infant mortality.

In addition, the discovery of riches in the form of natural resources and productive power has pulled developing nations into the maelstrom of the widening economy of the industrialized world and has enabled them to establish their own industries and new areas of agricultural production that give their peoples work and food.

But these positive developments are as ephemeral as drops of water on a hot stone.

IKEDA: All forecasts are, of course, based on the assumption that the current rate of population growth will continue unabated. In parts of Asia and Africa, where large segments of the population stand on the brink of starvation, birth rates continue to rise. This means that hunger may replace disease as a population-regulator. Even if the world manages to escape nuclear warfare, it must still face the obstacle of hunger.

DERBOLAV: Population in the Third World is growing by from 3 percent to 4 percent annually, while food production rises by only 1.3 percent. This means an entire and apparently endless horde of horrors. For instance, the developing nations may have to anticipate famine on an unimaginable scale by the years between 2025 and 2050. In connection with this, massive unemployment will constantly increase. Although exact figures for these phenomena are difficult to obtain (data and analyses employed in calculations about the future vary) all indications point to apocalyptic times.

IKEDA: In the name of what is called development, the great Siberian and Canadian coniferous forests are being destroyed, as are the tropical rain forests of the Amazon basin. American troops sprayed defoliant on the Vietnamese mangrove forests, which may never recover.

Of course, such apparently vital reasons are advanced as the essential nature of timber exports to financial stability, or the importance of clearing forests to open more agricultural land and, thereby, contribute to the feeding of the world's population. Nonetheless, since it is certain that continued deforestation of the world may well lead to an absolute insufficiency of oxygen, these reasons seem at best of secondary significance.

Do you agree that all peoples everywhere must be made aware of the danger loss of our forests poses and pool all efforts to save and, if possible, increase our priceless cover of greenery?

DERBOLAV: You quite rightly comment on the importance of forests and call for their preservation. Forests do far more than provide timber and energy. They store and renew water supplies, help create climates, purify the air, arrest erosion, and enrich the soil. In addition, in cities they shield us from traffic noise and are increasingly popular as places in which to spend leisure time. Finally, aside from all such utilitarian considerations, they are the homes of plants and animals that have their own right to live.

According to Eugen Drewermann's *Der tödliche Fortschritt* (The Deadly Progress; Regensburg, 1983), in 1974, 41 million square kilometers of the Earth's surface (about 32 percent) were covered in forest. But, since that time, this area has been drastically reduced. First the Philippines and then India, Malaysia, and Indonesia began ruthless deforestation to provide timber for export to Japan, the United States, and Europe.

West Germany produces enough timber for only one cubic meter per person per year; all the rest of the timber used in the nation must be imported. To meet such needs, the rain forests of the Amazon Basin are being cleared at a rate of a million hectares annually and will probably have been completely destroyed by the year 2000. In this deforestation, no consideration is given to the indigenous human population or the flora and fauna of the forests.

Many similarly disturbing instances might be cited. In Nepal, between 1964 and 1975, the forest area was reduced from 63 thousand to 32 thousand square kilometers. As a result of this deforestation, monsoon rains have caused catastrophic erosion, possibly related to the extraordinary flooding of the Ganges in India and Bangladesh in 1978 and again in 1980.

IKEDA: Some scholars claim that forests serve as reservoirs retaining the waters of heavy rainfalls and gradually allowing them to flow into rivers. When forest cover is removed, however, deluges suddenly flood into streams, causing the kind of catastrophic erosion you mention as having taken place in India and Bangladesh and thus taking a heavy toll in loss of crops and life among people who live in the lower reaches of the rivers. By stimulating an increased demand for timber for use as fuel and building materials, and by making it necessary to bring more and more land under the plow, population growth stimulates the rapid advance of deforestation.

DERBOLAV: Industrialization doubled the demand for lumber as a raw material between 1950 and 1975. Since 1945, Latin America has forfeited 37 percent of its forests; Africa, 50 percent; and Asia, 40 percent. In developing countries, even today fire is used to clear forest land. Industrialization and population growth have enormously increased the consumption of water, and this in turn has stimulated the tendency to allow deforested land to degenerate into desert.

Areas of arable land do not necessarily increase to meet continuously growing needs for space. On the contrary, desert areas are growing, especially where pressure from an increasing population is greatest. Clearly, then, the argument for clearing forests to open up more arable land is not only misleading, but also false. In fact, deforestation impoverishes the soil and leads to climatic alterations that, although difficult to assess, are most certainly extensive.

Still another disturbing phenomenon is the dying out of forests in the industrialized nations. Though this has been recognized for a long time, its causes have yet to be explained fully. In West Germany, forest areas are quantitatively increasing, although not in densely populated urban centers where they are most needed. Interest in profit determines forest cultivation in Germany. For this reason, spruce forests, which make money, are given preference over deciduous forests. It has been shown, however, that spruce forests are in danger of being destroyed by acid rain, to which they are especially vulnerable.

It seems clear that surviving forests must be given protection or at least that reasonable restrictions must be put on their use, while forests already in danger–for instance, the German Black Forest, the Austrian Vienna Woods, and the forests along the Danube at the Austro-Hungarian border–must be afforded appropriate care. Of course, as long as no restraints are put on the commercial-profit interests of large industrial enterprises and as long as international regulations are not established for air pollution (how difficult this is has been shown in Germany by lengthy debates about the compulsory introduction of low-exhaust automobiles) the attainment of these aims will remain an empty hope.

IKEDA: In the past, in Japan too, mixed forests were often cleared to make way for the cultivation of more profitable timber like Japanese cedar (*sugi*) and cypress (*hinoki*). Later, however, when it became apparent that shallow-rooted cedar and cypress contribute to landslides in times of typhoons or heavy rain and that they are subject to illness and insect damage, some people began calling for a reconsideration of this kind of reforestation.

Human society exists because of the mutual cooperation and support of diverse individuals. Similarly, forests and the entire natural environment depend on an organic inter-weaving of many different elements. It is, consequently, most desirable that the wholesome, overall operation of the world of nature be kept in mind when conservation policies are evolved.

2. Poisons Around Us

IKEDA: In the preceding section, we discussed briefly the importance of preserving forests, one of the things on which life on Earth depends. Now, I should like to turn our attention toward pollutants, things that must be eliminated because of the harmful effects they have on life. In the 1960s and 1970s, the pollution problem became acute in industrialized nations, where it stimulated fiery debates. We Japanese were made especially painfully aware of what environmental pollution can do to human beings by two widely publicized cases. A factory polluted the waters of a bay on the island of Kyushu by pumping into it waste materials containing mercury. Fishing families who ate fish contaminated with these pollutants were afflicted with grave, even fatal, illnesses. Another factory, in the Japan Sea region, polluted the environment with cadmium, which caused many people in the area serious bone damage and excruciating pain. During the several years that elapsed while investigations and debates were being carried out about the causal relation between the factories' practices and the pollution-connected illnesses and while trials took place to determine compensation for the victims, the public eye was directed toward the issue, the government revised environmental legislation, and business enterprises improved their waste-disposal practices. In other words, the overall situation took a turn for the better. Still, a complete solution has not been achieved. Pollution continues, if at a slightly retarded rate. The government has established laws setting forth permissible concentrations of pollutants in wastes. But, even though the factories abide by these laws, they are still pumping wastes into the environment; and, in the long run, the quantities they disgorge and the damage they do will be very little altered.

DERBOLAV: A German parliamentarian named Gruhle wrote a book entitled *Ein Planet wird geplündert* (A planet plundered), in which he advocated the total halt of economic growth as the only way to stop the plundering or destruction of Earth. He received few laurels for his efforts in Germany in general, and his idea won little approval among parliamentary factions.

Certainly economic restraints of the kind he advocates would only aggravate the already threatening increase in unemployment. Furthermore today economic growth is considered worthy of higher social esteem than a clean environment. Nonetheless, Gruhle was right in his identification of the ultimate causes of the disasters facing our world: there can be no doubt that the primary source of the environmental pollution and destruction taking place today is to be found in economic activity and specifically in expanding competition and pursuit of profit.

Other causes (like, for instance, hunting and sports), though of lesser importance, must be taken into consideration. The population explosion, too, cannot fail to have its effects on pollution as a result of the growing needs for housing, food, and consumer products it generates. Greater masses of humans demand more timber and fuel wood. They make necessary more intensive cultivation and exploitation of land, and increase the demand for consumer goods. This, in turn, stimulates expansion of the world economy (together with the bad side-effects of such growth), which naturally results in the greater generation of polluting wastes and rubbish.

(Clearly, disposing of wastes–both nuclear and ordinary– poses serious problems. In 1970, West Germany created 200 million cubic meters of waste and sewage. By 1972 the amount had increased to 260 million cubic meters, or enough to bury Greater Munich to a depth of one meter.)

Agriculture faces both domestic and international competition and the need to feed increasing numbers of people. In this realm, too, profit has long had the upper hand over simply satisfying needs, as is witnessed by the European Community's shameful destruction, for commercial reasons, of foodstuffs that could have been used to help famine-stricken Third World countries.

IKEDA: The same problem frequently arises in Japan. Farmers overproduce crops that promise to bring high profits and then, when transport charges surpass the crops' market value, virtually with tears in their eyes, plow them under with tractors. In such instances, liability is all that remains of the farmers' investment.

DERBOLAV: In addition, pursuit of profit alone in agriculture has had far-reaching, baleful influences on the natural ecology. Increased agricultural production is costly in terms of the quality of not only the soil, but also indigenous flora and fauna. Between 1938 and 1966, German agricultural production doubled. It increased by another 50 percent between 1960 and 1969. Together with this growth occurred a rise in the use of fertilizers and pesticides, in what amounts to an ecological vicious circle. Drastic cutbacks–for economic reasons–in crop rotation depleted the soil. This made necessary application of artificial fertilizers, which impoverish the metabolic processes of animals and disrupt those of plants. Plants became more susceptible to increasingly frequent insect plagues. Dealing with the insects demanded application of biocides, which put a further burden on the soil and inhibited the actions of natural fertilizers. With this, the humus soil structure was destroyed; and erosion set in, making it imperative to clear additional land for agricultural use. In short, agriculture was forced to make further incursions on forests.

Felling forest land and converting it to agrarian use has a tremendously impoverishing effect on the land itself. For example, in a hectare of forest land live roughly 250 thousand earthworms, whose combined weight is greater than that of all the mammals living on the same expanse of land. In addition, there are billions of micro-organisms in each square meter of forest land. When forests are cleared for farming, much of this life is lost; and the soil is made correspondingly poorer. Nor are these biological riches restored by reforesting with conifers stretches of cleared, insectless, bird-forsaken land that was once deciduous or mixed forest.

In Germany, 100 hectares of agricultural land are lost daily to plans for cities, express highways, and concrete airport facilities. Other expanses of our soil are being poisoned by such toxic industrially produced materials as nitrogen oxide. But to comment on such things is to touch only one dimension of the pollution to which our environment is being subjected. Our rivers, lakes, and seas are being contaminated. And substances equally as poisonous as those sullying other parts of the environment are poisoning the air, harming nature, and lowering the quality of life.

Incontestably industries in European countries are pouring wastes into the Earth and rivers. From the rivers–or directly from the industries themselves–these wastes find their way into our seas. Today, our rivers are transporters of vast quantities of dangerous toxic wastes; and our seas are among the greatest garbage dumps on the planet.

IKEDA: The cradle of humanity and the source of our continued existence is a natural environment in which countless creatures coexist in a harmonious whole. In a forest, the actions of insects, worms, and microorganisms convert fallen leaves into fertilizer enriching the soil. Insects thrive and become food for forest birds. The same relations of mutual support exist in the planet's bodies of water, the origin of life.

But human civilization today is introducing into this chain of life toxic substances that ultimately find their way back into human bodies. Thus we are destroying both nature's powers of self-recovery and the foundation of our own existence.

DERBOLAV: Inadmissible waste-control practices on the part of industry; oil-tanker catastrophes; and the well-known habit of transport ships–most notably those of fleets operating on low budgets–of dumping oil wastes, with no controls of any kind, directly into the water have polluted the oceans beyond their powers of self-purification. In Italy, 60 percent of all beaches are considered to be severely polluted. During most of the swimming season, from as early as 1961, large oil slicks have been washing up on the beaches of the North Sea. Moreover, in Germany alone, every year about ten thousand seabirds are killed as an outcome of oil pollution.

Environmental pollution is not the only tragedy befalling the world of animals. On a commercial basis, extermination of animals proceeds according to plan. West Germany is one of the greatest Western centers of the fur and leather trade, which costs the lives of millions of baby seals, otters, nutrias, beavers, and wild cats.

Human beings are playing fast and loose with the limited stocks of fish in the planet's oceans as well. For instance, the North Sea was once very rich in herring. In the 1950s, the stock was fished out in the English Channel. Thereafter, fishing methods were improved with the result that a record catch of herring (1.5 million tons) was taken. This quickly fell, however; and today the catch has leveled off at 3,000 tons instead of the former annual average of 200,000 tons. Ruthless overfishing brought a similar fate to schools of herring between Greenland and Norway.

In an analogous situation, in the Humboldt current, off the shores of Peru, fishermen took an annual haul of 15 million tons of anchovies until 1968. By 1973, however, the annual haul had dropped to 1.4 million tons. The fish-meal industry, which depended on the anchovy catches, has now completely closed down.

Until recently the unwillingness of the Soviets and the Japanese to limit their whaling operations, which they claim give work and bread to thousands of people, threatened whales with extinction.

IKEDA: As I said in the dialogues I shared with the late Aurelio Peccei, I believe that scientific investigations must be made of whales and that pertinent measures must be taken at once to protect endangered species. This may be hard on people who have made their living whaling, but the situation would be irremediable if whales became extinct. Whalers often insist that the danger of extinction is not as great as is claimed. But, by the time these people get around to recognizing the real peril, it may be too late.

Perhaps whales face the fate of the once common, Japanese ibis (*toki*). Today, because of the use of agricultural chemicals, only a few specimens remain, and there is little hope for their survival since, in spite of all human assistance, the birds seem unable to breed successfully.

DERBOLAV: It is not only commercial needs and interests, however, that threaten the world's wildlife: hunting and sport do so too. For instance, in Europe–mostly in Italy, but in Belgium, France, Spain, and Greece as well–the hunting of hares and especially of birds is widespread. In Italy alone, 500 million birds are killed annually during their migrations southward and back. In the other nations mentioned, 200 million are killed. Shrikes, redstarts, warblers, and song thrushes have, to a greater or lesser extent, been wiped out by Nimrods in these lands.

The 2,000-kilometer Great Barrier Reef in northeastern Australia, too, has been endangered, or at least seriously damaged, by human action. Sports divers have drastically reduced the number of blowfish, which till then had regulated the number of the somewhat-rare crown of thorns starfish. Once their natural enemy had been largely eliminated, the starfish reproduced drastically and devoured more than a fourth of the animals whose skeletons make up the coral reef.

Human meddling sets up chain reactions that disturb the natural balance in still other ways. For example, jack rabbits were introduced into Australia in 1788; and their numbers were kept in control by the dingo, the wild dog that is the continent's sole predatory animal. The dingo's main prey, however, was the large nonflying bird called the emu. At a later time, human beings introduced sheep into Australia; and the dingo began killing them. This inspired both farmers and shepherds to hunt and kill dingos, allowing the jack-rabbit population to increase so freely that today it has assumed plague proportions.

Human contamination of the seas and the atmosphere inevitably causes illness and other grief. You mention two dramatic instances of sea pollution that have caused great suffering in Japan. Surely the pollution of the air, too, is an extensive cause of sickness.

Motor vehicles are a major source of such pollution. Exhaust fumes from them not only cause a variety of human ailments, but also serve as indirect sources of many environmental disturbances. They decrease temperatures through the process of sunlight reflection called albedo. They menace cities with smog; produce carbon dioxide, which lowers climatic temperatures; threaten the vital ozone layer; and damage or even destroy art works.

We have experienced similar difficulties in connection with the Rhine. Although in this case chemical pollution did not directly endanger human beings, it did eradicate the river's rich fish population. As recent developments have shown, however, radiation damage caused by the kind of accidents in nuclear power plants, observed on a small scale in the United States and on a much larger scale at Chernobyl in the Soviet Union, is much more serious. Contamination of the soil and the Earth's atmosphere by such atomic isotopes as iodine 131, cesium 137, and strontium dramatically illustrates the dangers of radioactive radiation to human and nonhuman life forms both near and far and has shocked the Western world enough to stimulate a widespread tendency–similar to tendencies manifest by the peace movement–to renounce all aspects of economy related to nuclear power.

Nonethless, everyone understands that such renunciation

could guarantee necessary security only if carried out on an international scale. At present, such a development is unlikely. Indeed, many European nations already depend too greatly on nuclear-generated electricity to impose a burden on their economies by closing down nuclear power plants. Advocates of abolition of all nuclear energy cannot possibly overlook the pernicious economic consequences of the step they recommend–for instance, increased unemployment, shortages of electrical power, and so on. The willingness they display to dispense with the amenities of life is obviously unlikely to be shared by the majority of the people.

For their part, the advocates of the use of nuclear energy realize, naturally, that efforts to perfect security measures in the nuclear industry cannot escape a risk factor–a residual risk–because of human error and faulty construction methods.

The Soviet analysis revealed that the kind of super nuclear contamination resulting from the Chernobyl catastrophe involved the accumulation of six cases of human error. The Vienna conference of experts on the same disaster revealed that, as late as August 1986, security deficiencies persisted at Chernobyl.

To remove ourselves from the nuclear dilemma completely would require that we renounce either the 1939 discovery of nuclear fission or the currently hotly debated nuclear fusion, which promises an energy supply without the dangers of atomic radiation. But it is impossible either to renounce or anticipate discoveries, which demand the appropriate amount of time to be purified of pernicious effects and brought to full, useful development.

IKEDA: Even though industrialized nations set up and improve such legislation, no similar steps are being taken to curb pollution in newly built plants in developing nations.

Nor do pollutants affect only the generations living at the time they are discharged into the environment. The defoliants the Americans sprayed on Vietnamese forests during the war there have apparently caused dreadful deformities in the unborn: babies with anencephalia and hydrocephalia, most of which were stillborn, and one set of Siamese twins who are still living, though one is ill.

Radiation pollution also has long-term effects. Tens of thousands of people died in the atomic bombings of Hiroshima and Nagasaki at the end of World War II. Those who survived suffered years of radiation sickness; and children who were in their mother's womb at the time of the bombings have manifested various related pathological conditions. The islands in the South Pacific, where the United States and France have conducted nuclear experiments, are now uninhabitable by man. The region in the central-western part of the United States where atomic experiments were conducted is, apparently, still lethal: actors and staff members who worked on a motion picture there have died of cancer.

We have no way of knowing the long-range effects on human life of ingesting liquids and foods contaminated with polluting substances. But of one thing we can be certain: pollution has not stopped. And, as more and more regions come to depend on nuclear energy to generate electrical power, disposing of nuclear waste is becoming an increasingly serious problem, one of horrifying potential with which we must come to grips for the sake of our children and grandchildren and the generations to follow.

DERBOLAV: The problem of environmental poisoning is all the more monstrous when we take into consideration the genetic effects it can have on unborn babies. You mention Agent Orange, which the Americans used as a defoliant in Vietnam. Actually, it was the dioxin in the defoliant that did the damage.

Dioxin causes many deformities in those not yet born at the time of their mothers' exposure to it. One of the worst is the otherwise rare condition called holoptic encephalitis, in which the child is born with an exposed spinal cord; one eye; no nose; a trunklike growth on the forehead; and cleft lips, jaws, and palate. Fortunately most such babies die shortly after birth.

We Europeans are familiar with the danger of dioxin as a

consequence of the Seveso disaster–a fitting addition to the *chronique scandaleuse* of the menace humanity is to itself.

Apparently through human error, in 1976, at the Seveso (Italy) plant of the Swiss firm Hoffman-La Roche, about two kilograms of dioxin were allowed to escape. The danger is seen to be enormous when one considers that the amount of dioxin that could fit on a pinhead is enough to kill an animal as big as an elephant. Understandably, fear of these dioxin emissions terrified the local population, who abandoned their homes and left Seveso unpeopled.

The Seveso tragedy was followed by the satirical comedy of a frantic and initially unsuccessful hunt for dioxin waste. Hoffman-La Roche had disposed of other drums of this toxic substance in one of the large European dumpsites and refused to say exactly where. Ultimately, the drums were discovered in France and rendered harmless.

IKEDA: Possibly the most dreadful aspect of this situation is the way in which some industrialists and business leaders have become depraved enough to attempt to evade responsibility for their deeds. It is lamentable when people conceal deeds that jeopardize the lives of large numbers of people. It is only human to err. But we must accept the responsibility of recognizing our mistakes openly and attempting to minimize the harm they cause. Concealing errors out of fear of reprisal is unforgivable. Establishing ethics that work against concealment of this kind is important in dealing with the many perilous crises confronting us.

DERBOLAV: The discovery of the drums in France was not the end of the dioxin scare. Recently, it was suspected that dioxin had been detected in the waste-incinerators of the Boehringer Company in Hamburg. Parallel with this, an increase in the number of children suffering from holoptic encephalitis was feared.

Ultimately, however, the difficulty of establishing clear, scientifically verifiable connections between dioxin damage and genetic malformations hinders the vigorous prosecution of offenders. It seems that we must be content with pointing out occurrences of certain pathological symptoms and indicating their assumed causes; that is, we must attempt to establish plausibility, which, I hear, is considered sufficient grounds for legal action in Japanese courts.

The situation is, of course, different in unambiguous cases like the recent disaster in Bhopal, India, where a toxic gas used in producing insecticides leaked from faulty containers, poisoning more than 10,000 Indians, of whom 2,500 have died.

IKEDA: As you point out, establishing verifiable causal connections is always a major problem in dealing legally with damage brought on by pollution. It takes time to determine whether new chemicals have altering effects on human health and genetic makeup. Experimenting is out of the question since the experimental materials must be human beings. Moreover, the legal tradition is not to punish as long as reasonable doubt persists. All of this means that nothing is done about toxic materials until their leakage or exhaust into the environment has made it too late. Although observing the tradition of not punishing as long as doubt remains is vital for the protection of human rights in ordinary cases, it would seem advisable at least to take measures to halt dubious proceedings as long as they threaten human life on a large scale.

DERBOLAV: Essentially, since overpopulation is one of their causes, dealing with the maladies of environmental pollution necessitates attempting to find ways to control the population explosion. Europe in general and West Germany in particular have demonstrated that improving the standard of living lowers the birth rate. (West Germany has one of the lowest birth rates in the world.) This is why the first conference on world population, held in Bucharest in 1974, recommended indirectly reducing the birth rate by fostering a higher standard of living in developing nations.

Unfortunately, even if they could achieve the desired aim in a reasonable period, in the light of current rapid, virtually unbridled population growth, such measures are already too late. As two proverbs suggest–"Children are the bread of the poor" and "The beds of the poor are fertile"–there is a close connection between poverty and overpopulation. Consequently, all experts agree that aid to developing countries must be coupled with family planning and population policies–in the form of contraceptives, not of enforced abortions.

By restraining its alarming population growth, China has shown what can be done. It is true, however, that the Chinese methods are too rigid to be acceptable in democratic nations. Still, politically motivated abstinence in China had the astonishing success of reducing the worldwide annual growth rate from 2 percent to 1.7 percent.

Whether the gentle coercion of attempting to restrain population growth by withholding aid from developing nations who refuse to adopt suitable policies will work remains to be proved. And, in the light of the connection between poverty and fecundity, the probability of success is not great.

IKEDA: There is no doubting the causal connection between the population explosion and environmental pollution and destruction. It is a fact, however, that regulating population growth in the developing nations, in which the explosion is most violent, is difficult. The only ways seem to be self-enlightenment on the part of each citizen and family planning as a permanent part of the life-style. We must be prepared for the achievement of these goals to take a long time. A revolution in the name of popular self-awareness and ethics among big-business leaders should take less time in the industrialized nations.

DERBOLAV: Simple appeals to big business are likely to be ineffectual. This is why we must have strict laws passed setting maximum concentrations of toxic substances that may be buried in the earth or dumped into the air and water. Where they do not exist, laws protecting animals from the capriciousness of hunters must be passed.

This may be relatively simple to achieve in Japan. It is much more difficult in Europe, where, in spite of the European Community, political divisions and sometimes conflicting economic interest make it difficult to agree on regulations protecting the environment. To give a simple example, the extent to which they will protect or befoul the Rhine depends on the sense of environmental responsibility felt by the four nations lying along its course from source to mouth. I have already mentioned the extended debate over introduction of low-toxic-exhaust automobiles–now taken for granted in Japan and in the United States–which is only one of the many environmental problems on which we find it difficult to come to terms with our neighbors.

But environmental laws alone cannot solve the problem. We must all undergo a change of mind. Gaining impetus in Germany, as elsewhere, the ecological movement is striving to achieve long-range aims for a new way of life, though admittedly its realistic approaches are coupled with utopian hopes.

In his writings, the expert on the subject Eugen Drewermann has made stimulating proposals for abandoning wood, such fossil fuels as coal and petroleum, and even nuclear energy (the finite supply of uranium precludes a permanent solution) in favor of solar energy. But the sun cannot be expected to meet all human energy needs unaided.

IKEDA: To protect the atmosphere, the source of the oxygen on which all life depends, it is vital to stop relying on wood and fossil fuels. Such problems as storing large quantities of uranium, the danger of accidents, and the disposal of radioactive wastes resulting from ordinary operations plague reliance on nuclear energy. Ideally, we should seek energy sources that produce harmless waste products that can be recycled in the natural rhythm of the planet.

DERBOLAV: Many of the other proposals offered for improving and cleaning up our way of life are semiutopian. It has been suggested that we all become vegetarians and exist on algae with a 50-percent protein content raised hydroponically. Others have suggest organizing our world in more pleasant, more wholesome ways by relying on railways to replace freeways and constructing systems of electro-cars, moving sidewalks, and electronic communications systems. In addition, the idea of saving forests from the ravages made on them to supply wood for paper by relying on electronic technology (television newspapers, computer printing, and microfilm for whole libraries) has been advanced.

Some of these ideas are fantastic and may, sooner or later, after an amount of examination and discussion, be shelved. Nonetheless, we must never under any circumstances lose the creative imagination to seek ways out of the apparently hopeless situation into which we have gotten ourselves.

3. Playing with Fire

IKEDA: Mankind today is like a child playing with fire beside a munitions dump. We possess sufficient destructive power to annihilate the entire human species; and, in addition to the United States and the Soviet Union, with their immense nuclear arsenals, the number of nations that either do stockpile or are capable of stockpiling nuclear arms grows year by year.

When we realize that the present destructive capabilities are equivalent to several tons of TNT for each of the more than four billion people on the globe, it becomes manifestly clear that we must avoid all actions that might lead to large-scale conflict. The destruction of civilization now is tantamount to the elimination of a future for mankind. Even should some few people survive in the African inland or on isolated ocean islands, radiation pollution from a nuclear war would probably reach them soon. And it is certain that the glorious civilization humanity has built over the ages would never rise again.

Since I believe that open dialogue is the only way to intensify efforts for peace, reduce tension, and in these ways avoid nuclear war, I have engaged in frank discussion on a wide range of topics with political leaders and intellectuals from the United States, the Soviet Union, China, France, India, the nations of South and Central America, and many other countries and intend to go on with dialogues of this kind.

All peoples of sound judgment desire peace. It is differences of ideology, economic friction, and racial prejudices that stir up hatred and mutual distrust, which stimulate people to arm themselves out of fear of others. Granted that ideological differences and economic friction may never be entirely eliminated, it is nonetheless vital that we all speak openly with each other and make it perfectly clear that, in spite of all differences, we intend to prevent disagreements from being tied in any way to war. All parties must state their peaceful aims and reinforce their statements with actual arms reductions or, ideally, total disarmament.

DERBOLAV: The worst possible kind of environmental pollution is, without doubt, that which would be caused by nuclear world war. It would result in the annihilation of humanity which, today, is a possibility not to be totally excluded since the conflicts smoldering between the two major blocs into which the political world is divided could flare up into warfare. As you aptly describe the situation, humanity does resemble a child playing with fire next to a munitions dump since, in the hectic arms race, a mistake at a switchboard or a false alarm could launch, irrevocably, nuclear-armed missiles that could ignite a chain reaction of strikes and counterstrikes.

Apparently recognizing the problem early and convinced of the pacific sentiments of all people of good will, you have spoken out for peace among outstanding politicians of the great powers and of many other nations. Your activities for this cause have justly won for you the Peace Prize of the United Nations, an organization that has made notable achievements in resolving international conflicts and that, like you, interprets world peace as, first and foremost, a matter of common sense and morality. Certainly religion too must be taken into consideration in this connection. No person of faith, no matter what his persuasion, can accept war as a form of political settlement.

IKEDA: I agree entirely. Buddhism and Christianity both condemn the taking of life. It is the first of the Buddhist precepts and, of course, figures in the Mosaic Ten Commandments: "Thou shalt not kill." Although war itself is not necessarily mutual killing, destruction of life is obviously one of its indispensable means. Professing Buddhists and Christians who approve of war are in effect turning their backs on Shakyamuni Buddha, Christ, and God.

DERBOLAV: Unfortunately, however, war and peace are never matters of morality and faith alone but in terms of origin, process, and outcome, are always affected by an economic-strategic-political dynamic. No one who is seriously concerned with preserving peace can afford to ignore this influence. When Karl von Clausewitz attempted to legitimize war, in a restrictive sense, by calling it an extension of diplomacy by other means, he was putting morals and religion in the private sphere of human activity and the politics of both peace and war in the sphere of reasons of state.

This remains so today as well. But now differing interests and the divergent ideological views of powers and power blocs have inordinately intensified the conditions under which reasons of state operate. The worldwide peace movement taking place today in an unprecedented form clearly reveals how much the world has changed since Clausewitz's time and how different a modern war would be from traditional armed conflicts.

IKEDA: For one thing, the nature of weaponry has completely

altered. Although they could wound very seriously, swords, lances, arrows, and even rifles did not invariably kill. This cannot be said of the nuclear, biological, and chemical weapons today possessed by the powerful nations of the world. In the past, a belligerent recognizing the inferiority of its side and surrendering could feel reasonably sure that life would be spared. Warring parties today are permitted no such comfort. Under these circumstances, Clausewitz's definition of war as an extension of diplomacy by other means is inapplicable.

DERBOLAV: From a philosophical viewpoint, two striking differences appear between attitudes prevailing in the past and those current today. From the time of Aristotle until fairly recently, human dealings were considered as means for the attainment of given goals; and means and goals were to an extent proportionate. In the past, goals of warfare included the securing of political spheres, self defense, victory over aggressors, and so on. Generally speaking, one warring party entertained no idea of annihilating the opponent but always kept in mind conditions for peace negotiations and later coexistence. In individual instances, conflicts were no doubt harsh and bitter. Nonetheless, the conquered party was usually given a chance for agreement and possible later cooperation with the victor. The idea seems to have been, as Schiller put it, that only the reconciled, not the merely conquered, enemy can be said to have been truly overcome.

In the modern political realm, however, this proportionate relation seems to have been destroyed. In relation to their efficacy, means have grown incommensurately more important than goals, with the result that humankind is in danger of losing self-control.

Of course, in the past as well, conflicting parties violated the rules of proportionate relations between means and ends. And, in doing so, they only sowed seeds for further contention and strife. Two relatively recent examples illustrate the effects of the two ways of dealing with defeated enemies. The Versailles dictate imposed on Germany in 1918 aided Hitler in his rise to power. In contrast, General MacArthur's peace treaty with Japan in 1945 illustrates the kind of reconciliation that Schiller had in mind.

IKEDA: There can be no victor in a nuclear war: both sides must lose. Consequently, such a conflict is not war but suicide. Even in conventional fighting, as in the Falkland Islands campaign, victory is horrifyingly costly in terms of money and loss of life.

The United Nations is the proper scene for peace-oriented dialogue. Acting always on the principle of nonbelligerence, all member nations must strive to assist other nations in resolving whatever stubborn differences may plague their relations in connection with ideology, economy, territories, and so on. The United Nations is the proper place for mediation because it can carry out such a function more easily than any other organization currently in existence.

DERBOLAV: In modern warfare, the excessive magnitude of means has created a notable tendency to generate radical goals. Since the appearance of nuclear weapons, which can annihilate the opponent, it seems to me that a return to conventional kinds of battle might be taken into consideration in international political-security conflicts. For instance, though atomic weapons were on hand, they were not used in the Falkland Islands incident, which was carried out in the traditional way.

In the same direction of a return to traditional ways of warfare, on a constantly widening scale, peace manifestos of churches and other organizations demand that the self-defense needs of opponents be respected and that measures inspiring trust be employed to encourage the desire for peace. Approaches of this kind, which are in line with what Schiller said, seem to lead closer to a policy of general mutual disarmament.

IKEDA: In other words, the use of nuclear, biological, and chemical weapons represents a deviation from the essential goal of war. A victory in which totally uninhabited cities are filled with intact buildings so radiation-contaminated that no living thing can enter them is meaningless. Although it might eliminate a menacing adversary, such a war does so at the cost of spreading radioactive fallout and fearsome pollutants and bacteria that gradually destroy the lives of the victors themselves. Because they realize this, possessors of nuclear weapons feel compelled to rely on conventional weapons.

DERBOLAV: One element of the economic, political, and strategic dynamic that serves as a primary cause of war in the striving for supremacy (once among national states but today more and more among whole power blocs). Still another is the compensatory device of the balance of power, which wise statesmen once wielded masterfully in European peace politics.

In the light of the altered nature of modern warfare, in connection with the question of means and ends, though still valid, this compensatory device has long been in danger of degenerating into what might be called a balance of deterrence. But the paradox of the strategy of mutual deterrence is that it threatens what can under no circumstances–especially since it runs the risk of self-destruction–be brought to pass: a nuclear attack, which must be made with the realization that a counterattack will inevitably come too late.

It is easy to see why political and strategic supremacy in relation to balance-of-power politics is today largely ineffective. The concept of balance of power posits some kind of behind-the-scenes superpower responsible for maintaining stable world peace. In the nineteenth century, Great Britain often played this role, though certainly not without imperialistic motives. In the present distribution of power, however, a superpower capable of diplomatically–perhaps militarily–establishing a peaceful order among nations is lacking. One clever politician claims that the only way of bringing together the world's opposing powers and of binding them together politically and strategically would be an attack on Earth by an extraterrestrial power, compelling today's opposing forces to unite as partners in a common resistance struggle.

IKEDA: Whereas I believe in the possibility of life on a high level similar to that of human beings elsewhere in the universe, I consider the idea that such beings would attack Earth to belong in the realm of fiction. Even granting some form of life on other celestial bodies, sophisticated forms are likely to be rare; and there is no reason to think they are situated close enough to travel easily to our planet. In the three and a half billion years over which life has evolved on Earth, humanity has been in possession of truly sophisticated scientific technology for only a few decades. The distance between us and another life form at a comparable stage of development in the universe must be bewildering.

Furthermore, since the possession of sophisticated intelligence is usually accompanied by the desire for power, I think it more probable that such beings would war among themselves and kill each other off before they would think of traveling to Earth.

DERBOLAV: If, as one side in the exobiology debate insists, there are no other civilizations in the universe, this possibility remains only fantasy. If there are other civilizations, on the other hand, extraterrestrial beings would certainly overcome the vast distances involved and either conquer or make friends with man before such an alliance could be formed. In other words, all such speculation is fruitless; and the inimical tensions separating superpower blocs will probably remain unchanged. This is all the more likely given the mutually exclusive, apparently irreconcilable political ideologies they support.

Still, as the case of China vividly illustrates, political concepts change, as do relations among powers. Consequently, it may be reasonable to hope that, through adequate and imaginative crisis-management, we may survive even acute conflicts. As we have said, morality and religion can play a part in this connection.

IKEDA: Though they are often mistakenly considered to be as old-fashioned, religion and morality determine the ways human beings think and live. It is the role of religion and morality to teach that destruction and slaughter are evil and that construction and work for the sake of increasing human happiness are good and to stimulate human beings to think and believe in this way. Because of the threat of total annihilation of the human race that modern war poses, the importance of religion and morality is greater now than at any other time in history.

DERBOLAV: Clearly the problem of a nuclear war overshadows all others. A world devastated by such a disaster would be unable to deal with the destructive practices of environmental pollution or to apply family planning to counter the population explosion. Questions of environment and population are beside the point when the existence of humankind in general is jeopardized.

Even if we avoid nuclear conflict, in considering the population explosion, we must take into consideration the likelihood of expanded war. Sooner or later, given the required arsenals, the nations of the Third World, suffering from poverty, hunger, and overcrowding, may be expected to attack the industrialized nations of Europe and America–or at least the United States and Asia–in order to obtain the things they lack. Increasing the possibility of such a turn in events are both the willingness of many of even the poorest nations to spend money on arms instead of on consumer goods and the constant readiness of some people to sell secret military technical know-how to developing countries. Even the most stringent vigilance and international control organizations would probably be unable to hinder such things.

IKEDA: For the developing nations to convert the money they

spend on arms to industry and welfare and for the industrialized nations to stop providing military aid and devote strength to encouraging education and welfare would contribute tremendously to world peace and the happiness of humanity. Poverty in the developing countries is usually related to revolutionary movements. Fearing revolution, the nations of the free world tend to provide arms to antirevolutionary elements. But this has the effect of driving the poor farther in the direction of revolution. Political and social stability are essential if the poverty and suffering that inspire revolutionary ardor are to be eliminated.

DERBOLAV: Currently developing plans for the use of outer space open up terrifying perspectives of a cosmic war. (Indeed, the so-called Star Wars project is now a hotly debated issue between the United States and the Soviet Union.) Instead of questions of this kind, however, it would be much more meaningful to try to find out whether, aside from its importance as an object of research, outer space cannot help relieve Earth's population pressure. Occasionally discussed United States' plans for space stations that could accommodate large numbers of human beings may seem no more than fantasy now. Nonetheless, they are much more sensible than the idea of carrying the conflicts of the super blocs into outer space.

4. Preserving Parts of the Past

IKEDA: Human civilization is like a tree rising skyward; putting forth branches, flowers, and fruit, but inevitably dependent on deep roots in the past for support and sustenance. In Europe, the past is respected and preserved in houses, churches, palaces, plazas, streets, and other historical monuments that stabilize and enrich life. In Japan, however, aside from some famous temples and castles, relics of the past are few in number and relatively remote from the lives of the ordinary people. Much has been destroyed in fire and war, and what little remained until recently has been ruthlessly destroyed in the past few decades in the name of modernization and convenience. The preference for modern comfort over traditional beauty is vividly illustrated by the way many rural people are having handsome old farmhouses torn down and replaced by insipid, but well-equipped, new dwellings. In spite of the popular stir caused by recent excavations of old temples and villages from primitive periods, the majority of Japan's tangible cultural heritage is falling before the onslaught of urbanization and modernization.

Do you agree that the wealthy and developed nations of the world ought to take the initiative in projects to save cultural treasures everywhere?

DERBOLAV: Relations between humanity and its history and tradition are more pleasing to contemplate than reports of current disasters. To regard human achievements as no more than technical civilization–as it perhaps might appear to an extraterrestial being–would be tantamount to eliminating history, or perhaps it would be better to say that such a view would remove all desire to be concerned with history. The natural-scientific approach suspends the historical dimension. Concerning itself exclusively with quantifiable structures and objective relations, it takes no thought of predecessors, sources, or historical geneses. Humanity in general, however, owing to the ability to reflect, can turn back to what has gone before and can cultivate with the past personal relations transcending scientific categories of means and ends.

IKEDA: In addition to the natural-scientific approach, the economic approach causes human beings to suspend the historical dimension. Things considered ineffective economically are abandoned and replaced by more effective ones. For instance, old houses are pulled down to make room for office buildings, which bring in more revenue.

DERBOLAV: Historical relics can, of course, be of various kinds. Generally, they include such architectural creations of past epochs as palaces, churches, plazas, and even whole towns preserving more or less their original forms. Other aspects of our cultural tradition include, of course, graphic arts, sculpture, poetry, other forms of literature, and music. These latter forms distinguish themselves from purely architectural monuments in that they are awakened to new life not merely as a result of visual presence, but also through sensual or spiritual comprehension.

If education may be called humanity's second nature, cultural property handed down through the ages may be referred to as our second home. Though he might think some architectural changes bewildering, a person returning to his home city after a long absence is sure to find many things to remind him of his childhood and even to assume in his eyes the qualities of beauty. As we are fondest of familiar foods, so we take maximum pleasure in those places, streets, plazas, and so on to which we are accustomed, even when they fail to conform to objective aesthetic standards.

IKEDA: I agree that we are fondest of old, familiar places. But in some instances, very little survives to remind us of childhood. For instance, the southern end of Tokyo where I grew up was once a quiet, rural region with some fishing villages. It has now been completely urbanized. The sea nearby is so polluted that no one makes a living from fishing and other sea products as they once did. There is practically nothing left reminiscent of the place as it was when I lived there as a child. Perhaps the loss of actual places reminiscent of the past stimulates people to want to collect things from the past, that is, antiques.

DERBOLAV: The fondness for collecting antiques, on the rise among urbanites in our highly reflective age, is a secondary expression of human ties with the past. In my youth, few people collected them; and antique shops, consequently, were largely empty. Today, it is considered chic and a sign of a high standard of living to be in a position to decorate one's home with baroque furniture, to adorn it with Gothic sculpture, and to hang paintings and engravings of earlier periods on its walls. In many instances, this might be either purely snobbery or the outcome of nothing but commercial calculations. But it seems increasingly to reveal a new attitude toward tradition–an attitude that might best be called historical consciousness. Furthermore, though it appeared at first to be no more than a fad, the fondness for antiques is now assuming a more durable character.

So great has the demand become that antique dealers have little of worth left to sell; and, when they have something, it is at exorbitant prices. In the meantime, the production of forgeries has evolved into a lucrative craft–if not a veritable industry.

Unlike the performing arts, which can be revived at any time with nothing but a change of style, artworks in actual physical materials–architecture, sculpture, painting, and so on–fall victim to the fangs of time. They may be damaged or completely destroyed by war or natural disaster. Drastic climatic changes and such things as exhaust fumes from automotive vehicles can wreak havoc on them.

They need planned upkeep, maintenance, and periodic restoration. As is often lamented, people capable of performing such work are in too short supply. This is why, in restoring German cultural monuments bombed in World War II, we found it necessary to call on Polish specialists to assist our masters of restoration. As a consequence of the efforts of these people, many buildings, plazas, and whole parts of cities have been renovated techno-architecturally and aesthetically to the extent that they surpass the originals.

IKEDA: It is not only in Japan that parts of a great cultural heritage are being destroyed, and for a number of different reasons. Angkor Wat and Angkor Thom in Cambodia and Mohenjo Daro and Harappa in Pakistan are said to be in grave danger and to require immediate restoration and repair. But projects of this kind are immensely expensive and time-consuming beyond the powers of developing nations with many pressing problems.

Relics of the past will stimulate the creativity of the future, and it is our duty to pass on as much of the human cultural heritage as possible to posterity. For this reason, it is desirable that nations with funds and skill pool their efforts to save endangered historical treasures, no matter where they are. Doing so is not for the glory of any particular nation state, but for the honor of all humanity. The international undertaking that saved Abu Simbel, on the Nile, points to one way in which relics of historical value can be protected from the wave of modernism. Moreover, concerted effort on such projects sponsors a sense of communality among all cooperating parties and thus helps reduce the danger of war.

It is especially lamentable that vestiges of cultural heritage are destroyed, since the tree of civilization must wither and collapse without the nutrition and stability it derives from being deeply rooted in the past.

DERBOLAV: As all this indicates, when maintenance and restoration of cultural monuments are essential, the public must assume responsibility not only for covering the enormous costs involved, but also for the establishment of appropriate building regulations to ensure the quality of the work.

In the Federal Republic of Germany, under binding legislation for the protection of historical monuments, budgets are available at the federal, local, and community levels for such maintenance. The year 1975, which was named Year for the Protection of Monuments, revealed a kind of pan-European sense of responsibility in connection with the general cultural heritage. I dare say laws protect Japanese historical monuments, too.

Clearly, not merely beauty and aesthetic quality, but also such historical considerations as rarity and unusualness make relics of the past worth protecting. Monuments worth saving on such grounds are often withdrawn from the grasp of both public planning and private enterprise; and this is a frequent cause for dispute.

IKEDA: Precisely. And for this reason, not only art appraisers, but also a wide spectrum of specialists in history and other fields should be called upon to deliberate and determine those works that should be designated as cultural properties deserving protection.

DERBOLAV: In West Germany today, two million edifices (500,000 monuments and 1.5 million buildings of various kinds), or 15 percent of all architecture in the nation, are protected. Obviously, public funds are insufficient to sustain so large a number of architectural works. State agencies must content themselves with supervising privately owned, protected buildings by prohibiting owners from taking certain steps. In addition, they appeal to the people for donations and, in this, generally meet with a good response. In addition, certain foundations help solve financial problems.

The state and others, too, are concerned to restrain willful, tasteless new construction, like the gigantic concrete-and-glass buildings erected by large business enterprises that deform even the hearts of urban districts. Increasingly the general citizenry is taking the initiative in the forms of demonstrations and forums to challenge the state to deal with works of architecture that, though not yet officially recognized as worthy of protection, the people themselves deem deserving parts of the tradition.

IKEDA: Unfortunately, in no small number of instances, the state is responsible for the destruction of cultural properties. War is the prime example of this. But, even in peacetime, states have few qualms about putting economics first and sacrificing cultural property for other facilities that are more financially productive. This is especially true in Japan, where those in power tend to be authoritarian and reluctant to lend an ear to the voice of either people concerned with culture or the general population.

DERBOLAV: Monuments are, nonetheless, better protected in

the industrialized nations than in the developing nations of the Third World. I agree with you entirely that all humanity must attempt to accept the responsibility for the preservation of edifices, monuments, and other cultural properties in nations that are unable to deal with the matter themselves. Once again, as you say, the restoration work at Abu Simbel, on the Nile, indicates that this sense of responsibility is alive.

But, in the light of immense need for restoration, no doubt European nations, too, will occasionally require financial assistance. I have two particular instances in mind. Increasingly remarkable erosion attacking the foundations of the celebrated buildings on the Athenian Acropolis demands urgent correction. Second, Venice is slowly sinking but is financially incapable of undertaking the extensive groundwork that is the only solution to the problem.

Achievements in the field of cultural conservation by international, local-state, and private initiatives are admirable; but we must now appeal to the potential spirit of patronage of the whole world to mobilize an awareness of the importance of human culture in a much more urgent way.

IKEDA: Of course, work in both directions is essential. But first we must put a halt to such things as the atmospheric pollution from exhaust fumes that is causing the erosion of the walls of the Parthenon and the pumping of underground water for industrial purposes that is causing Venice to sink. Unless the fundamental causes are eliminated, symptoms, like the erosion of the marble and the sinking of land, will only recur. It cannot be overstressed that widespread cooperation is needed to achieve the desired goal.

DERBOLAV: In connection with public cooperation, I know from experience that, in the United States, whole floors of large museums are filled with rich collections provided by people who have presented their incomparable treasures to the public solely that, in return, the room accommodating them will bear their names. In this they follow the practice of feudal rulers, emperors, princes, and nobles, who, at death, often bequeathed their extraordinarily valuable collections of art works to state museums.

Cooperation between the public interest and donors determines the richness or poverty of the cultural heritage and the more or less complete representation of style epochs in museums. Sometimes the capacity of the state is overtaxed as when, at the end of feudal times (1789 in France and 1918 in Germany and Austria), the palaces and castles of the nobility became properties of new republics either as gifts or as the result of dispossession or confiscation.

In the case of such manors and palaces, it is most sensible not to leave the buildings to stand lifeless, but to permit them to fulfill their original purposes, as is usually the case with famous churches and temples. Even palaces and castles can be, at least partly, inhabited or can serve political, diplomatic, or artistic purposes or could house museums.

Though among tourists are some knowledgeable, well-read individuals who are able to connect real life with their long studies by visiting various places, it would be a great pity to make historical relics nothing but tourist attractions.

Therefore, to intensify relations between ourselves and our artistic heritage–both on the worldwide and the local-state level–we must refer to the sense of historical awareness and its cultivation that I mentioned earlier.

And this brings us to the historic-literary aspect of school learning–a topic perhaps dealt with too briefly in our discussion of education and cultivation. I spoke of the practical relevance of school-imparted knowledge and of the need for moral training. But historical-literary knowledge, without remaining always merely a burden on the memory, should awaken in students an understanding of our cultural heritage–what you call our cultural family tree, connected with the roots of life.

The pursuit of literature and music opens ways to the spirit objectified in the form of the poetic and musical heritage, which is a central part of our culture. This kind of education seems especially appropriate for two reasons. First, it compensates for the lack of historical material in curricula oriented toward technology and the natural sciences. Second–in the kind of positive terms you employ–it stimulates the creativity of young people and makes them sensitive to genuine cultural values.

5. Life-technology

IKEDA: Still another present problem with important bearings on the future is the rapid advance of scientific technology, especially in connection with genetic engineering, cellular fusion, embryonic fusion, and embryonic transplants–all matters intimately connected with the fundamental elements of life and closely related to the survival of humanity.

Having called forth revolutions in a wide field including medicine, biology, agriculture, pharmacology, ecology, and energy, life-technology, which is based on life-science, has assumed overwhelming importance in the latter half of the twentieth century. Since it tampers directly with genetic materials to improve or even create life, it ranks on a par for importance with the splitting of the atom. But if misused in wrong manipulations of natural operations or in upsetting genetic order, it could produce inhuman monstrosities and result in man's self-destruction. To prevent this, a system of bioethics must be established; and philosophers and religionists as well as scientists and legal specialists must participate in its compilation.

DERBOLAV: The time has come for us to attempt to discover the extent to which our dialogue truly represents a search for a new humanity. In our examinations of the future to this point, we have failed to draw up an outline for such a search since we have seen that, in spite the unprecedented intenseness and breadth with which our reflective ability enables us to enjoy our cultural heritage, our entire world is not only polluted, but also threatened with total annihilation through nuclear war.

It is, however, our technological capacities–frequently

condemned because of their economic commercialization and military consequences–that, for a decade, have provided us with a new source of satisfaction and pride by opening up wider, heretofore unknown dimensions of practical efficacy.

Like awareness of history in general, insight into his own natural history sets man apart from other animal relatives. By *natural history* here is meant the evolutionary process that, according to Darwin and his followers, places humanity at the pinnacle of creation and ultimately enables him not only to survey the geneses of all life forms, including his own, but also to influence them and, by means of genetic manipulation, to guide them in the directions he wishes them to follow.

Successes in the field of medical and surgical technology make less astounding what might have been the euphoric vision presented at the so-called Ciba-symposium, entitled Man and His Future, held in London in 1962. At this symposium, Social-Darwinism, long considered obsolete, celebrated a late triumph. The vision of the meetings united all kinds of possibilities: the idea of a bacteria-free world that, later, would become free of all infectious diseases; the idea of an endless, pain-free life resulting from the complete substitution of all bodily organs with transplants; and, finally, the idea of continuous qualitative improvement in man by controlled, accelerated eugenics.

IKEDA: In 1962, when this rosy forecast was made by the Ciba symposium, most scientists and a large segment of the general population believed blindly in scientific progress.

DERBOLAV: Clearly, the Ciba-symposium vision cannot be interpreted as the same as what we mean by new humanity. This all the more so since we must not forget the setbacks that can occur even in the virtually magical progress of genetic technology. One such setback is the consistent failure that till now has greeted all attempts at transplanting artificial hearts.

Although many contagious diseases have been either totally or partially conquered by means of this kind of technology, in recent years a new, dangerously infectious scourge has come to plague humanity in the form of the AIDS virus (LAV/HTLV-3), which, supposedly introduced from Africa, has spread widely in Europe and on the American continents.

Victims of the illness include homosexuals, drug addicts, and recipients of transfusions of infected blood. Not all those exposed to the virus, however, have developed full-blown AIDS, which attacks the immune system and is invariably fatal. Unfortunately, owing to incorrect publicity and insufficient information, an anti-AIDS mood among the general public—similar to racial prejudice and xenophobia—hinders communication with those who test positive for AIDS.

I mention no figures because the empirical basis is too small for reliable estimates and because findings are constantly changing.

In principle, it is apparent both that medical measures cannot overcome all contagious diseases and that other of the Ciba-symposium assumptions rest on shaky ground. Obviously, even in its most positive aspects, the picture of the future developed here cannot be interpreted as what we, in our discussion, have called the principle of new humanity.

In your own lectures, dialogues, and conversations you have left no room to doubt your belief that the goal of a new humanity must be achieved by a revolutionary spiritual and mental transformation that ultimately can be controlled and realized only through religion and philosophy.

IKEDA: Yes. Scientific technology, though an important means, must remain subservient to the human spirit.

DERBOLAV: Others have been in sympathy with your approach. In the 1970s and 1980s, hopes in Social-Darwinism, which had run high in the 1960s, were considerably dampened. Significantly, by casting doubts on their own hopes, the Social-Darwinists themselves displayed an astonishing sense of distance from a development that might otherwise have seemed to mark their triumph.

IKEDA: This distance reflects an ability to step out of specialist technical fields and view the issue from the viewpoint of all humanity. I suspect, however, that a voice from within requiring self-examination resulted from the difficulty outsiders have in understanding the long strides of progress made in these specialist fields.

DERBOLAV: Modern achievements in genetic technology and engineering are often compared to the splitting of the atom because of their revolutionary significance for the future. But a noteworthy difference between the two must be taken into consideration. Immediate strategic demands during World War II wiped from the board all the scientific scruples of the fathers of the atomic bomb. In the case of genetic engineering, however, as early as 1974, eleven leading molecular biologists made public a letter in which they pointed out the dangers of new combinations of genetic substances (DNA). Hardly a year later, in a rare example of functioning self-regulation, 140 scientists in related fields agreed on security guidelines to which they voluntarily subjected their own research. Put into effect in the United States in 1976 and in West Germany a few years later, these guidelines were only broadly formulated and have since been revised frequently. In addition, they apply only in cases of state-funded research projects. No doubt, we will be hearing of the difficulty involved in giving these guidelines legal form.

IKEDA: I dare say we shall. But to expand our discussion, I should like to consider the following points, which seem important to me in connection with life-science.

(A) Biological problems

Genetic engineering has produced especially noteworthy achievements in the field of pharmaceuticals. It has become possible to manufacture hormones, interferon, and even colon bacilli in large quantities. In the field of agriculture, genetic interchange can now improve plant and animal stocks. To reduce environmental pollution, microorganisms capable of breaking down petroleum and organic mercury are being developed. In addition, research is being conducted on vegetable masses that can generate methane gas. But, on the negative side of the picture, the danger exists that genetic engineering will produce harmful biological forms. The U.S. National Institutes of Health guidelines drawn up in the past have now been almost entirely abolished.

Second in this category, I might mention influences on evolution. At present, there is no way of knowing what such influences will be, although the recent claim that insertion of human genes (DNA of a nuclear form of life) into colon bacilli (pronuclear life form) does not break down evolutionary barriers seems optimistic.

And, finally, there is the fearsome possibility of biological warfare.

(B) Problems related to human beings

First in this category come genetic investigation and genetic therapy, which are indispensable techniques in the treatment of various hereditary defects. But DNA diagnosis reveals that there is no such thing as a genetically perfect human being, and this introduces doubt as to how far it is permissible to tamper with genetic makeup in the name of therapy. Furthermore, genetic therapy might be misused in connection with ideas of eugenics in attempts to improve the human stock.

Next, in relation to artificial insemination and so-called test-tube babies, it is enlightening to take a look at the following eight techniques by means of which insemination can be assisted medically.

(a) Artificial insemination employing sperm from the prospective mother's husband (AIH).
(b) Artificial insemination employing sperm donated by a man other than the prospective mother's husband (AID).
(c) Transplantation of an ovary or an ovum from

another woman's body into the body of the prospective mother, followed by artificial insemination employing sperm from the husband or from another donor.

(d)   Insemination outside the body (in a test tube) and then transplantation into the prospective mother's womb.

(e)   Genesis of the embryo outside the body (true test-tube baby).

(f)   Parthenogenesis.

(g)   Cloning.

(h)   Embryonic fusion.

Method (b), which seems to be a realization of ideas of the late eugenics specialist Herman Müller, has elicited much interest for the possibility of using sperm from outstanding persons, like Nobel Prize winners. In the numerous examples of the fourth technique (test-tube babies) the major problem arises in connection with the surrogate mother and, in the United States, has already caused legal troubles. For instance, if the child is discovered to be hereditarily defective, should the surrogate mother and father claim responsibility for it?

The production of cloned mice–that is, mammals–opens the way, in theory at least, to the cloning of human beings. Parthenogenesis, too, has been successfully perfomed on mice. Embryonic fusion results in children with four or more parents, all of whom can accept–or refuse–responsibility for rearing.

DERBOLAV: Your characterization of the extent and efficacy of life-technology in its various possibilities is brilliant. But, if I may, I should prefer to list the items in a different order: bacterial production of various proteins for pharmaceutical purposes (vaccinations and drugs); the use of genetically altered micro-organisms to make possible processes for protecting plants or reducing toxic elements in the environment; development of new kinds of nitrogen-fixing plants that use energy more efficiently and give higher percentages of nutritional value; methods for the genetic production of highly useful animal stock; contributions to the solution of the energy problem through the genetic alteration of various hydrogen-producing algae; genetic therapy for hereditary diseases and genetic defects; and, finally, intervention in human reproductive biology for eugenic purposes.

IKEDA: Various categorizations are possible. But in all of them, the greatest concern and caution must be exercised in applying these techniques to human beings. Recently, Japanese scientists, too, have been working with human genes. At the present stage, they have combined them only with mouse genetic structures; but some day it may be possible to produce apes possessing human genetic material.

Biotechnology is already rapidly and increasingly affecting the human sphere. And genetic engineering seems to be opening the way to so-called improvements in the human stock. Are we going to be able to put a stop to this kind of manipulation? Can we see to it that genetic engineering goes no farther than curing hereditary defects?

Biological warfare is a horrible prospect; but, if ever given the political backing eugenics once enjoyed, biotechnology could lead to incalculable human tragedy.

The attempts men of religion and philosphers are making to establish bioethics to control biotechnology and life-science only make more apparent the double nature–both good and evil–of scientific technology. What standards should we adopt for dealing with these issues, all of which are of the greatest moment to the humanity of the future? I am interested in hearing your comments on these points in relation to Christianity and Western philosophy.

DERBOLAV: Mendel and others identified chromosomes in organic cells as hereditary carriers. But it was not until recently that the code of genetic information has been cracked, making it possible to coordinate the ways genes and their combinations produce certain characteristics. It seems to me that the possibility of recombining genetic material has broken down the formerly insuperable barriers among species. This is the new and at the same time alarming aspect of recent developments in genetic engineering.

The wonder of genetic combinations has always taken place in natural species in the begetting of individuals and generations through the combination of the sperm cell and the ovum. Since combination of genetic materials could not be anticipated in these natural ways it is scarcely surprising that life-technology programs include the transferal of this process from the mother organism to the test tube and the retort.

Originally, because they reproduce rapidly asexually (through cloning), bacteria and viruses were considered most suitable for genetic experiments. Indeed initial medical and pharmaceutical achievements in the field were made with such materials: production of human insulin, formerly obtainable only from animal organs; production of the growth hormone somatostasin; and the development of vaccines protecting humans and other animals from viral diseases.

Gradually, more complex procedures led to the breeding of new plant and animal species expected to give better crops and larger herds and to be less dependent on climate. It became possible to correct such genetic anomalies in humans, other animals, and plants as sickle-cell and Cooley's anemia. Unquestionably, a wide spectrum of possibilities and developments that are now difficult to imagine remains open to life-technology. But, though in principle transparent, the procedures are so complicated to execute practically that they remain largely inconceivable to laymen.

IKEDA: As you note, complex procedures have led to crop improvement. For example, rice, the staple of the traditional Japanese diet, is originally a tropical plant and formerly would not grow in northern Japan or in other cold or mountainous regions. Chilly summer weather brought danger of very poor crops. Stock improvements, however, have produced strains yielding average crops even under extremely bad climatic conditions.

Similar strain improvements have produced sweeter apples and oranges and a hybrid called the pomato, which yields both potatoes and tomatoes. Small breeds of chickens have been developed to reduce feed costs.

DERBOLAV: I have already noted that molecular biologists themselves so clearly recognized the unparalleled risks and perils implied in the achievements and accomplishments of life-technology that they were willing to propose safety measures to be imposed on their own work. Nonetheless, scientists, too, are only human and, though committed to the truth, do not hesitate to make commercial use of their discoveries.

Herein lies a great danger. When their safety measures were about to be converted into federal law in the United States, scientists immediately sensed an unallowable infringement on their freedom and stopped at nothing to neutralize and render innocuous their own proposals. At the same time, intensive commercialization of molecular-biological discoveries got under way and scientists took a lively part in it. Researchers took out patents or accepted positions as advisors or designing engineers in commercial companies. None of this set a good example for the European nations who had followed the American lead with regard to legal safeguards in genetic engineering.

IKEDA: The case is similar in Japan, where all of these things are done on a commercial basis giving sole precedence to economics. In extreme cases, no thought is given to long-term results if immediate profit is forthcoming. The theory is the same as the one that results in industrial pollution.

DERBOLAV: From this it is clear that, owing to its extensive socio-economic consequences and relations with political security, genetic engineering requires not only a juridical framework, but also a set of definite moral standards and regulations. You rightly mention a bioethics that must include not only all of the points we have already discussed in connection with medical ethics, but also a full range of other matters that we can only touch on here.

Actually, in this discussion we are not breaking new ground, since a form of regional ethics in this connection has been evolving for a long while in the developed nations. One of the numerous institutions devoted to this cause is Hastings Center; that is the Institute of Society, Ethics, and Life Sciences, in Hastings, founded by the Catholic philosophers Daniel Ghallaghan and Willard Gaylin. From twelve to fifteen experts in the fields of philosophy, law, medicine, and theology work at the institute.

Other similar institutions include the Joseph and Rose Kennedy Institute for the Study of Human Reproduction and Bioethics, at Georgetown University, in Washington, D.C., which similar to the Hastings Center, has published the Encyclopedia of Bioethics and issues its own periodical. The Northwest Institute of Ethics and the Life-Sciences and the Institute of Human Values in Medicine of the Society for Health and Human Values, in Philadelphia, also publish relevant periodicals. Similar organizations, with a partial philosophical-religious orientation, may be found in San Francisco, Los Angeles, St. Louis (Missouri), Charlottesville, Chicago, and Houston (Texas).

Nor has Europe remained idle in this field. The Society for the Study of Medical Ethics, established in London in 1972, publishes the *Journal of Medical Ethics*. Important work is being done at the Deutsches Institute für ärztliche Mission, in Tübigen, which works closely with the Christian Medical Commission of the World Council of Churches. These organizations, many of which publish periodicals, discuss a wide range of subjects from human experimentation, gene manipulation, artificial insemination, organ transplants, abortion, and euthanasia to the just apportionment of medical resources among the world's peoples.

IKEDA: This is an important issue. Done in the name of

relieving human suffering, all of these things have positive aspects. But they have other aspects that violate human dignity as well, and a very delicate line separates the two categories. As a single example, the recipient of a heart transplant is granted an extension of life free of suffering, whereas the very operation is posited on the death of the donor.

The danger in these matters is that the human body can come to be regarded as a kind of machine. Coping with this issue necessitates investigation into the essential nature of the human being.

DERBOLAV: Since, within the general frame of our search for a new humanity we are attempting to discover the role human beings, as inhabitants of this planet, can and must fulfill in the future, I should like to set forth the whole area of biotechnical problems in a systematic way.

I follow my own conscience in these matters. But, if asked my personal opinion, I must remember that, in addition to juridical treatment of this highly difficult problem (an embryo-protection bill exists in the Federal Republic of Germany), on February 22, 1987, in its instruction about respect for new life and the dignity of human reproduction, the Catholic Church made binding statements on the topic.

Since, in the end of their instruction, the authors–the Congregation for Doctrinal Instruction–address state authorities, in an advisory instead of a demanding way, their work is expected to produce effects in the political sphere.

Mankind continues to expand its capabilities. And it is now essential to ask whether we *ought* to do what we *can* do, or whether we should not have certain rules to restrict our arbitrariness and orient our actions. If such rules are required, technical planning must be subjected to moral principles, that is ethics, or, in the case of genetic engineering, bioethics.

Instead of being something unique and apart, bioethics is an offspring of general ethical principles applied to a specific field of activity: that is, life-technology. As ethics, it follows general principles. As bioethics, it is a casuistic method of illuminating concrete problem situations arising within a particular area of action.

A fundamental principle–virtually a natural law–of bioethics is this: it is wiser to prevent harm than to help and do good if helping and doing good involve too great a risk. In short, in a field as explosively dangerous as genetic engineering, the first requirement must be *primum non nocere* (first, do no harm). This is why safety regulations occupy a central place in genetic-engineering legal codes in all lands.

IKEDA: Ensuring safety is tantamount to prizing life. And prizing life is to place maximum importance on its natural rhythms and operations.

DERBOLAV: But genetic-engineering measures fall not only under ethical, but also under juridical norms as well. Between the two there exists an uncircumventable relation. Since the law rests on a moral consensus, nothing illegal can be morally demanded. But morality takes pride of place over the law since legal conflicts arising from morally founded decisions must not inhibit those decisions but must be decided on the juridical level.

IKEDA: The law is applied only when some harm has actually been done. Questions of morality arise when it is clear that, unless averted, something will result in harm. Once done, harm, at any rate from the victim's standpoint, cannot be undone. And this is why morality must be given precedence in such instances.

DERBOLAV: A case involving Australian genetic engineering illustrates my meaning. A wealthy American couple, who were killed in an airplane accident, had previously had an ovum from the wife inseminated with the husband's sperm and then frozen in a nutrient fluid at temperatures of 200 degrees below zero. The question after their death was whether the fertilized ovum should be implanted in a surrogate mother or should be, so to speak, killed. This question is a moral one and must be decided independent of the issue of inheritance of the unfortunate couple's considerable property. Inheritance is a legal matter and must not be allowed to influence the moral issue of life or death for the fertilized ovum.

Bioethics belongs to what Max Weber correlated with responsibility in that it not only must evaluate aims, motives, and outcomes of actions, but also must take into consideration possible undesirable side-effects. For instance, it is correct always to give thought to the irreversibility of the effects of genetic-engineering on immediately succeeding generations, although it is doubtful if this is indeed always taken into consideration in actual practice.

In the early stages of experimentation in this field, it was felt imperative to warn that the bacteria and viruses being used in research might conceivably escape from laboratories, make an ecological niche for themselves in the outside environment, multiply out of control, and thus constitute a serious health-hazard to humanity. It was argued as assurance that only a concatenation of highly improbable conditions could bring about such an accident and that researchers restrict themselves to breeding viruses that can survive only in laboratories and perish in the normal environment. Both arguments noticeably dampened initial discussions about the risks of genetic engineering but were little consolation in the light of even the remote possibility of an occurrence of this kind.

Some people advocate employing bacteria that can digest such substances as oil and organic mercury dumped into the oceans of the world. But surely, once in the waters in great masses, these bacteria would severely burden oceanic ecology with their metabolic wastes.

IKEDA: Nothing is more perilous than thinking on the basis of optimistic forecasts. Dealing with life demands much stricter predictions, because the damage caused by steps like dumping bacteria into the oceans–even with the optimistic aim of dealing with polluting oil and organic mercury–can be irreversible. Similarly, genetic mistakes introduced into a strain, even with the noblest motivation, can persist throughout succeeding generations.

DERBOLAV: Finally, anyone even slightly concerned with the ecology must ask whether new production of insulin, vitamins and hormones, antibiotics, and interferon is truly necessary and whether it would not be possible for us to get by with the materials we already have. A recently published report by the World Health Organization claims that 210 medicaments would completely satisfy all the world's needs. Still, in such rich nations as the United States, 20,000 medicines based on from 2,000 to 3,000 substances are marketed. In this instance, would it not be wise to restrain genetic technology from further contributing to the already sufficiently threatening overdosing of humanity with various medicines?

IKEDA: Factors other than genetic engineering contribute to the plethora of drugs on the market in places like the United States and Japan. Taking advantage of the universal human desire for health, longevity, and vigor, pharmaceutical companies produce virtually countless medicines, many of which overlap or ludicrously duplicate chemically and pharmaceutically the products of their rivals. Skillful advertising is then employed to stimulate consumption. In Japan, in spite of legal restraints, each year such companies market huge varieties of medicaments and related so-called health foods. The stimulus of a free economy aggravates competition among the producing companies to stimulate consumers both to buy and to take more medicine than is actually good for them. And, as you infer, overdosing with medicaments has detrimental effects on human health.

DERBOLAV: The most upsetting aspect of the production of medicines through genetic technology is the nature of its motivation. From its very inception, such production has been inspired not by research interests and the desire to be of assistance alone. Instead, from the outset, motivations have been increasingly adulterated by the profit interests of the industries involved. And this has blurred the distinction between genuine needs and artificially generated needs.

Of course, political considerations influence the issue of genetic engineering and medicine. One of them is the just apportionment of the products such engineering is now producing or may produce in the future. Because of their close relation to the future of humanity, the achievements and triumphs of genetic engineering should benefit all peoples.

As to genetic engineering and human reproduction, we must take many unknowns into consideration and must attempt to avoid making rigid judgments.

Removing the fertilization process from the physical womb to the test tube and later replanting the fertilized ovum in the true, or in a surrogate, mother, as is done in extrauterine fertilization, represents so radical a shift from traditional views of human sexuality and reproduction that it is scarcely surprising that the leading Catholic theologian Karl Rahner, who attributes the instinct to faith to all human beings, considers it sinful on the basis of its being a detachment of physical sex from personal love. His view may be countered easily by pointing to the numerous acts of procreation occurring in either extramarital affairs or in church-sanctioned marriages devoid of personal affection. Unlike Rahner, I raise no moral objections to these modern practices since they frequently enable barren women to become mothers.

The longing for children is natural and noble and is part of a woman's role in life. Correcting organic imperfections or hereditary impairments hindering childbirth seems laudable under all circumstances.

Still relations between the woman supplying the ovum and the surrogate mother can cause complications. It seems best to operate on a purely commercial basis, as is generally the case. In such instances, the surrogate who carries and gives birth to the baby is paid on the basis of an agreement, as used to be the way of hiring wet-nurses. Closer relations between the two women can result in emotional problems after the birth of the child.

It remains to be seen, however, whether–even given the kinds of legal and bureaucratic barriers encountered in Germany–adoption is not the more natural way of correcting what might be called the genetic lottery, which sometimes results in genetic shortcomings hindering conception, pregnancy, and birth. In many instances, women hesitate to adopt because of false pride and vanity stimulating them to want only children they can say are of their own flesh and blood.

IKEDA: The insistence on blood connections seems to me to be a narrow carry-over from some primitive belief in the magical efficacy of blood itself. It is far better to attempt to make a scientific or medical correction of the faults causing barrenness than to resort to surrogate mothers, since it is a cruel blow to force a woman to give up an infant with whom she has developed profound affection during the nine months during which she has carried it inside her body.

DERBOLAV: Other possibilities are suggested. For instance, embryonic fusion producing children who are the offspring of multiple parents–who, as you have pointed out, may or may not care for them or who may even reject them outright–is sometimes discussed, as is the idea of freezing fertilized ova to be thawed later and to develop into children who may look back on parents who lived decades or centuries earlier. I find such processes disturbing and could consent to them only after examining their goals. For example, I would not veto the idea of embryonic fusion employed to correct hereditary impairments or to restrain outbreaks of hereditary illness. Otherwise, I would have serious reservations.

IKEDA: I agree entirely. These techniques should be used only to prevent suffering and must never be attempted solely out of–even scientific–curiosity.

DERBOLAV: Finally, I should like to deal with the concept of eugenic tampering with the aim of improving humanity. The Nobel-prize winner Hermann Johann Müller seriously contended that it is possible to improve human genetic material. Together with other critics of genetic engineering– among whom I believe you may be numbered–I am of the opinion that, even with the loftiest Social-Darwinian dreams of the future, such tampering is to be neither acknowledged nor justified.

Even setting aside the question of whether the humanistic claim for human improvement can or should be carried over into biology, we lack all standards for defining what *better* means in this field. Throughout the course of history, standards have changed and have adopted different forms as the spirit of the age has altered. This means, of course, that the human historical substance is plastic and formable. Biological transformations, however, even in the name of so-called improvements, would be irreversible and uncorrectable and would channel development in single, definite directions.

In general, in attempting to define convincingly the meaning of a "better future," we only grope in the dark. Naturally, we can use genetic technology to combat pathological hereditary factors and the organic defects they produce. We find ourselves in an embarrassing position, however, when we attempt to define an optimum state of health on which to base health policies.

We are in a still greater dilemma when we try to breed intellectually superior beings. Where should we put priorities? In keeping with current educational policies aimed at merely stuffing children's heads with information, should we strive to increase intelligence connected with theoretical knowledge? Or should we attempt to cultivate multiple talents? And, if this is the case, what talents should be especially emphasized? Or should we try to make the new human being more productive, creative and imaginative than his predecessors and thus give him the chance to develop total self-control and self-negation?

IKEDA: As many science-fiction writers present the picture, in the future, theoretical knowledge will probably be monopolized by computers; and only multiple talents–in such fields as art and literature–will be left to human beings. Though no one can predict which of these fields should be emphasized, I doubt that artificial promotion should be attempted. Instead human beings should put their innate, natural powers of application to use in developing their abilities. Even in their naturally cultivated states, talents often come accompanied by faults. Artificially promoting the amplification of talents could amplify the faults as well; and this could lead to the annihilation of the human race.

DERBOLAV: The temptation to want to improve man morally by altering his character, or his habitual moral-motivation system, encounters problems of no less difficulty. What characteristics should we attempt to breed into human beings when evidently moral values alter from nation to nation, from epoch to epoch, without providing any eternal, universal standards?

A biologically controlled and directed evolution of this kind would anticipate and trespass in historical development. And the only outcome of such a process would be the kinds of monsters Aldous Huxley forebodingly depicted in *Brave New World*. In the 1920s, when he wrote this novel, Huxley knew of cloning (asexual reproduction and multiplication of fertilized ova) but not of manipulation in the form of combinations of genetic material.

Although he therefore had to make do with cloned, in-vitro embryos in developmental stages to typify the new generations of human beings, the consequences are gruesome enough. In his brave new world, children are not conceived and born in the natural way, which is considered disgraceful.

Instead they are developed from ova fertilized in test tubes and biochemically manipulated to produce beings that are geotypically and phenotypically identical and may be assigned in groups to given professional or political tasks.

Huxley perceived that a society rigidly hierarchically structured by means of genetics and biochemistry could contain elements of conflict. But he attempted to minimize this danger by genetically programming into the social and functional groups a sense of satisfaction with their lots. This involves a point of irony: the idea that eugenics could ever produce a happy humanity seems never to have occurred to Müller, the zoologist. Had it occurred to him, he would have found himself hopelessly entangled in the philosophical definition of happiness, a definition that still remains ambiguous.

IKEDA: Huxley's genetic programming of satisfaction with their lots in social and functional groups is an unsettling concept implying the loss of basic humanity. The desire to improve and the strength and wisdom to actualize that desire are the most dignified aspects of human nature. I am vaguely frightened by the idea of manipulating genetic material to deprive us of these characteristics.

DERBOLAV: Today, attempts to combine human genetic material with that of the apes, our closest relatives, indicate that we are moving in the direction of visions of omnipotence. Creation of new species and subspecies, by now common practice at the level of such unicellular organisms as viruses and bacteria, assumes a different appearance when carried over to higher forms of life.

Nature has hindered cross-breeding by setting up barriers among species. The most common exception to the rule, the mule, which is a cross between a mare and a jackass, pays for his unique position by being sterile. We are accustomed to the mule, but how would we react to semihuman apes with incipient abilities to speak and reflect? The creation of such beings would amount to breaking into evolution by producing intermediary species that, with a blow, could change our entire cultural and political civilization.

Owing to the great complexity of necessary conditions, the probability of successfully combining genetic materials at this extraordinary level appears slight at present. Nevertheless, because of the rapid advances being made in this area, future prospects are frightening.

IKEDA: Genetic engineering to produce species superior in certain traits that then use their superiority to seize power over natural human beings is another horrifying concept. There are many examples of manipulation of human beings for the purposes of powers in authority. For instance, I have heard of a group of desperate assassins, in the Arab world, who are controlled by narcotics. The Western nations and Japan remember all too vividly the tragic consequences of patriotically indoctrinated young people who sacrifice their lives for the sake of a nation or a political party. Manipulation of a similar kind brought about through genetic engineering would be irreversible and would certainly lead to the total destruction of humankind. This is all the more certain because of the great destructive and killing powers of modern weaponry.

DERBOLAV: In your opinion, biological warfare would be the worst possible abuse of biotechnology. Should a nuclear war occur, even those who escape the bombings themselves would unavoidably be victims of such side-effects as radiation, which affects health and genetic make-up. But, as we have already seen, future military clashes could well be conducted in conventional, non-nuclear ways. And, if this is the case, biological warfare could become a foreseeable reality. The effects of the poison gas used in World War I, of the defoliant Agent Orange employed in Vietnam, and of the chemical weapons reportedly used by the Iraqis against the Iranians clearly show what we may expect. Now that the very idea of what was once called a righteous war has lost its meaning, it must be stated emphatically that chemical weapons have no place in conventional conflict. (It is pertinent to note that, at present, East and West Germany are negotiating the establishment of a Central-European zone, even extending beyond the Iron Curtain, in which chemical weapons will be forbidden.)

In conclusion, I should like to pose this question: In the light of the jeopardy in which our future stands, is there any point in discussing the chances for a new humanity? The kind of humanity that is meant here is not to be found in horizons of a brave new world of the kind Huxley depicted. Nor it is to be attained by attempting to correct the genetic lottery, according to which distribution of natural characteristics has been left to coincidence. That humanity is not to be found in the self-satisfied conviction that our technological and cultural achievements–which we are, however, responsible for strictly protecting from damage and destruction–are the first decisive steps on the way to self-perfection. Finally, it lies in neither progression toward an awareness of freedom, according to idealistic philosophical formulas, nor in the willingness to strive for self-perfection, although as both Europeans and Asians insist, such endowments are essential and praiseworthy.

The quality that will be most essential to the new humanity is the ability to criticize and control the self in relation not only to the human environment, but also to the general biological and perhaps geological environments. No generation has ever been in such great need of self-control as the present one. The specific task of all human beings today is strict, constant self-control.

IKEDA: I agree. Today, as human beings, we are most urgently required to be aware of our responsibility to the whole world, including animals, plants, and inanimate matter. Taking this awareness to all peoples requires a correct understanding of the relation between human beings–ourselves–and the rest of our world. Objective, scientific thought is of the utmost importance in stimulating such understanding. It is not enough for us to impose standards on our world, since standards operate effectively only when based on an understanding of the causes for their necessity.

The moral and ethical standards Buddhism establishes against such things as taking life, lying, and deception are meaningful because they are founded on a philosophy that comprehends the universally applicable Law of Cause and Effect and that explains the relation between human beings and the environment as one of unity and interdependence (the doctrine is referred to as Eshō-Funi in Japanese).

Awareness of our responsibility to the rest of the world imposes on us the demand for self-control. In all our actions we must consider the needs and conditions of the beings around us. An automobile that has been speeding along at 100 kilometers an hour on an express highway must decelerate to ten kilometers an hour upon entering a narrow, ordinary road filled with pedestrians. Obviously the driver must obey red traffic signals. In addition, however, he must stop even when he has the green signal if a pedestrian is crossing.

Human beings must demonstrate a similar attitude of concern for all animate and inanimate creation, including natural resources, water, and the air. We do not operate alone on the planet and could not survive without the support of all the other beings around us. They are the foundation of our existence. Destroying them is tantamount to cutting away the ground under our own feet.

We must strive to preserve harmony with all phenomena in our environment and, in doing so, must take the future into account. Sacrificing the natural resources of the world to the satisfaction of our own selfish desires and polluting the environment with toxic wastes threaten the very existence of our children and their children and grandchildren. Surely, no one likes to entertain the prospect of starving and poisoning posterity.

Moreover, in the light of the Buddhist doctrine of transmigration, in future existences, we ourselves will be forced to suffer the consequences of the depletion of resources and the environmental pollution we commit in this life.

I am convinced that, granted a correct understanding of true relations between humanity and the environment, most of us would be willing to view our own actions critically and to exercise self-control.

We have called this final section of our dialogue *For the Future*. In defining the future, we must take into consideration all the generations who will come after us. In addition, in accordance with Buddhist teachings of transmigration, in existences to come, we too will participate in the future, as will all things animate and inanimate. In everything we do, therefore, we must remember that the fate of one part of the universal whole is inseparable from the fate of all other parts.

DERBOLAV: No one today can neglect critical self-examination, a prerequisite of which is systematic education. Only by gaining a differentiated insight into his entire situation, through experiences with family, school, the mass media, and adult education all together, can a person expertly and responsibly carry out such examination.

It would be as absurd to attempt to overlook the dark sides of our present existence as it would be, like a bird mesmerized by a serpent, to despair in the imagining of all manner of evils and apocalyptic visions of the end of the world. I can only repeat what I have already indicated: man would totally surrender to fate if he failed to believe in himself and if, in Karl Rahner's expression, he lost trust in his own moral instinct and allowed the small plant of hope rooted in him to wither and die.

Religion, no matter what its form and kind, offers assurance that such hope is founded and justified by something deeper, transcending the bonds of ordinary life. Both Christianity and Buddhism can be abundantly helpful in this connection. I am sure you will understand that I am not advocating flight from bankrupt human intelligence into the merciful realm of religious faith. Instead, I am taking the path that we have proposed since the outset of our dialogue: relentless analysis of our current situation of life and faith and examination and elucidation of all the problems arising for human beings, who must not only reflect on their technical creations and spiritual achievements, but also preserve open access to the saving experience of religion.

The "weathermark" identifies this book as a production of Tanko-Weatherhill, Inc., publishers of fine books on Asia and the Pacific. Composition: Photography Publishing Company, Seoul. Printing: Yamagata Printing Co., Ltd., Yokohama. Binding: Makoto Binderies, Tokyo. The typeface used is Palatino.